FERRIES TO FIRE ISLAND
Captain Edwin J. Mooney

Printed in the United States of America
C.E.M. Inc. P.O. Box 2188
North Babylon, NY 11703

FIRST EDITION

Cover Design by Brian Mooney
Computer Assistance by Brendan Mooney

DEDICATION

In memory of Captain Elmer Patterson, founder of most of the present ferry system to the west end of Fire Island. Captain Patterson dedicated his life to his ferries and had little time for much else.

In memory of my late 21 year old grandson, Brian Mooney, who passed away a few days after completing the cover for this book. He is dearly missed by all who loved him.

Elmer Patterson at the open helm of FIRE ISLANDER (circa 1953)

ACKNOWLEDGMENTS

I have collected pictures of local ferries for over fifty years and was greatly rewarded with old pictures from Wally Pickhard. Wally had been going to Ocean Beach for over eighty years, was wounded on December 7, 1941 at Pearl Harbor, and his mother was on the village board in 1947 when Fire Island Ferries was awarded its contract.

Captain Luke Kaufman shared his collection of ferryboat pictures.

Billy Berka lent me his album of great black and white pictures taken while he was my deckhand and later when he was one of our captains.

I also received pictures from long-time beach residents Bob and Geraldean Stretch, Walter and Bea Thornberg, Bruce and Jen Kahler as well as summer residents John Dircks and John Hann plus picture postcards from Ray Demaria. Postcards are a great source for pictures of past history, and they were in common use as a way to stay in touch with family before telephones were introduced into every home.

I have a portion of Captain Patterson's pictures from Shirley Patterson and a few from Artie Weis. Artie grew up and went to school in Kismet and Ocean Beach. After World War II, he was the Kismet ferry captain.

Warren James gave me pictures as well as the history of Fair Harbor.

Russ Mayer of Kismet sent me copies of the logs Felix Dominy kept as Fire Island lighthouse keeper.

I thank everyone else who gave me some of these pictures, stories, and information. There are so many people, I could not list all of them. Many of these photos just sat in a drawer for years until I began compiling this book in 1999.

I have to thank my wife of 53 years, Pat, and my children Michael, Tim and daughter Casey for putting up with me while I worked long hours, weekends and holidays.

AUTHOR'S FOREWORD

This book focuses on the ferries that ran to the west end of Fire Island (the area between Fire Island State Park, now known as Robert Moses State Park, and Point O'Woods), Long Island, New York, on scheduled trips beginning in 1856 to the Surf Hotel, to the present (2004). I have also included the history of the owners and operators of each company and their vessels.

When I arrived in Bay Shore in 1948 and began working as a deckhand for Fire Island Ferries, Clyde Best was running ferries from Babylon to Fire Island State Park, Gus Pagels from Bay Shore to Fire Island State Park and Fair Harbor, the Weis family to Kismet from Bay Shore, Saltaire village operated their own ferry, Elmer "Pat" Patterson had just replaced Azariah "Cap" Robinson on the Ocean Beach run, the Zegel family ran to Seaview and Ocean Bay Park, Point O'Woods had their own boat, and Dunewood and Atlantique communities did not yet exist.

I became a captain during the summer of 1948 and kept a camera close at hand; many of those pictures are found in this work. Much in this book is from firsthand observations, stories from other captains, engineers, and deckhands who were here when I arrived, records and files of Fire Island Ferries, and information from Gus Pagels. Also included are notes I filed away, and information I obtained from visits to the Mariners' Museum, Newport News, Virginia; Babylon and Bay Shore historical museums; Suffolk Marine Museum; and picture exhibits at Ocean Beach, Saltaire, and Point O'Woods.

Much of the data about older ferry vessels came from books printed by the US Government, titled *Merchant Vessels of the United States* (MVUS). A few of these books were found at the Suffolk Marine Museum in West Sayville. Frank Braynard of Saltaire (historian, artist, author, and best known for organizing the first New York Op Sail in 1976) lent me his collection of MVUS, and Luke Kaufman lent me one as well.

CONTENTS

Page

FIRE ISLAND AND GREAT SOUTH BAY

Long Island and Fire Island are made up of sand and gravel left over from the last ice age, which occurred 10,000 to 25,000 years ago. Fire Island is a 32-mile long sand bar with an average width of about a quarter mile. The shallow Great South Bay is about five miles wide, and its sandy bottom separates Fire Island from the south shore of Long Island. Charts from the 1600s have seven inlets between Jones Inlet and Montauk Point. In the 1930s, there were four inlets: Jones Inlet, Fire Island Inlet, Moriches Inlet (I read one report that stated Moriches Inlet opened during a northeaster in March 1931 along with a loss of dunes and houses in Saltaire), and Shinnecock Inlet (which broke open in the 1938 Hurricane).

Beach sand moves along the ocean from east to west and flows into the inlet where it builds up on the east side of the inlet while the inlet stays open by moving to the west. The prevailing summer wind comes from the southwest, and fog comes in off the ocean from the southeast. Major destructive storms that cut away the beach howl in from the northeast. The northwest wind and its high pressure bring in the cold Canadian air and lower the ocean and bay water level in the winter. If the high pressure area brought in by the northwest wind lingers and temperatures are in the teens or lower, we can start to have ice, which first forms in the East Bay and along the Fire Island bay front. We can be clear of ice in Bay Shore and not see any ice until we get to West Fire Island. When there is another day or two of cold weather, the whole bay can freeze.

January 1918 set a low temperature record for Long Island of -14°. It was to be followed a month later by a new record of -16°F. Sam Pastorfield told of ice in the bay until May of that year. He and others remembered driving Model A Fords across the bay to obtain food and other supplies. To prevent the car from sinking if they hit soft ice, they lashed extra long 2" x 10" boards under the Model A. Also used on the frozen bay was an odd type of ice boat called a pumpkin seed or South Bay scooter, which originally was a duck boat with steel runners added to the bottom. They were extremely fast and could sail across small openings of water. If they broke through the ice or had to sail over open water, they carried a pike pole with a sharp hook for boaters to pull or push themselves back up onto the ice.

Small Great South Bay scooters (1903)   Hal Fullerton photo

Northeast storms have done more damage to the beach dunes than hurricanes, except for one hurricane that I have been told hit in 1910. However, one report stated that no violent hurricanes hit Fire Island between 1900 and 1938. Destruction to the Saltaire beach occurred in 1931 during a prolonged northeaster that took away much of the beachfront, leaving low dunes for the storm surge of the 1938 Hurricane to wash over. A three-day northeaster on March 5-7, 1962 destroyed 100 houses on the oceanfront and took away sand dunes.

During a storm (1962)   Ed Mooney photo

Other major storms on Long Island were Hurricane Donna on September 12, 1960, Hurricane Belle on August 9-10, 1976, Hurricane Gloria on September 27, and the October 31, 1991 Halloween storm.

EARLY HISTORY OF FIRE ISLAND

In 1693, William Smith, a Long Island resident, was given a large area of Long Island as well as all of Fire Island by Governor Benjamin Fletcher, who was the representative of the English Crown. Much of Fire Island remained in the Smith family until about 1900. There were no year-round residents on Fire Island prior to 1900, except for the lighthouse keeper and his family plus a few fish factory workers and squatters. Other than the Surf Hotel, there were only a few buildings that were used in the summer as bars and restaurants for groups that sailed over for a day at the beach and a clambake party. The lifesaving servicemen stayed at the numerous stations during the stormy winter season; the rest of the year they fished, farmed, or tended to their trade on the mainland.

After a storm (1962)   Ed Mooney photo

FIRE ISLAND LIGHTHOUSE

Fire Island Lighthouse (circa 1960) Ed Mooney photo

The first Fire Island lighthouse was built in 1826 and was replaced with the present lighthouse in 1858. In 1974, the lighthouse was abandoned, and a strobe light was installed on the Robert Moses water tower to take its place. In 1986, the lighthouse was restored with a new beacon.

DOMINY HOUSE

Felix Dominy was the Fire Island lighthouse keeper from 1835 to 1844. He purchased land east of the lighthouse and in 1847 built one of the island's first summer resorts, a small inn called Dominy House near what is now Kismet. The hostelry was built with shipwreck lumber. (I am unable to find any record of ferry service from the mainland to the Dominy House.) At that time, the Fire Island Inlet was closer to Kismet with great fishing of blues, weakfish, and bass plus duck hunting. Boaters would stop in for dinner after fishing in the deep water not far from the bay front at Kismet. Felix died around 1891 and his wife Phoebe moved to Bay Shore and opened the Dominy Hotel on Main Street.

SURF HOTEL

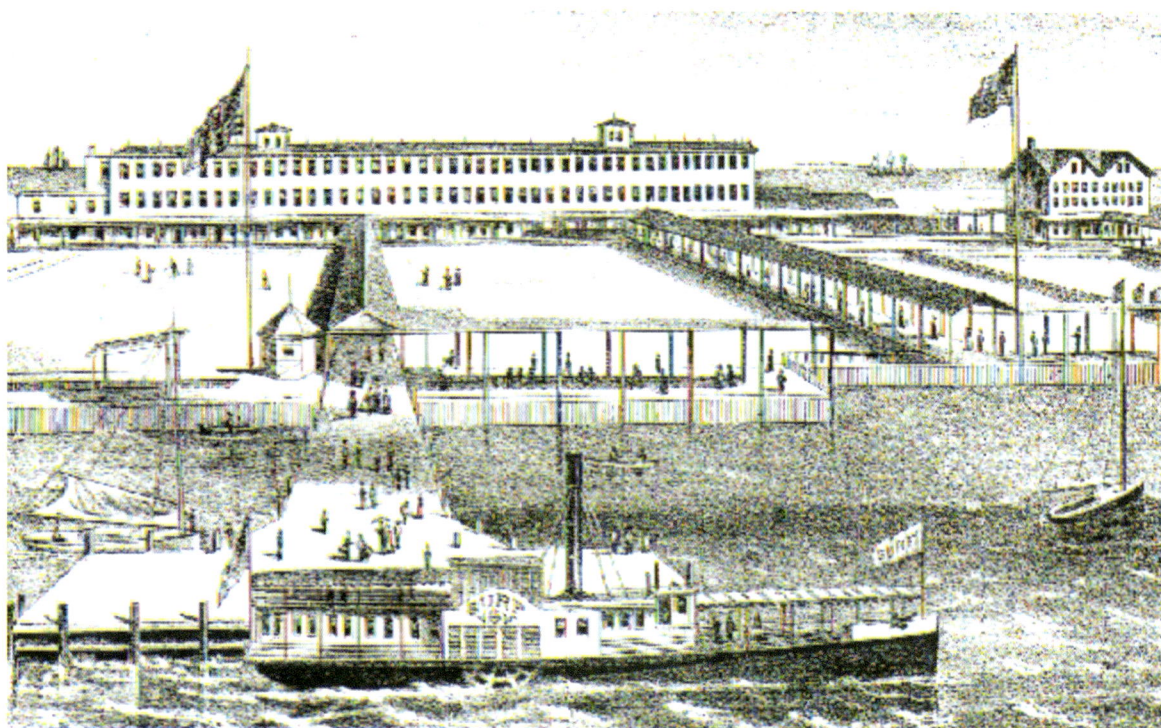

Surf Hotel (circa 1875)   This picture appears in several books on the early history of Fire Island

David Sammis began building the Surf Hotel just east of the Fire Island Lighthouse in 1856 on 120 acres of land he owned, or thought he owned. The ownership of the land would be debated in court for many years and finally settled in 1925. By the 1880s, the resort hotel had rooms for 1,500 guests and was serving many important political people from the city and state government as well as a few people from Washington, D.C. Prior to the construction of the railroad to Deer Park in 1843, travel to Long Island from New York City and Brooklyn meant a long ride by wagon or stagecoach, or a long sailing subject to wind, waves, and tide out in the Atlantic Ocean. Before the railroad came into Babylon, Sammis brought his guests from the Deer Park railroad station to the Babylon dock by stagecoach, a four-mile trip.

In 1859, New York State gave Sammis an exclusive license to operate ferries on the run to his dock to prevent baymen and other boaters from using his docks. It also gave him power to acquire terminals by eminent domain on Fire Island or the mainland.

When the Southside Railroad came to Babylon in 1867, Babylon became known as the Gateway to Fire Island. On the side of the station in large letters it stated "Babylon" and under that in large letters "Fire Island." The guests then had a short ride to the steamboat dock by horse and carriage or stagecoach.

The South Side Railroad reached Patchogue by 1869 and was formally absorbed by the Long Island Railroad in 1889. In 1871, Sammis built the Babylon Railroad, a trolley from the Babylon station that ran down Fire Island Avenue to the steamboat dock. At first, the trolley car was horse-drawn, then steam powered, and finally electric powered.

Based on the size of the hotel and the distance and travel time from Babylon, there must have been a fleet of boats serving the hotel. There is an old picture of the steamboat dock taken before automobiles were in use, and it shows eight horse and carriages on the dock alongside two smaller boats of about thirty feet long, but only about eight feet wide. The boats had a single deck and a canvas awning, and did not have a smokestack necessary for steam power, so they may have had early naphtha or gas engines.

Sammis's hotel business had started to decline in the early 1890s. In September 1892, New York State bought the property (120 acres) for $210,000 to use as a quarantine station for a shipload of people from the Mediterranean on the **SS** *Normannia*, and it was reported to have some passengers with cholera. The *Normannia* passengers, who numbered about 500, were loaded onto the vessel *Cepheus* in New York Harbor to be transported to the Surf Hotel. The hotel never recovered from all the bad press about guests with cholera. The state then leased it out to private innkeepers, who failed to make money. The hotel was sold at auction in 1907 and dismantled.

A group of influential residents of the south shore area went to the state to have the west end of Fire Island (those 120 acres) made into a park to prevent development. This land was to become New York State Fire Island State Park in 1908. Robert Moses had plans to build a road on Fire Island as early as 1922. Many years later, in 1964, another group was successful in having the undeveloped areas of Fire Island become a national park to stop a road from being built and to halt further development.

FIRE ISLAND STATE PARK/ROBERT MOSES STATE PARK

In 1908, the governor of New York signed a bill authorizing the creation of the Fire Island State Park. The following year, state park buildings and boardwalks were built east of the lighthouse and were destroyed in a 1918 brush fire. (I did not find any record of ferry service from 1909 to 1918 to the park.) In 1922, the state park had ferry service run by the Weis family from Bay Shore and used the Kismet dock; the round-trip price was 50¢.

In 1926, Camp Cheerful for handicapped children was built east of the lighthouse by the New York City Rotary Club; destroyed by the 1938 Hurricane, the camp was never rebuilt. The park, too, was destroyed in the hurricane, but rebuilt shortly afterward.

Before the Captree Bridge was built from West Islip to Captree Island, the ferries *Roamer II* and *Mischief* departed from the Babylon town dock, and *Running Wild, Atlantic* and *Cherry Grove* from Maple Avenue dock in Bay Shore to the state park. After the causeway from West Islip to Captree was completed in 1954, Babylon and Bay Shore service ended, and a ferry dock was built in Captree Boat Basin, just a short boat ride to the state park. Because of the popularity of the park, the *Miss Fire Island* and *Miss Captree* were added to the *Roamer II* and *Mischief*; all four were needed on nice summer weekends. This service ended when the Fire Island Bridge (Robert Moses Bridge) joined the state park to Captree in 1964. (I found agreements between Gus Pagels and the Long Island State Park Commission for ferry service from Bay Shore to the park from 1944 through 1954; Gus may have run there prior to 1944.)

In the 1940s, 1950s, and early 1960s, the state park had boat basins, a ferry dock, a state police house, a shipwreck shelter, a bathhouse, lifeguards, and a great beach. The Robert Moses Bridge over Fire Island Inlet (1964) and parking fields were added later to complete the state park facility and ended ferry service. In 1964, Fire Island State Park was renamed Robert Moses State Park

FIRE ISLAND NATIONAL SEASHORE

After a group of Fire Islanders prevented Robert Moses from building a highway from Jones Beach Causeway across the inlet and down Fire Island continuing over Moriches Inlet all the way to the east end of Long Island, they then worked to have Fire Island become a national park. President Lyndon Johnson signed the bill in 1964 to create the Fire Island National Seashore. With this came the end of rapid development that we had seen in the 1950s and early 1960s. In 1985, the Fire Island National Seashore aquired the 120 acres of New York State Park land east of the lighthouse, which was the old Sammis Surf Hotel location.

Without the National park, the undeveloped land west of the Summer Club, the track of land by Lonelyville, the area by Robins Rest, and two tracks in the Kismet area would all have been developed. The national park also put an end to commercial building.

COMMUNITIES ON WESTERN FIRE ISLAND *(from west to east)*

KISMET

Kismet dock, view from the bay (circa 2001)   Ed Mooney photo

"Live and let live" was the motto used in Kismet for many years, but it no longer applies today. Kismet slowly turned into a family community with many small children playing on the beach and fishing off the ferry dock.

In 1876, a 90-foot tall Western Union telegraph tower was built on the beach between Kismet and the lighthouse with a man stationed there with a powerful telescope to identify ships headed for New York Harbor. He would telegraph agents in New York City to have a tug meet the ship and line up stevedores to unload the ship, giving from five to ten hours advance notice of the ship's arrival. This service ended in 1920 when radios became common on ships.

Kismet became a community when Fred Weis and his two sons, Herb and Cliff, and the family formed Kismet Park Corporation, bought a 359-foot wide tract of land, bay to ocean, from the Sammis Estate in 1925. They opened a restaurant and store and began ferry service from Bay Shore using the ferries *Kismet, XL,* and *Mischief.* The boats *Kismet* and *XL* were built in Bay Shore and owned by Cliff Weis and the Bay Shore Boat Company. They also serviced Camp Cheerful, West Island, and Fire Island State Park.

The story that Kismet was named after the ferry *Kismet* is partially correct. Frederick W. Weis was an active Mason, and the name comes from the Mason Temple shrine in Brooklyn.

When the 1938 Hurricane struck Long Island, the eye of the hurricane passed over Kismet, and the storm surge destroyed twenty of the twenty-two existing homes by washing them off their foundation posts.

Artie Weis was the Kismet ferry captain after World War II. Around 1950, the Weis family gave up ferry service and sold their interest in Kismet. Also around this time, Dick Greenamyer bought the Kismet Inn and boat basin.

In the early 1950s, Kismet went without ferry service for a few years, and the Saltaire boat began to stop at Greenamyer dock in 1954. The present Kismet ferry dock was built in 1961, and ferry service was combined with Dunewood from the main ferry terminal in Bay Shore. Saltaire service was required to operate directly to and from its own terminals during the summer. Passenger loads were light during the week when the ferry, usually the *Fire Island Flyer*, went from Kismet, passing Saltaire and Fair Harbor to Dunewood. Until Captain Elmer Patterson built his own dock at Kismet, the Kismet ferry loaded and unloaded at the Kismet boat basin entrance, then owned by Dick Greenamyer. Combined Kismet-Dunewood service left from the main ferry terminal until 1973.

After buying Fair Harbor Ferries in the winter of 1972-73, Fire Island Ferries Inc. (FIFI) moved the Fair Harbor service to its Main Terminal (after thirty-eight years from Maple Avenue dock), and moved Kismet service to Maple Avenue dock. During the week, Kismet was combined with Saltaire from the Saltaire terminal. On weekends, the Kismet ferry left from Maple Avenue dock, which had no covered waiting area, and the Kismet passengers complained about the move. Fair Harbor passengers complained that the Main Terminal was too crowded. However, it took only a short while before everyone was happy, and service was improved with more trips and shorter travel time.

Some of the early FIFI ferries to Kismet were the *Islander, Roamer II*, (first)*Flyer*, and (first) *Fireball*. Captain Elmer "Pat" Patterson, a FIFI partner, had a ten-year lease on the bay front property on the east side of the dock beginning in 1969, with an option to buy the property at the end of the lease. With just two weeks left on the ten-year lease and option, the landlord tried to break the lease and option and remove Patterson. Bob Royce, Patterson's and Fire Island Ferries' attorney from about 1960 to 1989, wrote to Kismet Park Corporation that the sale/option would take place at his office (119 East Main Street, Bay Shore) on Monday, July 2, 1979, for the seller to convey title as pursuant to the agreement, or an action would immediately start in New York Supreme Court. The sale took place, as per the option, on June 29, 1979.

Patterson had the present ferry dock widened to eighteen feet in 1963, leasing the dock area from Kismet Park Corporation. Around 1969, he had the Kismet house barged from Bay Shore and used it during the summer. The present building on the dock was also barged from Bay Shore and originally used as a freight house. Later it was converted into a hot dog and ice cream stand operated by Shirley Patterson (Pat's second wife) and her family. Patterson sold the Kismet dock and house to Fire Island Terminal (FIT) in 1982. In 1981, Warren Lem, owner of Kismet Out restaurant (which had been built in 1974) operated the hot dog stand for a few years after Shirley gave it up, and when he left, Billy DeNatalie opened it as a pizza shop.

Patterson also sold gasoline on the outside of the west side of the entrance to the boat basin, but stopped doing so; regulations, logistics, and safety were not worth it. At first, the gasoline was brought over in fifty-five gallon barrels and pumped into an underground storage tank, which met Coast Guard transportation regulations. Later, Patterson mounted a 1,000-gallon tank on the deck of the ferry *Fire Island* after she was no longer in use as a passenger ferry. This worked fine, but was dangerous and against USCG regulations. One of the ferry captains notified the Coast Guard of the large gas tank on a non-tank vessel, and the gasoline service ended. Greenamyer sold gasoline at Kismet basin years before Pat, but he quickly ended the dangerous business the day he had a barrel of gasoline go on fire while pumping into his large storage tank.

Kismet has deep water close to its bay front requiring only short piers out into the bay. It's not too far from the Fire Island Inlet, and it has a strong current at the dock.

Kismet has a general store, which is also the post office. Ocean front lifeguards are from the town of Islip lifeguard district. Kismet has a strong, active homeowners association. Its main attractions, other than its beautiful beach, are Kismet Inn and Kismet Out restaurants, Billy's Pizza at the ferry dock, and its very friendly people.

SALTAIRE

Saltaire dock (1998)   Ed Mooney photo

Fire Island Beach Development Company sold building lots in Saltaire, beginning about 1910. The development company cut down the high dunes at the oceanfront to give new homeowners a view of the ocean. There were 100 houses in Saltaire by 1911. They even had an ad campaign back then: "The Summer Home for Sensible People." By 1917, there were about 200 bungalows, but World War I slowed development. A 1918 map of Saltaire has the ocean walk "Ocean Promenade" and a row of lots on its ocean side. A major loss of beachfront took place in a winter northeaster of 1927 that washed away dunes, seven houses, and Ocean Promenade. On July 5, 1928, an auction was held for 293 Saltaire lots. A March 1931 storm took away the rest of the houses on Ocean Promenade and the Western Union tower (thus, a row of houses was gone before the 1938 Hurricane).

The village of Saltaire was incorporated on November 10, 1917, which was also the date of elections and the first village board meeting. This meeting was held on the way to Bay Shore on the ferry *Eladio* that left early to get ahead of a snowstorm.

The yacht club opened in Saltaire in 1912. Saltaire had telegraph service from 1923 to 1937, its first post office opened in 1924, its first telephone and telephone booth were installed in 1937, its first phone in a cottage in 1949, and first electric service in 1936. The permanent filled ferry dock at Saltaire was constructed in 1936.

If you hear of a house in Saltaire called a "Coffee House," the name refers to any house that Michael Coffee built in Saltaire. Mike arrived in Saltaire in 1913 and worked for the development company for one year before going out on his own. He built over 100 houses, 3 churches, and the Village Hall. He was the major builder in the village, noted for his excellent buildings, and a man of fine character.

Under a New York State law of 1918, an Incorporated Village could operate its own ferry, but Saltaire did not at that time. The following is from the minutes of a village of Saltaire meeting of January 20, 1922: "The boat service has been maintained under a joint ownership of two men who reside in Bay Shore. It has been uncertain and unsatisfactory at times, and the village officials have been notified that the service will not start up again in the spring under private ownership, which makes it necessary for the village to operate."

The village began to operate its own ferry service in 1922 with the vessels *Stranger* and *Eladio* (*Eladio* served the community for thirty-five years). Other vessels that followed were the *Saltaire*, *Saltaire II*, and *Saltaire III*. From 1910 through 1931, Herbert Patterson, Captain Elmer Patterson's father, was a Saltaire ferry captain and later the ferry manager for the village. When Captain Herbert Patterson lived in Bay Shore he walked about twenty minutes to and from work, always dressed in khaki pants, shirt, jacket and captain's hat. He was also a licensed real estate broker in Saltaire; he died in 1949.

Prior to 1931, Saltaire ferries departed from the west side of Maple Avenue dock along with the Point O'Woods and Ocean Beach ferries until the village of Saltaire bought property for their present terminal and built the ferry slip, parking field, and garages. The garages were later removed to expand parking.

The village of Saltaire bought the Bay Shore property for their ferry terminal in 1931 from Spencer Aldrich and his wife, Harriettte, for $20,000. It consisted of two parcels: the 50' x 100' entrance, and a one-acre parking and dock area. The first parcel, referred to as the right-of-way to the inside piece and which could not be built on, resulted in a court case when the restaurant to the south used it as a right-of-way for deliveries and garbage trucks and at times blocked the entrance to the ferry and parking. A few years earlier, the restaurant had added cesspools, a retaining wall, and an addition on the side of their building that required getting to the back door of the building using Saltaire property. The court found in favor of Saltaire since the restaurant had frontage on Maple Avenue that could be used for their service. The deed restriction did not call it a right-of-way, only that it could not be built upon.

On September 21, 1938, a hurricane passed by Cape Hatteras, North Carolina, out in the Atlantic Ocean, and the weather bureau lost track of it. Its forward speed of advance went to an unheard of fifty miles per hour, passing directly over Saltaire about ten hours later without advance warning. (It was called the 1938 Hurricane because they didn't name hurricanes at that time.) Long Island had not had a major hurricane in some thirty years, and that day, Saltaire had ninety homes washed into the bay off their foundation posts and seventy-five others were heavily damaged. Four Saltaire people died, and the toll would have been much higher if it had taken place three weeks earlier when all the summer people were there. The *Eladio* was at the Saltaire dock, and many people took shelter on her during the storm. She could not leave the dock during and after the storm since she was locked in place by houses and wooden boardwalks that washed up against her. Also at the dock was an ex-Navy battleship tender, *Sea Horse*, that served as a shelter for people and was stuck by floating debris.

The question has been asked: Would the *Eladio* have survived the crossing to Bay Shore if she had left the dock with a load of passengers just before the storm hit? Someone who was there during the storm didn't think so! During the storm, the village dock was underwater, and that is the highest dock we use. A report of Fire Island after the 1938 Hurricane recorded a loss of 265 houses while 922 survived, Saltaire lost 90 out of 150, and Ocean Beach and Seaview only lost 4 out of their 700 houses. The tidal surge with the wind-driven waves was at least thirty feet high when they hit the beach and washed across the island into the bay.

Hurricane Donna was approaching on September 12, 1960, and Suffolk County called for the evacuation of Fire Island; Saltaire began to comply at 1 A.M. The storm went through twelve hours later, and Fire Island had the ocean wash over the dunes in twenty locations.

A three-day March northeaster storm in 1962 destroyed 100 homes on Fire Island. As a result, Robert Moses unsuccessfully revived his dormant 1924 plan to build a road down Fire Island to protect the island from the ocean.

After World War II, the village bought an 85-foot ex-Navy PT boat that was cut down to just under 65 feet (cut twenty feet off the stern) to comply with United States Coast Guard (USCG) regulations regarding "Rules for passenger vessels under 65 feet." The boat was extremely slow, had one 6-71 diesel engine, drew six feet, and had a load of cement in the stern under the deck to correct the trim and get the stern down after replacing three large gas engines with one small diesel. She had two decks, dark green side curtains that were rolled down in bad weather, she was hard to handle in the wind, could not get to the fuel dock at Gil Clark's at low tide, and just was not a good ferry.

At the board meeting of May 27, 1950, the village board voted to have the ferry operation run by professionals. The village and Captain Elmer Patterson, with Bill White and Bill's cousin, Dr. Eldridge Smith, signed a ten-year ferry contract on December 18, 1950. FIFI began to make stops at Saltaire on November 1, 1950, before the contract was signed. Patterson, as president of the newly formed (July 3, 1950) Saltaire Ferry Inc., signed the contract, agreed to buy the village's ferry *Saltaire III* and their barge for $15,000, to be paid for over the ten years of the contract, build a new, faster ferry for 125 passengers or more, transport new home construction material for the first two years or first twenty houses of the contract at no cost, and give a 25% discount to transport major construction material after the first two years until the end of the contract. (Interestingly, two new houses were built the first year and only a few the second year, and then a building boom started in Saltaire and on the rest of Fire Island.) The one-way fare at that time was 85¢. Patterson retained Al Skinner, the Saltaire captain. Patterson and White's Saltaire Ferry Co. Inc. (*Islander*, *Saltaire III*, *Fireball*, and scow) merged in 1967 into FIFI, which actually ran the service, but kept its own set of books.

During World War II, the Navy and Air Force used a 63-foot air/sea rescue (ASR) boat to pick up downed pilots. After the war, many ASRs were for sale by bid from the government and were obtained at low cost. Most of them were located in Norfolk, Virginia's Naval Base but Patterson found a good one in Florida with running Hall Scott gasoline engines, and it was all ready to go. The boat was brought up from Florida by Fred Scopinich and his cousin; they had one engine quit on the trip north and got hell from their fathers for spending too much time in Florida. The boat was converted at Freeport Point Shipyard by the Scopinich family and entered ferry service in 1952 as the ferry *Fire Islander* (called *Islander*). With her gasoline engines, she crossed the bay in fifteen minutes, but used twice the amount of fuel as other ferries. At that time, gasoline was about 30¢ a gallon, while diesel fuel was about 15¢ a gallon, making her fuel cost per trip about four times as much as other ferries, but she was fast.

Air/sea rescue boat FIRE ISLANDER at Brewster's (circa 1954)   Ed Mooney photo

Gus's air/sea rescue boat as it looked before conversion (1957)   Warren James photo

At this time in the early 1950s, Patterson's Ocean Beach competition at nearby Seaview still used gasoline engines while we were all diesel until Pat ran the *Islander* with gas engines. The *Islander* would sometimes make a trip to Ocean Beach in violation of the contract to use diesel only. After the *Islander* began going to Ocean Beach, we had to remove the "Ride the Safe Diesel Way" posters at our terminals. The gas engines required special care and had to be carefully tuned up and constantly checked for gasoline leaks. They could blow the porcelain center out of a spark plug. After two years, the gas engines were replaced with a new Detroit Diesel engine series, 6-110, manufactured only for trucks at that time. Adapter rings were machined in Sayville by master machinist Carl Pausewang. The rings were needed to mount the old reverse marine gears from the old engines to the new engines. The old mechanical gears were engaged with a four-foot lever at the pilot station or bridge (there was no pilothouse on the *Islander* at that time; you piloted out in the weather).

The first Saltaire ferry contract called for direct service during the summer, and off-season for the Ocean Beach ferry to drop off passengers on the way to the beach. If someone wanted to be picked up by the Ocean Beach boat going to Bay Shore, they had to put up a flag at the dock house. Most of the time, the flag worel wasn't taken down when the passengers got on the boat so it was still up for the next trip and of course when the incoming boat stopped, no one would be there. On a cold winter day, the boat would slow down, see no passengers, and so continue on to Bay Shore (we had no radios at that time). You would dock and secure for the night, and later find out someone was waiting out of the cold wind behind the dock house. There were also days when it was too rough to dock and make a pickup.

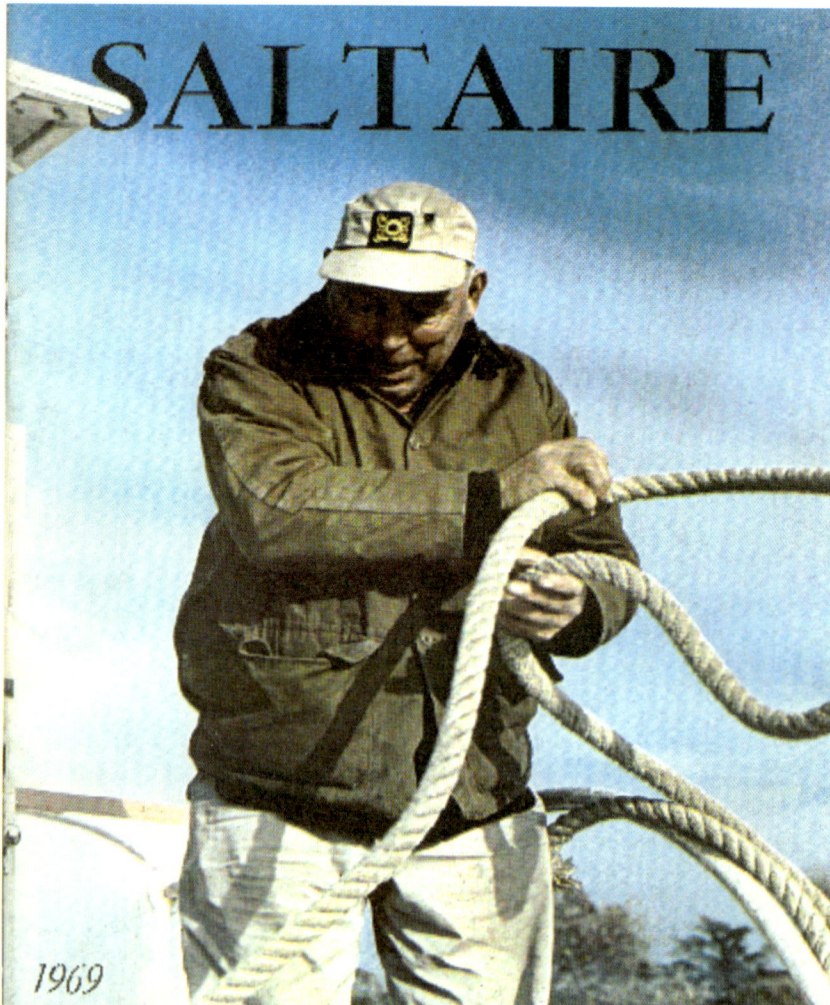

Captain Al Skinner   From a picture book of Saltaire

Before the bridge to Fire Island was completed, Captain Albert Skinner, who ran the Saltaire ferry, lived in a small building, the famous "shim shack" at the Saltaire ball field, from May to October. Al called it that because he always asked his friends to come over to help him put a shim under his refrigerator to level it; they had drinks first and forgot about the shim. Adults and kids of Saltaire loved Captain Al. He played the accordion, sang, told jokes and stories, and paid for soda, hot dogs, and watermelon for his mid-summer birthday party for the kids at the ball field. Captain Skinner was one of the last true bay men, who made their livelihood from the bounty of the bay, fishing, clamming, eeling, catching bait, scalloping, shooting ducks for market, and cutting salt hay used for packing dishes. He was a guide for duck hunters, and ferried people to Fire Island during the summer. Al, a

14

self-taught naturalist, could identify any duck, bird, bird's egg, fish, mammal, turtle, or any living creature in the bay area. Al started to work for the ferry in 1951 and retired in 1969 and moved to Florida where he had spent his winters for years before retiring.

Captain Dick Ivey worked for Fire Island Ferries on weekends for thirty-five years, most of that time on the *Islander* and later the (second) *Stranger* on the Saltaire run. Dick was well liked and respected, but firm on safety and regulations and would not take wagons or bikes on the passenger ferry. On a busy Sunday afternoon, a man put a wagon on the Kismet ferry loading to go to Bay Shore, and Dick asked him to take his luggage off the wagon and leave the wagon for the freight boat the next day. The passenger refused, and Dick would not leave the dock until the wagon was removed. They were at an impasse and getting nowhere when a friend of the unbending passenger unloaded the contents of the wagon on the boat, threw the wagon in the bay, and called out to Dick, "Everything is all set. We can now go to Bay Shore."

While loading the *Belle* at Maple Avenue dock (before I went into military service and before we moved up to the new Main Terminal, about the spring of 1951), a man told me he did not have fares for his family to go to Saltaire, where he had just been hired by the village as a maintenance man. Mr. Cornelius Hummel's English was perfect, but his wife and three children did not speak English. (They were from Holland, but during World War II, he had been in England where he learned to speak English.) They had come to the United States without a job and little money, which was now gone, and everything they owned was in a few suitcases. Through Catholic Charities in New York City, he had obtained this Saltaire job that also provided a house. He showed me his hands that had never done hard work before. He had been a policeman, and now he was going to dig ditches and bury water pipes and install boardwalks. He and his family would ride free on the ferry under the Saltaire contract (village workers and family received passes).

Mr. Hummel and his family were well liked. Mrs. Hummel took in wash, and they bought a bigger hot water heater and an electric ironing machine for sheets and pillowcases, expanded the business, and saved their money. When the ice cream store in Fair Harbor was put up for sale, the Hummels bought it and expanded it into a restaurant. When New York State made additional liquor store licenses available (the state had not issued new liquor store licenses for a long time), Mr. Hummel obtained one for a Fair Harbor location. After things were going well in Fair Harbor, he quit his Saltaire job. During the long winter with his Fair Harbor operation shut down, he tended bar in Bay Shore.

Mr. Hummel made many trips on the ferry with me when I was a captain and pointed out that you had to work for yourself to make any real money and that this country had plenty of opportunities to do that. He traveled around the United States looking for the best place to retire. On one of his last visits to Fire Island, he told me that he had found the best place to live to be Laguna Beach, California, and he moved there.

On the way to Ocean Beach west way on September 2, 1968, I used the Saltaire black water tower and a house on the bay front as a reference point to make my shortcut turn inside buoy Crazy Charlie. On my next trip, I could not find the tower; the village had dropped it to the beach and replaced it with a pressurized ground tank - what a relief to know it wasn't my eyesight.

In March of 1974, Fire Island Terminal (FIT) entered into agreement to operate the Saltaire parking field. The village office on the other side of the bay had little control of the parking operation in Bay Shore. All too often, FIT had to send a parking attendant down to open the lot when the Saltaire attendant was late.

FAIR HARBOR

Fair Harbor dock (circa 2000)   Ed Mooney photo

After Gus Pagels (1897-1977) sold his business and retired, he sold his house at 40 Maple Avenue in Bay Shore to Warren James, who had been a deckhand and captain for Gus in the 1940s and early 1950s. (Warren was sixteen years old when he started as a deckhand.) While cleaning out the attic, Warren found two plastic bags of ledgers and papers left behind by Gus and gave them to me. Much of the history that follows comes from those papers.

Gustave J. Pagels incorporated the Cherry Grove Ferry Corporation in Sayville on March 5, 1931, with his wife, Gertrude, and his brother, William Pagels, to run ferry service from Sayville to Cherry Grove in competition with the Steins. He appears to have run this service from 1927 through 1947. At first he ran from Patchogue and stopped at Blue Point for more passengers, then over to the Grove. Gus bought a piece of bay bottom just west of the present Cherry Grove ferry dock in 1931, but it doesn't appear that he ever had a dock built on it.

In 1923, service started to Fair Harbor and for about twelve years was run by Captain Charles J. Smith on the *Zuzu*.

The Fair Harbor Development Company Inc. was incorporated in 1923 by Isabella H. Clock and George W. Weeks, Jr. On March 1, 1935, Gus signed a two-year contract with Fair Harbor Development Company to provide ferry service between Maple Avenue dock and the foot of Broadway, Fair Harbor. There were some interesting points in the contract: rates one-way 35¢, round-trip 70¢, commuter 100-ticket book at 25¢ a ticket, freight charges not to exceed Saltaire rates, use of *Atlantic* or other suitably equipped boat, rent or fee to the development company of $150 per year, and a requirement to post a sign on the boat stating "No Drinking of Liquor." In March 1937, Gus signed a new three-year contract with the same terms as 1935. In March of 1940, they renewed the agreement for five years with new fares: one-way 50¢, round-trip $1, ten trips for $3.50, children half fare, monthly ticket good for the purchaser-only $10, and the fee to the development company dropped to $100 for the first three years and went to $150 for the last two years. Looking through Gus's old files and logbooks, I found that Gus had a summer mail contract shortly after beginning service to Fair Harbor. His motto was "Service Makes Us Grow."

Gus used the same clothbound ledger starting in 1935 for twelve years; he never spent a penny if he didn't have to. (These were hard times with one of three men out of work.) In this ledger: gasoline 13¢ a gallon (Gus got a tax refund of 4¢ a gallon for off-highway use of the fuel), postcard stamps 1¢, deckhands were paid $5 a week, captains $25 a week, a gallon of copper bottom paint cost $3.25, and spark plugs 50¢.

I have been told that Gus lent Fair Harbor Development Company $2,500, and when they could not pay him back, they gave him 100 Fair Harbor lots which he later sold at a nice profit.

Gus generally started service each year on the second weekend in March and ended in November when homeowners drained and turned off water to protect pipes from freezing. Terry and Gibson handled his insurance (the same firm that had Fire Island Ferries' insurance for more than fifty years).

Fishing in Great South Bay during the 1930s and 1940s was heavy with flounder, weakfish, bluefish, fluke, and bass. Gus ran the **Running Wild** and **Cherry Grove** on many fishing trips from April to June, and the *Atlantic* for charter picnic trips to the beach. Times were tough, and he did whatever he could with his boats for income. Captain Patterson chartered the **Running Wild** from Gus at $15 a trip for thirteen trips in 1938 (I assume for Seaview and Ocean Bay Park) and a few times in 1939-1941, and again in 1948-1951 for Ocean Beach.

Some of the early crew of the ferry to Fair Harbor were: Gus's nephew, Fred Pagels, who was on the payroll most of the time from 1937 through February 28, 1941 and returned again in 1946, with his last pay in 1947, W. Ryan, Whinny, Solan Tolson, Collins, Morris Johnson, Fred Abrams, Kenneth Baldwin, Ken Lee, J. McElvee, Lawrence Balwin, Aldwin, Gordon Rider, K. Bihler, Walter Chaskel, Tom Brown (my brother-in-law), Fabe Saxes, Ed Gangloff, Cliff Weis, Bruce Burns, and Clyde Oakley, who first shows up on the payroll in June of 1939, then went into the military service in June of 1942 and returned in March of 1946. Clyde continued to work for Gus until 1972 when Gus sold the ferry line to Fire Island Ferries, and FIFI did not hire any of the crew from the old Fair Harbor ferry. Clyde Oakley was the only year-round crew that Gus had at that time. For the first ten years in the Fair Harbor ferry business, Gus kept his pay records in his ledger without much more than the person's name and the amount he was paid. By the 1940s, captains were paid $35 a week, deckhands rarely showed up in the ledger, but when they did, they were paid about $3.50 to $5 a week. By 1946, captains were up to $60 a week, and gasoline was 15¢ a gallon and by 1948, 19¢ a gallon.

In November 1940, Gus entered into a contract with Thompson Construction Corporation of Albany, New York for the charter of the **Running Wild** and **Cherry Grove** to transport workers from Greenport, near the east end of Long Island, to Plum Island and Great Gull Island. Thompson Construction had a War Department contract from December 1940 to March 1941 for the construction of gun emplacements at Fort Terry (Plum Island) and Fort Michie (Great Gull Island). The captains were Clyde Oakley and Fred Pagels. The charter rates per day with captains were $25 one boat, $45 two boats. The boats were back in Bay Shore by May of 1941. In February 1942, new gas engines were installed in the **Running Wild** by Brewster's Shipyard for $664.86. In 1942, there were 8,750 round-trip passengers to Fair Harbor.

The Fair Harbor census of October 1947 listed eighty-one houses. Logbooks of the late 1940s indicate the largest one-way trip out of Fair Harbor on a Sunday or holiday was about 150 passengers. By the mid 1950s, a large trip off the beach on a Sunday afternoon hit 233 passengers; all three of his boats were used on that trip. In 1955, they carried a total of 31,000 passengers with the *Atlantic*, *Cherry Grove*, and *Running Wild* making a total of 528 round-trips. There were 398 round-trips to Fair Harbor in 1945. Only one letter of complaint from the homeowners association was found, asking him not to carry freight and passengers together on the passenger boats (since Gus did not have a freight boat or barge, many times he loaded freight on the *Atlantic*, leaving little room for passengers). The grocery store had its own freight boat; Ernest Grassnick had the *Souvenir* and later Eddie Lipinski had the *Chesapeake*, which he bought from Patterson.

Gus's books start to show income from the Fire Island State Park run in 1944 of $5,625 and in 1945, $4,433. The *Running Wild* and *Cherry Grove* loaded at Maple Avenue dock in Bay Shore and ran to the park by way of the Babylon Channel or Wig Inlet. In Gus's contracts with the state from 1947-1953, service was from June 15 through Labor Day with at least one trip daily, fares were $1 round-trip, children half price and under five free, no charge for state employees on duty or business, and no fee due from Gus to the state. The contract was renewed yearly without a change until 1953 when adult fares became $1.25, children 60¢, and required insurance coverage went from $10,000 and $20,000 to $20,000 and $50,000. In 1954, when the bridge to Captree was completed, the state park ferry from Babylon moved to Captree Boat Basin, and Gus gave up the Bay Shore to Fire Island State Park run. Clyde Best was the Babylon to Fire Island State Park operator, and his son-in-law Ed Gangloff, who had worked for Gus in 1947, later took over the operation. It was a short run and became a four-boat operation. Gus reported his 1948 assets as thirty lots and two cottages in Fair Harbor, two lots in San Carlos, California, 90' x 1,000' of bay bottom at Cherry Grove, vessels *Cherry Grove*, *Running Wild*, and *Atlantic.*

Gus had his own ferry basin and freight house built at Fair Harbor during the winter of 1954 and the spring of 1955; prior to this, he used the town dock. Ivar G. Olsen did the dock building at a cost of $14 a foot for bulkheading 242 feet, twelve pilings at $12 each, and nine tie poles at $5 each. The 32' x 80' basin cost $3,673.

Gus had the Fair Harbor mail contract until 1957 when he somehow lost it to Patterson. There were logbook entries in Gus's boats of Patterson's crew unloading mail and carrying it over Gus's docked boats to get to the Fair Harbor post office.

In 1953, Gus started to look at an air/sea rescue boat after seeing how well the *Islander* worked out. Papers show that Gus bought two 63' ASRs without engines at Norfolk Naval Shipyard, Portsmouth, Virginia. In December 1956, Clyde Oakley towed them to Bay Shore with the *Cherry Grove*. The first ASR became *Isle of Fire*, rebuilt as a ferry at Freeport Point Shipyard by the Scopinich family. Two new GM 6-110 diesels with hydraulic 1-to-1 gears were installed, and the *Isle* entered service in the spring of 1958. (I found an invoice dated October 22, 1957 signed by Mirtos Scopinich for $11,669 and a past-due letter on November 10, 1958 of $4,169.64.) The *Isle* was a great ferry for her cost and provided service to Fire Island for thirty-two years. She was sold in 1990 and was still in use (not as a passenger boat) near New York City in 1999. The second hull that Gus bought was sold to Zee Line, Inc., but the work required to pass USCG inspection was too extensive; it was sold to Al Olsen, who, by pre-arrangement, re-sold it to Patterson. The hull was painted bright red and was decked over into a barge, badly needed at that time to carry building materials to the beach.

Richard Taubler was the naval architect of the *Isle*, *Isle II*, *Zeelion*, *Zee Whiz* as well as the ferry *Captain Patterson*. The *Isle II* was also a converted ASR with her pilothouse mid-ship raised high enough for the operator to see over the passengers seated and standing forward. It was not a good arrangement, unpopular with the crew and passengers. She had three 6-71 GM diesels, which was not enough power to maintain speed when carrying a large number of passengers. The bottom was distorted under the engines. She was sold by Fire Island Ferries to Fred Sherman, owner of Davis Park Ferry, about two years after FIFI bought her as part of the Gus Pagels purchase. They made good use of the boat by winning the bid to Watch Hill from Patchogue, part of the Fire Island National Seashore (someone else wanted the run, but did not have a USCG-inspected vessel). The *Isle II* was later sold to Sayville Ferry for the Sunken Forest run; they later sold her to Jack McCormack for use on the Finger Lakes in upstate New York. (Jack bought the *Seaviewer* from FIFI for use on the Finger Lakes a few years before buying the *Isle II*.) After getting to the lakes, she did not pass the local USCG inspection, and the *Isle II* was decommissioned.

Gus was getting on in age and took his son-in-law, Homer Baumgarten, into business with him. They made an effort in 1959 to buy waterfront property between Ocean Avenue and South Clinton Avenue for their own ferry terminal that was now sheltered by the new Bay Shore Marina, built in 1958. From the few letters I found, no one would sell or lease property to them.

Homer did a poor job of running the operation, buying things they didn't need, not sending out bills, etc. Gus's daughter, his only child, divorced Homer. Gus, his wife, and his daughter had controlling stock and removed Homer from the business, which by then was in financial difficulty. By the spring of 1972, Gus was in his mid-70s, had things under control and offered the business for sale. Fire Island Ferries made a written offer with a price, decent down payment, interest, and ten-year payment schedule. The offer would be withdrawn if not acted on by October 31, 1972, the last day of our fiscal year. This would give Fire Island Ferries the winter season to upgrade the Fair Harbor operation. Three weeks before the offer was to expire, Gus came to my office to inquire as to what we had decided to do. After explaining to him to take our offer as it was or the offer would not be there after October 31, he said he had two better offers. I told him to pick the best one of the two since I was not going to match them. Gus went on to explain that the other parties had no money to put down. I know he was concerned about a down payment after the way his son-in-law had run the business, and a new owner could take all of the summer income, not pay bills, not maintain the boats, and leave Gus to take back the business and try to recover again at his advanced age.

A few days later, Gus's wife, Gertrude, brought Gus to our office, and she said, "I understand you boys made an offer to buy the assets of Cherry Grove Ferry." They agreed to accept our offer, and the deal was quickly done. We paid the down payment to Gus and made ten years of payments to Gus's daughter, who had remarried and lived in Maine.

Gus had retired the old ferry *Atlantic* a few years before we closed the deal. When they hauled her out on the marine railway at Brewster's for USCG inspection, a plank dropped off the bottom. The inspector wanted to see the frames, which weren't accessible from the inside. It was reported that she had a hull built out over her original hull; this was possible as she was also reported to have been a steam side-wheeler. If that was true, then when they made her into a gas engine, screw propeller driven, they extended the hull out to the guards or the area that contained and protected the side paddlewheels.

FIFI bought the *Running Wild*, *Isle of Fire*, *Isle of Fire II*, and the *Cherry Grove*. We never used the *Cherry Grove* and within a few days after the closing, we sold her to Barry Barton of Sayville. Barry converted her into a freight boat for service to Cherry Grove and the Pines.

Gus's deal included the ferry basin and freight house at Fair Harbor, but nothing in Bay Shore. Gus always used Maple Avenue dock for ferry service and tied up the boats in the canal behind his house on Maple Avenue when the boats weren't in service. We moved the ferry operation to the Main Terminal with its parking lot, rest rooms, sheltered waiting area, ferry office, and, at the time, Porky's restaurant. A few people complained about the move, thinking the Main Terminal would be too crowded. We moved the Kismet run down to Maple Avenue so we could combine Kismet with Saltaire during the week and back up each run when needed on weekends. With the Fair Harbor ferry at the Main Terminal, we combined weekday and some weekend trips with the Dunewood run.

I heard criticism that we had paid too much for four old boats, but we weren't as interested in the boats as we were in the Fair Harbor dock and freight house. On weekends, one large ferry now takes the place of the *Running Wild, Isle*, and *Isle II*, and on weekdays Dunewood is added as a second stop. Off-season Fair Harbor freight is combined with other stops on the *Vagabond* or

America, and during the summer, perishables are loaded at Maple Avenue dock on the 10 A.M. Atlantique ferry, leaving Maple Avenue in time to make the trip from the end of the marina directly to Atlantique and then over to Fair Harbor.

There were about 300 houses in Fair Harbor in 1983, and now there are around 400. Fire Island Ferries transported the garbage from Fair Harbor to Bay Shore on the *Turtle* from 1981 to 1985.

DUNEWOOD

Dunewood was the last community developed before the Fire Island National Seashore Act of 1964 prohibited further development on Fire Island. Murray Barbash, the developer and builder, had a canal dredged into a docking area in the shallows east of Fair Harbor in 1958, building fifty houses over the next four years. The second phase of fifty houses was built from 1962 through 1964. Fire Island Ferries had the dock built and transported all the building materials for the houses. The first dock was only eight feet wide.

After unloading a load of cement block onto the dock by hand from the *Fire Island Maid* (we did not have a crane or fork lift at that time), Captain Lenehan expressed his concern to the foreman about the weight on the dock. He was told that the builder's crew would take the block off the dock right away, but something more pressing on the job site was done, and the work crew left on the passenger ferry before moving the block. That night, the dock collapsed. The next day the block had to be recovered from the shallow water under the dock and the dock repaired. Years later, the dock was widened to its present eighteen feet.

Dick Block and Billy Leyrer took over the ferry service to Dunewood during 1968 and 1969 under the corporate name Fair Harbor Ferry, hoping to buy out Gus and take over the Fair Harbor run. Gus never changed his corporate name and it was still Cherry Grove Ferry Corporation; it cost money to change corporation names. Block and Leyrer bought two old rumrunners, Zee Line's 59-passenger *Artemis*, which they renamed *South Bay Courier*, and Robinson's 85-passenger *Margaret*, which became *South Bay Challenger*. Because Dunewood is a family community, everyone who goes over for the weekend in the spring and fall leaves the beach around the same time on a Sunday afternoon, and the two passenger boats could not handle that traffic in two trips.

After their first spring, they bought a crew boat and had her converted into a ferry by a yard in the Morgan City, Louisiana area and named her *South Bay Master*. She made about the same speed as the other ferries when she was almost empty, but lost speed with over fifty passengers on board. She also had more draft and wake than the other ferries. They ran from what was called Ball Parking Field, operated by Bob Ball (owned by Morty Bushard) on the west side of Maple Avenue (just south of the Zee Line ferry terminal), the same dock that Robinson used for many years to service Ocean Beach. Dick and Billy had a tentative rent agreement that became much higher when they went to sign the lease, and they were stuck since they had no other dock from which to operate. They were unable to pay their bills and went out of business after two years. They sold the *Master* back down in the Gulf; a major hurricane had damaged many crew boats there, and she went right to work. Dick Block moved to Houma, Louisiana where he operates a marine industry book distribution business. Bill Leyrer went into the large tanker brokerage business and died in the 1988 Pan Am, Lockerbie, Scotland plane bombing.

Three or four years after they were out of business, a tax agent came to my office looking for the operators of Fair Harbor Ferry. I informed him that that was us (by then we had bought out Gus and we were operating to Fair Harbor). He asked about back taxes owed by Fair Harbor Ferry Inc. I told him he was looking for the Fair Harbor ferry company that went to Dunewood and that the Cherry Grove Ferry went to Fair Harbor during the tax years under investigation, and that we, Fire Island Ferries, now went to Dunewood and Fair Harbor. The agent thought I was pulling an Abbott & Costello "Who's on first" routine, and I had to prove to him that Fair Harbor Ferry Inc. went to Dunewood, Cherry Grove Ferry went to Fair Harbor, not Cherry Grove, and that we now went to Dunewood and Fair Harbor. I understand that Dick Block made good over the next few years on all the outstanding bills and taxes.

Fire Island Ferries resumed Dunewood service in 1970, combining it with Kismet from the Main Terminal. Many Dunewood people walk the short distance to or from their house to use the Fair Harbor boat since they have more trips per day.

FIFI had a written contract from 1961 to 1967 with Dunewood South Beach Development Corporation, owned by Murray Barbash. I do not know why Patterson and Barbash did not renew the contract, and FIFI was out of Dunewood at the end of 1967 until it resumed service in 1970.

ATLANTIQUE, TOWN OF ISLIP BEACH

Before the bridge to Fire Island existed, beach lovers from the Suffolk County area had to take a ferry to Fire Island State Park from Maple Avenue dock in Bay Shore or Babylon public dock or drive to Jones Beach. The car ride was long and traffic could be heavy on a hot Sunday. The boat ride was a pleasant and popular trip. Islip boat owners had few docks available to them at the beach, except the boat basin at Fire Island State Park, which was always full on summer weekends. In 1962, the town of Islip created the large Atlantique boat basin, bathhouse, snack shack, and lifeguard swimming area for Islip town residents. Ferry service to the Islip town dock at Atlantique started in 1962 by Gus Pagels for the town of Islip, from the new Bay Shore Marina.

The town of Islip was asking for bids, as follows: one year, plus three-year renewable, service to start June 9, 1962, town to keep all fares, adult round-trip $1, child under 15 for 50¢, depart from the east end of the new Bay Shore Marina, and service must be direct. Patterson bid $12,000 and lost to Gus Pagels. For the next bid (1965), Patterson let it be known that he was not going to bid on Atlantique again and was going to run the *Queen* to Jones Beach. (We lowered the pilothouse one foot on the *Queen* to pass under the bridges around Jones Beach Theater without having to wait for them to be raised.) Patterson fooled everyone when he put in a bid and won a three-year contract.

Beginning in 1965, the town was to pay $21,500 a year to FIFI, and the town kept all fares. The contract also called for four round-trips per day and five on Sunday, the total combined capacity of all boats to be not less than 600, a passenger number which Gus Pagels found hard to fill. Later contracts had the ferry pay the town a fee, but the ferry operator collected and kept the fares. On a nice day, traffic often exceeded 600 passengers at Atlantique to return to Bay Shore in two trips, at 3:30 P.M. and 5:30 P.M., requiring a backup boat for the *Queen*. We always had to have a boat ready to back up the 10 A.M. to Atlantique until the Robert Moses Bridge and parking fields were finished being constructed. Then traffic fell off, and after the late 1960s, we never had to back up a trip. Most of the passengers were middle school children, too young to work, too old to stay around the house during summer vacation; Atlantique was the place to hang out with others their own age. At the peak of popularity, the *Queen* ran most of the service, with backup and lighter trips by the *Flyer*, *Belle*, (first) *Bird*, (first) *Ball*, or *Roamer*. On May 24, 1977, Town of Islip Supervisor Peter Cohalan wrote FIFI a letter of permission to take freight to Atlantique.

Atlantique, the small community just to the east of the new basin, was founded by Carlton Brewster and Dr. George King in 1912, and now has about fifty houses.

Atlantique community has no ferry dock of its own since it's too small to support a ferry. The homeowners petitioned the town of Islip for more service to the town dock at Atlantique. The town then requested Fire Island Ferries to provide additional trips from our Main Terminal to Atlantique town beach, but not as part of the contract. A scheduled trip leaves from the Main Terminal and stops at the marina to pick up the scheduled beach trip, and on the way back stops at the marina and then the Main Terminal. On Friday evenings, Saturdays, and Sundays, Atlantique service is combined with Dunewood from our Main Terminal. It's not too far to walk from Dunewood or Fair Harbor to Atlantique.

LONELYVILLE

Lonelyville is a small community of about fifty houses and a dock for homeowners' private boats. Lonelyville started as a fishing village in the 1880s, established by the Fire Island Fishing Company, which had a long pier out into the ocean. One of the founders was Captain Selah Clock of the **Blue Nose** schooner, winner of the Lipton Cup race. The other founder was the famous local Dr. George King.

ROBINS REST

Robins Rest is a small community of about forty houses started by the Robins family in 1925. It has a bay front restaurant with its own dock. The community uses the Ocean Beach, Atlantique, and Dunewood ferry. The new restaurant owner started his own ferry service in 2002 with a small, fast, shallow draft boat.

FIRE ISLAND SUMMER CLUB

The Summer Club consists of two streets, bay to ocean, adjacent to and west of Corneille Estates (just west of Ocean Beach) and uses the Ocean Beach ferry. The main clubhouse building is the old Coast Guard Station from Lone Hill, Fire Island. The community has their own water system, sidewalks, and bay and ocean swimming. Some of the members who formed the club and built their houses on club property were originally homeowners in Ocean Beach. Together with the Corneille Estates, the Fire Island Summer Club consists of about ninety-five homes.

CORNEILLE ESTATES

Corneille Estates is a narrow strip of land, bay to ocean, on the west side of the last walk in Ocean Beach, and its residents use the Ocean Beach ferry. The Fire Island School, built in 1954, is in Corneille Estates.

Ocean Beach ferry basin (1948)   Shirley Patterson Collection

It's been reported that there was only one house in Ocean Beach in 1905. The main east-west channel was close to the bay front where only short docks needed to be built, an advantage other communities, except Kismet, didn't have. Zee Line built the ferry dock out into the bay at Ocean Bay Park, which needs to be dredged almost every year.

John Wilbur of Ocean Beach Improvement Company began selling lots in 1908. His motto was "Ocean Beach, where health and happiness go hand in hand." Mr. Wilbur sold all 1,000 lots within five years, mostly to Brooklynites, who were lured to Ocean Beach with a free sail across Great South Bay. The community boasted that it was free of hay fever, and at that time it was since the only plant life was beach grass, and many homeowners burned it to discourage insects. Most of the vegetation now growing was brought over on the freight boat to be planted in Ocean Beach. In 1914, the main portion of the Olympic Club at the end of Saxon Avenue in Bay Shore was barged to Ocean Beach and was added to the Ocean Beach Hotel. The village was incorporated in 1921, joining Wilbur's development with a smaller area to the west called Stay-A-While.

Ocean Beach had the first sewer system on Long Island east of Jamaica, Queens, and also had an incinerator. In the 1920s, the wooden boardwalks were changed to cement walks. In the 1930s, a water system was added to the village, LILCO (now LIPA) brought electric to the island in the late 1930s, and in the 1940s was the onset of telephone service, which replaced the popular telegraph office that was at the site of the present police station.

Captain Azariah Robinson was awarded an exclusive franchise for ferry service to Ocean Beach in 1927. During the course of renewal of this franchise, the village and Robinson were unsuccessful in having the owner of the private ferry terminal repair and enlarge the basin to meet the needs of the public. Robinson complained of private craft entering the basin and interfering with the safe operation of ferryboats. On one occasion, the ferry *Ocean Beach* rammed and sank an expensive yacht. The story was that the ferry captain and engineer weren't getting along. When the captain signaled the engineer by ship's telegraph for full astern (or reverse) after entering the boat basin, wanting the ferry to slow to a stop with a spring line at her normal unloading spot, the engineer gave him full ahead instead of full astern. The yacht they hit was tied up at the freight dock and was cut in half; luckily, no one was on the yacht.

The village bought the ferry basin from John Wilbur on October 16, 1937 for $10,000. They bonded the purchase and $8,000 for improvements, and in December 1937 signed a lease with Robinson for $2,000 a year rent. On October 25, 1937, the Suffolk County Board of Supervisors voted in favor of a resolution to authorize the village of Ocean Beach, New York "to issue its bonds in the amount of $18,000 for ferry terminal purposes." The purpose of the bond money was to purchase for $10,000 from Ocean Beach-Fire Island Company the existing ferry terminal, and to improve, enlarge, and repair the same. The bond was to be repaid in ten years. Prior to the issuance of the bond, it was approved by the voters of the village. The action was recorded by the clerk of Suffolk County on January 21, 1938. In 1945, they issued a bond for $47,000 for another basin improvement, waiting room, and freight house. The Bono ran to the end of Robinson's franchise, April 30, 1948.

Ocean Beach now has about 550 houses, 14 restaurants with bars, 2 hardware stores, 2 grocery stores, a bake shop, 3 ice cream shops, a few boutiques, a movie theater, a deli, pizza shop, its own police force, courtroom, jail, fire department, and automatic telephone switchboard building for the entire island. There are no cars or auto taxies, just sidewalks and wagons since everything is within walking distance to the ferry, downtown, and the beach.

After the Fire Island National Seashore was established in 1964, beach taxies were not allowed on the oceanfront, eliminating the popular way to travel between beach towns. Fire Island Ferries filled the void by running lateral service (Suffolk County lateral ferry license was signed in 1966) to the towns between Kismet and Fire Island Pines. Using a ferry on this service required going halfway across the bay to avoid the shallows after passing Point O'Woods to get to the Grove and the Pines, adding considerable time to the trip. There had always been water taxi service doing cross-bay trips at odd hours when the ferries weren't running. These smaller shallow draft boats entered the lateral trade, making the trip much faster, and the ferries cut back to a reduced schedule, only serving towns between Kismet and Ocean Bay Park.

After World War II, Ocean Beach had growing problems with too many bars attracting younger people from the mainland and other communities looking for a good time, while the homeowners wanted a quiet family downtown. Many homeowners rented their houses to families for a month or two, and others rented them out to a group of unrelated persons, who were willing and able to pay a higher rent.

Fire Island is attractive to New York City dwellers who don't own a car. They take a subway to Penn Station, a one-hour train ride to Bay Shore, and finally a half-hour ferry ride. Then, no more traffic, just walk to your home with your luggage and whatever else in a little red wagon, and it's just a short walk to the beach, stores, and restaurants.

If you watch the Saturday 9 A.M. trip to Ocean Beach, you will see some passengers wearing white shirts, jackets and ties, carrying a briefcase, looking very much out of place. They are going to the small courthouse to represent their ticketed clients, in most cases, they lose their case and pay a $50 to $250 fine for breaking village ordinances, or the rules of "NO." The present Mayor and board of trustees are business friendly and you can now eat ice cream on the walk outside the store, you can ride a bike outside the business district before dark, and there is a new sign at the ferry terminal: "Welcome to Ocean Beach."

The first Fire Island school opened in Ocean Beach in a rented store front building owned by George Stretch, Sr., and ten students attended. Later, a one-room schoolhouse was built in 1924 in Ocean Beach. The present brick school was built on the west side of the last walk of Ocean Beach in 1955. All the building material was taken over by FIFI on a small scow and freight boats, with just about everything loaded and unloaded by hand and delivered to the job by two Model A Fords and one Model B Ford. At the same time the school was being built, we transported and delivered material for twenty-six houses under construction between Ocean Bay Park and the Summer Club. Zee Line also delivered material for about twelve houses during this period.

Prior to 1958, Fire Island School District paid to have about twenty students above eighth grade live on the mainland with room and board, and attend Bay Shore or Islip schools. Beginning the school year of 1958, Captain Patterson was awarded a three-year contract to transport about twenty-seven high school students at 7:30 A.M. from Ocean Beach to Bay Shore by ferry, where they were picked up by a school bus and taken to local schools, returning to the dock for a 3:30 P.M. boat back to Ocean Beach. When the bay froze, the boat ran between the Coast Guard Station and Captree. A second contact was awarded in 1961 to June of 1964, the year the Fire Island Bridge opened, and the children were then bused off with four-wheel drive vans.

The beachfront lost sand in 1952 and 1953, and when it built back up a little in the summer of 1954, the village scraped the new sand off the beach and used it to build up the dunes. After the bridge and parking fields were built at Robert Moses State Park, the day crowd going to the beach at Ocean Beach dropped to almost nothing. Why pay for parking and a ferry when you could go to the beach by car and not worry about a schedule?

The 1976 village board was composed of homeowners, who did not want off-islanders or day-trippers using their beach, walks, water, police, etc. They even referred to the restaurants as "their restaurants." To try to cut back on these people, the "Land of No" signs were put up in Bay Shore as well as at the Ocean Beach dock. Laws were passed to prevent groups of unrelated persons from renting a house in order to maintain peace and quiet.

They also made FIFI cut back its schedule. Beginning in July, we could not have a boat land in Ocean Beach between noon and 1 P.M. on Saturday. We would have so many people on the Bay Shore dock by 12:15 P.M. that we loaded a boat and went slowly across the bay, not landing until 1 P.M., followed by another boat as the slow boat pulled out. We also had to discontinue the 12:15 A.M. Sunday run and have no trip leave after 11 P.M. Saturday. Some people walked through Seaview and took the Ocean Bay Park ferry that left later, some took a water taxi, and others just hung around on the walks after the bars closed at 4 A.M. and came off on the first boat out of Ocean Beach, a sorry looking group of young people. In 1991, Ocean Beach required a beach bathing permit to use the beach area by the lifeguards. In 1993, the board became pro-business, and they strongly requested that we add a 1 A.M. Sunday trip out of Ocean Beach. We added the trip, and on holiday weekends use three boats on that trip. It is profitable, but it's a difficult situation; the trip requires extra manpower, equipment, and security as well as lower limits on the number of passengers on each boat for crowd control.

After the village incinerator was shut down in 1976, FIFI began to bring the Ocean Beach garbage to Bay Shore. In 1976-1977, a contractor tore down and took away the old sewer plant and incinerator to make room for a new sewer plant, which was needed to meet the latest water quality standards of water discharged into the bay. We contracted to transport the material. The job was so big that we bought a very old, 100-foot wooden barge (someone said she had once been a steam dredge). The barge worked well, taking the large crane and other construction equipment over. We

25

tied her up at the bay front at the east walk in Ocean Beach for the contractor to load the broken up old incinerator and sewer plant, and we would tow her to Bay Shore.

We gave them careful instructions not to overload the barge and have her aground. When we arrivedto tow the barge to Bay Shore, I told them the barge was overloaded and to remove some of the load. The jobsite boss said the barge didn't go down that much and didn't see a problem; the barge could not go down because she was on the bottom, and we could not pull her off. They unloaded enough from the end near the shore that was in shallow water and with great effort, we pulled her off and started west way to Bay Shore. With this extra heavy load of broken concrete, steel, bricks, etc., some of the dry planks were now well underwater and leaking. A portable diesel pump was kept running and had no trouble staying ahead of the water leaking in.

After passing buoy number eight, only about a mile and a half off Bay Shore, the barge sank. It wasn't that deep where she sank. She was only a few feet underwater at the aft end, and the forward end had a sealed tank that kept that part above water. We had to mark the barge for the night, and the Coast Guard set a wreck buoy nearby.

We hired a local dive company to determine why she had sunk (they were no use at all, but sent a big bill). Before we could pump out the barge and raise her, we had to unload and clear the deck enough to seal it with a large sheet of plastic. Ronback Marine, which did all our dock building at that time, used a crane and bucket to remove the material and load it into roll-off containers on the *Turtle*.

The fair weather helped, and when we cleared and sealed the deck, Ronback used all the pumps they had and all of our pumps as well. At low tide with all the pumps running, the water level inside the barge started to go down, and the barge began to rise (the end with the tank was always floating and gave us a place from which to work). As the pumps slowed down a little and suctions had to be cleared, the tide started to rise, and the barge began to take in more water than we were pumping out. We could see it would take a bigger pump rather than several small pumps. Ronback rented a four-thousand-gallon-a-minute de-watering pump. With the pump running wide open with its governor control by-passed, the barge came up off the bottom. A search for the leak found nothing, and back in Bay Shore, a more careful look also found nothing.

We used the barge a few more times on this job with much less weight, and one last time to bring the large crane and all the other construction equipment back to Bay Shore. We now no longer had a use for this oversize barge. While we tried to get rid of her, we let her sink on the east side of the Saltaire dock in Bay Shore where we could always pump it out with our own pump. With the help of some Captree fishermen and the New York Department of Environmental Conservation, we towed the barge to a deep hole inside the sore thumb along Oak Beach and sank her for a fish reef in 1979.

SEAVIEW

In the early 1900s, Gilbert G. Smith had a fish factory at "A" Street in Seaview that was supplied by his fleet of bunker menhaden boats. They would land the fish on the beach and bring them overland to the factory for processing. The factory closed in 1907. He also had a fish factory just east of Point O'Woods. In 1907, Seaview lots were being sold by Gil Smith with a deed restriction banning fish factories (you could never sell a lot for a residence anywhere near a fish factory since the smell was so overwhelming). The lots were gradually sold, and now there are about 340 houses in the community. The first map of Seaview streets was made in 1918. Ed Davis's family built the fifth house in Seaview in 1921.

Seaview ferry basin (circa 1990)   Luke Kaufman photo

Seaview is on the east side of and shares the last walk in Ocean Beach. Many of its residents use the Ocean Beach ferry service, and they all use the Ocean Beach business district since Seaview only has a grocery and liquor store operated by the third generation of the Wes Little family.

Dick Woodhull, the one-room schoolteacher at Ocean Beach, was also a real estate broker in Seaview. He strongly advised me to buy vacant, unimproved lots in Seaview about 1953 before walks and utilities were installed, but not having money, I declined. He urged me to borrow the money since the lots would increase in value, but I didn't. The lots were quickly sold and built on as the building boom took off (and the value did increase quickly).

The average beach cottages and most of Seaview's growth came during the 1950s and early 1960s. Walter Wiesman owned a large portion of Seaview during that time, including the house on the west side of the entrance to the Seaview Basin.

Luke Kaufman gave me this picture of the VAGABOND on her way out of Seaview with a load of passengers on the upper deck. The upper deck was later removed. (circa 1938)

27

In 1934, a ferry named *Fire Island* sailed from Babylon to Seaview. From 1936 until 1942, Captain Elmer Patterson used the ex-rumrunners *Vagabond* and *Artemis* as the Seaview ferries. They both had two Liberty aircraft gas engines converted to marine use, and they would speed by Captain Robinson's slower Ocean Beach ferries. Passengers in a hurry would walk over from Ocean Beach and take a fast Seaview ferry. In 1938, Patterson hired Gus Pagels to help him out for a few trips.

Tonis "Snyde" Zegel was granted the right from Gil Smith to run ferry service to Seaview in 1942 when Patterson left to take a commission in the Navy during World War II. It has been reported that Patterson was in debt and Smith wanted to end the relationship. Zegel bought the boat basin in 1958 from Gil Smith, owner of Great South Beach Improvement Company, which had been formed in 1915. Zegel bought 22 acres of bay bottom off Ocean Bay Park in 1959. During the season from mid-May through late September, the ferry crew (usually the Zegel family) that made the last trip of the day to Seaview would stay overnight in the crew house on the dock between the two basins. They then made the early trip in the morning, arriving in time for passengers to catch waiting cabs and rush to the train station to catch the 7:22 A.M. to New York City. On Monday morning, an earlier trip left at 5:50 A.M., often called the "death boat" because the passengers looked dead that early in the morning from the long weekend, and if they missed the boat, they were dead, late for work. People also took this boat to beat the rush hour traffic. I believe we had more people commuting to work off the island in the 1950s and 1960s than we do now.

Seaview Ferry was also bringing loads of material on a wooden scow and the *Osceola*, all having to be loaded and unloaded by hand. In 1947, when Patterson was awarded the Ocean Beach contract, he still owned the *Vagabond*. He replaced the gas engines with 6-71 diesels, removed the upper deck seats, and changed the name to *Fire Island Miss*.

When the Zegel family, Robert (Bob), Elwood (Pep), Snyder (Brud), and Fred sold the ferry basin to Fire Island Ferries in 1984, they put the Seaview pleasure boat basin up for sale as a separate property, but FIFI was not interested in owning or operating it. The Zegels offered to sell it to the Seaview Association, but they turned down the offer as being too high and said that no one else would pay the price. They were wrong.

Lee Pokoik of Ocean Beach, well known for his legal actions with the village, paid the asking price. Seaview Association brought unsuccessful legal action to stop the sale. Then Mr. Pokoik would not rent slips to Seaview residents and only rented slips to boat owners from the mainland. The association tried to prevent overnight living on the boats. They tried to get the federal government to buy the basin and lease it back to the association. They tried to get the Suffolk County Health Department to shut down the dock house used by the dockmaster. They wrote a threatening letter to the owners of the dock house (that was me) stating it had to be rented to the association for their lifeguards.

Mr. Pokoik loved his battles with them, and nineteen years later still has ownership and control of the basin. It has been reported that Seaview Association spent as much fighting Mr. Pokoik as the original asking price of the basin.

OCEAN BAY PARK

A subdivision survey map of 1909 by Eugene R. Smith shows all the streets and lots laid out as they are today. In 1920, a development company built twenty houses, but went broke. The main east-west channel runs about 400 feet out from the bay front as it passes the Park (as it is commonly called), then turns north at Point O'Woods, and the bay front is shallow from there east. It's been

Ocean Bay Park dock (1983)   Luke Kaufman photo

reported that during Prohibition, liquor was transported from the Park oceanfront to the bay by horse and wagon to waiting boats at the bay front.

Tonis Zegel (born in West Sayville in 1893 and died at the age of 86) began ferry service in 1928 or 1929 from Maple Avenue Dock and moved to 108 Maple Avenue, an eighty-foot lot he bought in 1942, where they built a shop with used lumber. John A. Flynn and sons renovated a bay front community clubhouse, "Casino," into a bar and restaurant in 1937. In November 1938, the Flynns bought underwater property in front of Lots 82 and 83, 1,000 feet out into the bay and 120 feet wide, from Fire Island Holding Corporation (which was formed in 1909 and who were the developers of the Park). In 1930, Fire Island Holding Corporation, consisting of Gleason and Dolan, built the Ocean Bay Park dock at the end of Cayuga Street on land they purchased from Long Island Oyster Farms, Inc. Today the third generation of Flynns runs the restaurant and boat basin.

The Park was a popular playground for Broadway stars before World War II. Anyone with a county license and a boat could rent the dock from the Flynns and operate a ferry from the Park to the mainland, and it appears both Patterson and Zegel did, Patterson with two ex-rumrunners *Vagabond* and *Artemis* (both were also used on the Seaview run). After the war, Patterson tried to resume service to the Park, but had to give it up to take care of his 1948 Ocean Beach contract that he had trouble handling and had to hire extra boats on Sunday afternoons.

New sidewalks and utilities were added in the 1950s and 1960s, increasing the need for more ferries. To the slow, one deck, single screw *Osceola* followed the *Artemis*, *Margaret*, *Seaviewer*, *Zeeliner*, *Zee Whiz*, and *Zeelion*. Zee Line bought twenty-two acres of bay bottom off the Ocean Bay Park bay front from Gilbert P. Smith, Great South Beach Improvement Company in May 1959. They did this to prevent other docks from being built into the bay and the owners from claiming ferry wake damage. Also, the purchase gave Zee Line bay bottom on which to later build their own ferry terminal at the Park.

The Zegels used Flynn's dock until 1964 when they built their own dock and terminal, the present Park ferry terminal. The story told by the Zegel brothers is that after attending a meeting with the five Flynn brothers, who had made demands for free freight and all their help riding free, the Zegels quietly began to acquire bay front property: two lots from Patterson and five lots from Elizabeth Gardiner (who owned Lots 51 through 55). The first the Flynns knew about Zee Line Ferry moving off their dock was when they saw the new dock under construction. I believe the Zegels would have built the new dock even if demands were not made because it's hard to run to someone else's dock.

29

The Park terminal was built just before the Fire Island National Seashore was created. Shortly after the Ocean Bay Park terminal was bought by Fire Island Ferries, four of the five upland lots were sold to the town of Brookhaven as a park district, with one lot kept by Fire Island Terminal as a right-of-way to the bay side walk. It took four years to be paid by Brookhaven town for the land and, in hindsight, the sale was a bad business move since the property was the last available commercial-zoned bay front property on the island.

Five of Captain Snyder Zegel's sons started to work on their father's ferries at a very young age, handling freight, baggage, painting, parking cars, selling and collecting tickets, working on engines, and so on. As soon as they were tall enough to stand at the ship's wheel and see over the bow, they were running the boats under the supervision of a licensed captain, and as soon as they turned eighteen, they took and passed the test to became captains. They worked seven days a week when not in school and began to make business decisions with no ownership in sight. They had a meeting with their father regarding ownership, and the boys formed Zee Line Inc., with Fred as President, Bob and Pep as Vice Presidents, and Brud as Secretary and Treasurer (the oldest brother had moved to Florida). As they expanded with new boats, they needed more docks and parking on Maple Avenue, Bay Shore. They bought four or five houses north of their terminal and moved the houses to the beach and sold them, clearing the empty lots into parking fields. Each time they bought a house, they believed they paid too much for it, but after a few years, they knew they'd gotten a bargain. They bought the last one December 1976 from Cliff and Belle Weis, the lot just south of the Point O'Woods Bay Shore ferry terminal.

Pat and Snyde were bitter rivals over Pat's loss of the Seaview run, and they competed for every fare (it's only a short walk between Seaview and Ocean Beach). Pat lived in Ocean Beach from May through September, and as captain made the last evening trip to the beach and the first one off in the morning, the same as Snyde did from Seaview. They both left the beach at the same time in the morning, and Pat would wait for Snyde to pull out of Seaview and chase after him with the *Belle.* He didn't care how fast he had to run the engines, he just had to race and beat Snyde. Most of the time he tried to get the shorter inside of the turn, even if he had to go into very shallow water, and at times the center prop was turning sand.

Except for the short time Pat had gasoline engines in the *Islander*, we had posters on the docks and ferries pointing out the dangers of fires or explosions of gasoline-powered boats. Zee Line replaced the 6-cylinder Hall Scott gas engines in the *Artemis* and *Margaret* with military surplus 6-71 diesels. During the early 1960s, Pat and Snyde did not speak to each other, but Pat did speak to Bob and Pep Zegel, and they made a deal to allow Richard Taubler, the naval architect, to redraw and use the bottom lines and plans of the *Belle* to build the *Zee Whiz* and later the *Zeelion* in Freeport Point Shipyard by the Scopinich family. The *Whiz* went into service in 1964 with three late model Detroit 6-110 diesels. She had seating for over 200 passengers, but the USCG rules would not let them carry over 150 passengers. She was made of wood and only metal boats would be certified for over 150. Two years later, in 1966, they built the *Zeelion,* using two early model Detroit 12v71N diesels that were new, but did not have cooling of the liner below the intake ports. They bought the engines at a good price, but they had a short life between overhauls. Years later, Fire Island Ferries replaced the block with updated ones with cooling below the intake ports. Because the USCG regulations limited the wooden boats to 150 passengers, Zee Line Inc. decided to build the *Zeelion* for passengers and freight. She has two decks forward of the engine room and one deck over the engines and aft with seats that are taken ashore during the week to allow for freight runs, and the seats are replaced on Friday, after her freight run, for weekend passenger service. The new ferries allowed them to sell the *Osceola, Artemis, Margaret*, and the barge.

In late April 1980, Zee Line, the Seaview, Ocean Bay Park ferry, applied for a 75¢ fare increase with the renewal of their county cross-bay license. They had gone three years without an increase that they said was needed to put money aside to build a new ferry. When the County Transportation Committee offered them only 50¢, they walked out of the hearing and suspended service the next day (since they no longer had a license) and didn't run for two weeks. Now it was May and the season was about to begin; May 15 always seems to be the turning point for warmer weather and an increase in ridership. The residents, some of who had spoken against the fare increase, now put pressure on the county to approve the increase. The county quickly passed the 75¢ increase, renewed their license, and service resumed. Zee Line never built another boat and sold the business four years later.

POINT O'WOODS

1908 postcard from Jen Kahler, mailed to Arthur Kahler, Islip

Point O'Woods community bought a piece of bay bottom sometime before 1939 that is now their boat basin and bay bottom on the west side of their main dock. Point O'Woods owns the first lot on the bay front west of their dock in Ocean Bay Park, which may have been purchased in 1939.

Point O'Woods began in 1894 as the Protestant self-improvement "Chautauqua Assembly." Frequent lecturers were senators, congressmen, actors, scholars, famous tour speakers, plus animal acts, concerts, musicians, exhibits, etc. It's been reported that 150 boats arrived on the Fourth of July, 1894. At that time, the Long Island Railroad round-trip ride from New York City with a transfer at Babylon to Point O'Woods was $2, and from Sayville it was $2.30. Just to the east of Point O'Woods is Oakleyville, where Gil Smith had his fish factory in 1898.

A few businessmen purchased the side-wheeler steamer *Connetquot* from William K. Vanderbilt for $4,500 in 1895 for service from Sayville to Point O'Woods, a run of about five miles.

ROW AND TOW. Point O' Woods ferry is shown being hauled at Rogers Shipyard, Ocean ave., Bay Shore. Background scene dates photo in the early 1900s. Aboard are Marshall and Albert V. Rogers, Jr. In the rowboat are Albert V. Rogers and Edward Crawson, Sr. Photo loaned by Sue Sabiston.

Picture from unknown newspaper (circa 1907)

In 1897, they had two ferries, the *Nancy Lee* and *Connetquot*. The *Connetquot* broke down mid-summer and was replaced by the ferry *Bay Shore* that also went to the Surf Hotel. Chautauqua failed to sustain itself financially, and the Point O'Woods Association was formed as a club and took over the area. In 1899, the association needed ferry service that it could control and depend on, and they set up Bay Point Navigation Corporation. The corporation has owned and operated their own ferries for over 100 years. Some vessels included the *Mosquito*, *Grace Shaffer*, *Bay Shore*, *Point O'Woods I, II, III, IV, V, VI and VII.* One of its founders was Captain Karl Kahler, first of the many Kahlers to work for Point O'Woods.

The association built the yacht club 1899, the Inn in 1900, and the large oceanfront club in 1910. No alcohol was served at the club or the Inn. Membership to the association is open only to families with children and includes strict requirements that limit membership. You don't own your home; you lease it from the association for ninety-nine years. A new house can only be built in the community when they lose a house to fire or storm. Over the years, northeast storms and hurricanes have taken beachfront homes, and other homes were moved back behind the dunes to save them. Three houses burned to the ground after a hurricane.

These storms also damaged the oceanfront club, first taking the dunes and deck out front in 1953. Each new storm took more sand and did a little more damage. The association decided to tear down the club due to its age and location, now almost on the beach. Fire Island Ferries got the contract, and with Russ Rielly and our garbage contractor "Get Rid of It," we completed the job in about two weeks. Rielly knocked down the club with an excavator and drove back and forth over it with a bulldozer until it was crushed to splinters. The material was then taken to the basin and loaded onto a large barge borrowed from Bob Conway. Steel sides were welded on the deck to hold the material. Five barge loads were towed to the Bay Shore west terminal where it was unloaded into a waiting row of 30-yard roll-off containers. The removal took a total of 36 container loads.

I have been told that most of the lumber used to build Point O'Woods was brought over on the steamboat *Turtle*. The date of her construction is right for this. I had heard from a few people of a large painting in a Sayville bank of the *Turtle* with a load of lumber on her deck. She had a smokestack and stern wheel.

WEST FIRE ISLAND

In 1900, a steam dredge pumped sand onto West Fire Island from the main channel and around to the east side of the island to make a channel and filled in the low areas of the island with the dredged material. A large hotel and streets were planned and water mains were laid. It was reported that a few boats ran service, but the project failed. Who would live on West Island in the bay when you could have both the bay and the ocean at Fire Island? The stock market crash of 1929 also ended the needed development funds and buyers. It's been told that the Weis family ran service to West Island before 1929, and they may have run there after that time. Snyde Zegel ran the *Osceola* to West Island before 1928 when he also ran to Ocean Bay Park.

THE MAINLAND

Bay Shore

Point O'Woods and Saltaire ferries loading at Maple Avenue dock (circa 1915)

In the 1800s, Maple Avenue was the location of Doxsee Clam and the Clock's oyster business. Wealthy Brooklyn and New York City people discovered the fishing and sailing in Great South Bay around 1840, and the south shore of Long Island became the place to spend the summer, away from the heat and smells of a large city with its many horses. Bay Shore, Sayville, and Babylon became summer resort communities with hotels and summer cottages. In the summer, you could always depend on a strong southwest breeze by mid-morning coming in off the cool ocean. There were only a few roads down to the docks and bay at that time at Babylon, Bay Shore, Sayville, and Patchogue.

A Long Island Railroad schedule of 1897 states: "For Fire Island, stages connect at Bay Shore for steamers to Fire Island with trains leaving Long Island City at 8:30 A.M. and 11:00 A.M. and 4:30 P.M. daily except Sunday while the Fire Island Hotel is open, until about September 1st." It also states: "For Point O'Woods, stages connect at Bay Shore for steamers to Point O'Woods until about September 1st."

J. Adolph Mollenhauer sold property at the end of Maple Avenue in Bay Shore to the town of Islip in 1903. Later, the state deeded some bay bottom to the town to extend the dock for use by ferries and commercial fishing boats. A 1930 map from Bart Ackerson Real Estate of the dock area has the old Maple Avenue dock plus the proposed drawing of the 225-foot addition as it is now.

The rumrunner *Maureen,* built in 1929 at Freeport Point Shipyard, was seized during Prohibition at Maple Avenue dock with 500 cases of liquor on board.

With the opening of the Southern State Parkway extension in 1949 to Bay Shore, you could easily drive from New York City without all the stoplights that made for a long trip on Sunrise Highway. The parkway helped to make Fire Island more accessible.

The United States Army Corps of Engineers issued Public Notice 29 on September, 1958 to dredge and build the Bay Shore Marina. Doug Brewster, owner of the Ocean Avenue shipyard, and Herman Hammer of Gibson and Cushman Dredging Company, located at the end of Homan Avenue, pushed for this project. The marina opened in 1959.

After the marina was completed, Gus Pagels and his son-in-law tried to buy bay front property, which became protected by the marina, for a ferry terminal. No one would sell so they continued to operate off Maple Avenue dock.

Zee Line, the Zegel family's operation, worked from the west side of 104 Maple Avenue at the present dock by the west terminal building. They slowly moved north as they bought the adjacent houses and moved them to the beach, buying the last one from Cliff Weis in 1965.

Penataquit Shipyard, Inc, organized in 1976 by Ed Mooney and Frank Mina, bought a 60-ton Acme rubber tire boat lift to service our ferries.

Assembling 60-ton Acme boat lift (1976)   Ed Mooney Collection

Purchasing it was a good move that was quickly copied by Sayville and Patchogue ferries as well as by Charlie Hart of West Sayville for his machine shop and boatyard operation. The new ferry terminal building was built in 1982.

Fire Island Terminal bought the Ball parking property in 1985 from Maple Avenue Waterfront, Inc. It was a mess after being damaged in Hurricane Gloria in 1985. The garages were falling down, junk was everywhere, there were sunken boats in the little basin, all the bulkheading was falling in, and the small slip was almost filled in with dirt and sand. The two-story house that Bob Ball had lived in was in bad shape, and when we started to repair the house, we found the lower part of the structure had been underwater so often that it was rotted beyond repair so we tore down the house. There was also an old steel building used as inside parking that we removed. We filled many 30-yard roll-off containers to clean up the place, and over the next ten years, we rebulkheaded the property.

Ball parking from ferry slip (1985)   Ed Mooney photo

Penataquit Shipyard bought 118 Maple Avenue, which was a restaurant building, from Ellie Corchran in April 1986. We leased it to Il Garafano as a restaurant in 1979. After a few years, the operator was so far behind in the rent that he was forced to close. The building was in poor condition, and the floor would go underwater in a hurricane or after a heavy rain when Maple Avenue flooded. In 1995, we tore down the building and added the property to the west terminal for parking. The south end of the west parking terminal was used in the clam and oyster industry from the late 1800s until around 1931. An old photo circa 1915 has the buildings in the background.

Penataquit Shipyard bought Bay Shore Marine Basin from Ken Carrode of Gibson and Cushman Dredging Company on December 29, 1986. At that time, it was a marina, a parking field in the summer, and dry boat storage in the winter, but one of its other uses was for storage of dredge equipment that took up much-needed parking and boat space. We cleaned up the place and removed buildings to increase parking and outdoor winter boat storage.

Ed Mooney bought out Frank Mina's stock in Fire Island Ferries, Fire Island Terminal, Penataquit Marine Construction, and Fire Island Cruises and as part of the transaction gave Mina the shipyard, ending their partnership on April 4, 1989.

Main Terminal of Fire Island Ferries

Main Terminal, Bay Shore (1990s)   Ed Mooney photo

When Fire Island Ferries began ferry service (May 1, 1948) to Ocean Beach from Maple Avenue dock, freight and lube oil barrels were stored in two garages in what was then next to, but part of Gil Clark's Clam Bar and Fresh Fish Market building. Gil Clark's was to become one of the most famous seafood restaurants on Long Island. These two garages later became the bar area of Gil Clark's, now Molly Malone's. By 1951, Gil had enlarged his fresh fish and dining area by converting three or four other garages that he had rented to year-round Fire Islanders. In 1952, Gil told Pat that he wanted the two garages that FIFI used. Also, the town was after Pat to remove the empty return bottles, beer barrels, bottled gas cylinders, and milk crates from Maple Avenue dock. The beach building boom was starting. The pressure was on Pat to get a terminal.

The *Fire Island Maid* loaded freight, unloaded returns, and tied up for the night at the west side of Maple Dock at the first dock nearest Gil Clark's. The *Belle* docked just ahead of the *Maid* and the (first) *Miss* ahead of the *Belle*.

As I look back at the whole picture of Patterson being awarded the Ocean Beach service contract and a few years later building the Main Terminal, I wonder when he first made plans to buy the terminal property.

November 1951, William White and Elmer Patterson made application to Islip town to rezone all the property lying south of a line 100 feet south of Aldrich Court for business purposes and to leave 100 feet north of this line Residential AA, as all of the property was at that time. The town planning board denied the change on December 31, 1951. Patterson and White acquired the terminal property from Spencer Wyman Corporation on February 28, 1952. Ward Ackerson handled the real estate transaction. The property was owned by Selah and Ellen Howell in 1885, Spencer Aldrich in 1889 along with an addition from Edward Landow in 1892. I had heard that Patterson had trouble raising the money to buy the property, so Spencer Wyman Corporation held one mortgage at 5% interest and White's cousin, Ethel L. Schuler, held another; both mortgages were repaid in September 1955. I have been told that more than a few people laughed at Pat for buying a swamp.

The zoning board held a public hearing on April 22, 1952. This time the town planning commission approved the application on May 27, 1952, based upon certain conditions. The conditions imposed were: Patterson and White record in the Suffolk County clerk's office a Declaration of Restrictive Covenants on the land north of the proposed parking field (100-foot-wide buffer zone) and ferry terminal along Aldrich Court, as follows: remain Residential AA; limit it for one-family private dwellings with a private family garage for not more than two pleasure cars; dwelling erected on plot with not less than 112.5 feet width fronting Shore Lane or Aldrich Court; not to disturb any natural growth until this property is sold for residential purposes; no buildings will be located along Maple Avenue; the ferry slips to be located on Penataquit Creek and the shoreline of the creek to be bulkheaded; the entrance/exit to be on Maple Avenue; the parking field to be fenced; if it becomes necessary, an exit-only into Shore Lane, not to be used as an entrance; and all improvements to be completed within 12 months. These covenants were signed on August 23, 1952.

On the rezoned portion, Captain Patterson cleared the trees, brush and other vegetation, had the local dredging company, Gibson and Cushman, dredge sand from the creek and slip area, and used it to fill in the property. They started dredging 24-hours a day, but nearby residents had the town make them shut down at night. After digging out the slip area, they just dug in one spot, east of the slips. In this way, they got only clean sand without old sunken boats, tree stumps, or thick, smelly bog and mud. The sand was then covered with fill or clean dirt, the first two piers and bulkheading were completed with a wooden deck ahead of the slips, they built an entrance/exit road and vehicle unloading area, which was tarred and covered with bluestone. The required fences were erected, signs, lights, railings, small parking office, and anything else needed to change a swamp and unimproved land into a ferry terminal. Bill White's cousin put up money to keep the terminal construction going and was a silent partner. Fire Island Terminal Inc. was incorporated on January 7, 1953.

The *Fire Island Belle* made the first landing into what is now Slip Number 5 on May 14, 1953, and the next weekend, the parking field was completely filled with vehicles. That weekend the weather was great on Friday and Saturday, but on Sunday it rained so hard that the parking field turned into a sea of mud. People had to walk through mud well over their shoe tops to get to their cars. Patterson had a tow truck pull out stuck autos, and he stayed right there and took all the abuse, but did not give refunds. Within a few weeks, the parking field was covered over with cinder or ash, the byproduct of coal, which was burned for electric power. Pat had the present shop built as a freight house and shop, and next to the shop he moved an old garage that became the first ferry office. There was also an office in the Ocean Beach freight house where the billing and other business was done. After the first summer, the small restaurant with rest rooms was built.

After two years in the new terminal, it was obvious that Pat needed the 100-foot buffer for parking, and he petitioned the town for a zone change to business of a 60-foot strip adjacent to and along the north side of the parking field, leaving a 40-foot. There were those who had foreseen the day when an attempt to grab off the remaining 100 feet would be made; they didn't have long to wait. Patterson badly needed that 100 feet because our parking area was filled, and we were turning away cars by Friday night or Saturday morning at the latest.

An answer to his petition addressed to the town board from all the residents of Maple Avenue, Aldrich Court, and Shore Lane by the Attorney for the Objectors, Joseph H. Flynn, dated October 11, 1956, stated: (1) The public welfare and convenience will not be served. (2) The neighboring property will be substantially and permanently injured. (3) The adjacent property is Residential A. (4) Land zoned business could have upon it, among other things, a penal institution, undertaking parlor, airport, cemetery, circus grounds, etc. (5) They want to prevent the encroachment of business into their neighborhood. (6) Patterson and White for Fire Island Terminal agreed in August, 1952 to leave this

100 foot wide property Residential A. Fire Island Terminal has violated the restrictive covenants on the parking field as follows: (a) Erected "A very unsightly row of garages in plain view of Maple Avenue." (b) "Erected a one and one half stories waiting room that towers like a barn over the surrounding area, which is brightly lighted by beer signs therein." (c) Put a 25-foot wide roadway out of the property into Shore Lane used by the public as both an entrance and exit. (d) The bulkhead on the easterly portion of the property has not been done. (e) Recently a bulldozer was grading in the Residential A zone. In 1955, Patterson graded a portion of Residential A as a staging area for taxicabs. (f) All the improvements were not completed in twelve months, the freight shed and office were completed in 1954, and the garages, which were never called for in the 1952 agreement, were built in the winter of 1955-1956. Mr. White and Mr. Patterson did not live up to a single covenant, except the first, the filing of them.   (7) When the application was made in 1952, there was a dire need for extra parking space for weekend Fire Islanders, and on this fact and Patterson's assurances that he would not encroach on the residential parts of Maple Avenue and Shore Lane, the town board granted the rezoning.

The Town of Islip Planning Board denied the rezoning of the 100-foot buffer on April 11, 1958. In August 1958, Fire Island Terminal made application to: give the town of Islip fifteen feet of the buffer zone, park cars on the remainder that had to be rezoned from Residential A to Business 3, FIT to install self-contained drainage, subject to approval of town engineer and superintendent of highways, erect and maintain a 6-foot stockade fence for the entire length, and plant evergreens three feet high every six feet. A vote was taken, and the application was unanimously passed on August 12, 1958.

In September 1958, a restraining order was filed in Riverhead Supreme Court to prevent the rezoning. The plaintiffs were Edward W. Antos, et al, Shore Lane, Maple Avenue, Aldrich Court residents. Their attorney was Joseph H. Flynn, who issued a summons against the town board, Patterson, White, and Fire Island Terminal. The attorney for the plaintiffs was Emmett F. McNamara. The defendants' attorney was George F. X. McInerney for the Town of Islip board, and Robbins, Wells, & Walser for Patterson and White and Fire Island Terminal.

The town and Patterson prevailed, and the parking field was enlarged to its present size. The town also had Patterson close down the exit out to Shore Lane and gave him room to install a sidewalk along the entrance/exit road.

Captain Patterson bought out all Bill White's interest in 1967. In 1974, Captain Patterson sold Fire Island Terminal Inc. (the main parking field and docks) to Fire Island Ferries Inc. (Ed Mooney, Frank Mina, and John Van Bree).

Babylon

Trolley from Babylon railroad station to steamboat dock (1871)   From Babylon Centennial Book

The South Side Railroad from Brooklyn and New York City went to Deer Park in 1843, and when the Surf Hotel opened in 1856, stagecoaches ran from Deer Park station to the Babylon steamboat dock. Sammis built a horse-drawn trolley line from the Babylon railroad station to the Babylon dock after the railroad extended its track there in 1867. (The trolley tracks were still visible in the road on Fire Island Avenue into the 1970s.) I read that steam from a steam house was loaded into tanks on the trolley allowing the trolley to run down to the dock and back; later it became an electric trolley.

Babylon steamboat dock (circa 1885)   From 1993 Babylon Village Directory

The Babylon dock was used by ferries to the Surf Hotel on Fire Island, Oak Beach, and to the Wawayanda Club, a popular sportsmen club on Captree Island.

Sometime around the 1940s, ferries ran from the Babylon town dock to Fire Island State Park until 1954 when they relocated and sailed from Captree when the first bridge was built. About 1898, Babylon had its first auto on the road. Guglielmo Marconi built a wireless station in Babylon in 1901, which sent and received Morse Code, the beginning of present-day radio.

Babylon dock (circa 1885)   From 1993 Babylon Village Directory

Patchogue

Patchogue was the deepwater port on the south shore of Long Island and in 1849 was much bigger than Mechanicsville, now Bay Shore. Patchogue had wool and cotton factories, paper mills and later, a lace factory and oil terminal. The railroad arrived there in 1869, and the federal government dredged the channel to ten feet in 1902. Some of the first large ferries were built and sailed to Fire Island from Patchogue.

UNPLANNED EVENTS

KEEP IN MIND AS YOU READ THE FOLLOWING THAT THESE EVENTS TOOK PLACE OVER A FIFTY-SIX YEAR PERIOD, MOSTLY WITH OLD EQUIPMENT AND LITTLE MONEY FOR REPLACEMENTS.

Fire on the (first) Fire Island Miss

The rumrunner converted into the Seaview ferry *Vagabond* by Captain Patterson in 1937 was renamed *Fire Island Miss* in 1948. She had a dry exhaust system that was too close to unprotected wood, which had dried out (the exhaust temperatures run 800°F; that's well above the temperature needed to ignite wood). The *Miss* came out of Ocean Beach on a hot Sunday late in the afternoon with a full load of seventy-five passengers. After passing West Island, in about the middle of the bay, a passenger, who was also an Ocean Beach fireman, reported to the captain that he could see a fire in the engine room through a small opening in the forward engine room bulkhead. The passengers were moved out of the area, and the captain raced to Bay Shore with black smoke and flames coming out of the exhaust stacks. The *Miss* had mufflers mid-ship on the cabin top, just forward of the engine room. The engine blowers pulled the air, smoke, and flames out of the enclosed engine room and blew it out the exhaust pipe, keeping the fire from getting enough oxygen to spread. Someone saw the smoke and called the Bay Shore fire department, and they arrived at Maple Avenue dock about the same time as the *Miss.* (This was before we had radios and before the marina was built.) The captain, a Bay Shore volunteer fireman, docked on the east side of Maple Avenue dock since it was closer than our terminal. The passengers got off quickly through the mid-ship exit, the pilothouse, and over the stern railing. No one was hurt, and the damage was repaired in a few days. Changes were made in the exhaust system to prevent a reoccurrence.

Small Fire on (first) Fire Island Miss

On a bitter cold day in the late 1950s or early 1960s with the bay frozen over and the school boat operating out of Captree to the Fire Island Coast Guard Station, Bill Madsen and I had to do repair work on the (first) *Fire Island Miss* over at Captree. The potbelly stove was at the forward end of the cabin, and we didn't get much heat aft to the engine room where we were working, so we opened the draft to make the stove hot. It was not long before the stove was glowing red in the low light of a dark winter late afternoon. Bill noticed some smoke outside. The canvas luggage cover had been pushed up against the stovepipe and was smoking and burning, but the snow on the canvas kept down the flames. We put out the fire with snow, and then disposed of the old cover that now had a few large holes in it; nothing else was burned. We were lucky that we were there and had not left for the night.

Fire Island Belle Hits Boat in Fog

Before radar was in common use, not many private boats went out in the bay in heavy fog. Sometimes fog rolled in around ten A.M. when a light offshore breeze ended, and the fog that was out in the ocean moved in. This would catch boats away from the dock that did not intend to be out in the fog. The *Belle* left Ocean Beach in thick fog and went east way, passing a Seaview boat also going at a reduced speed to Bay Shore. After the *Belle* passed buoy number three off Ocean Bay Park, she ran into a private boat, causing a small amount of damage. Besides the fog, improper crossing signals by the private boat added to or caused the accident. It was my day off so I did not know much about it other than what the crew told me the next day. As time went by, I thought we would hear more from the USCG, an attorney, or at least the boat owner, but nothing happened. Months later I found out why: There was a woman on board with the owner, who was not his wife.

Belle Broken Planks Entering Ocean

During the three-day northeaster of March 5-7, 1962, which slowly washed away the beach and oceanfront houses on each high tide, the *Belle* made all her three daily scheduled trips. The entrance to the ferry basin looked like the ocean, with waves going over the east and west sides of the entrance. It was too rough to lay on the west face, and we broke lines tying up on the north face. At times the tide was level with the top of the dock, the walks were all knee-deep with water, and it was cold. The first day of the storm, with seas running over the west side of the entrance and ice still inside the basin in the southwest corner, I went into the basin at a fair rate of speed to avoid being set down against the west side. As I was going in, a sea lifted the *Belle* and then dropped her down against an entrance riding pole. It felt like a pretty hard hit and on checking, we found two planks just above the water line were broken and one frame was cracked, but we were not taking in any water. On our return to Bay Shore, not a drop of water came in. I expected to get yelled at by Patterson when I told him what I had done. Instead, he told me you have to expect things like this to happen if you run in bad weather. We were able to use the boat during the rest of the storm before making repairs.

Belle Broken Exhaust Pipe

At one time the *Belle* had exhaust pipes made out of asbestos water pipe, the same pipe buried underground in city water systems. It took exhaust heat and water and was approved for use as wet exhaust. On a busy Saturday morning with a full load to Ocean Beach, the boat felt heavy as we neared the Ocean Beach basin and slowed down. After docking and unloading, I checked the stern section. We had water entering through the starboard engine exhaust pipe that had broken in half just aft of the engine room. By hanging on a rope tied between the stern bits, I plugged the pipe with rags and crumpled newspapers at its outlet at the transom. The starboard engine ran the bilge pump and now could not be run. With a borrowed pipe wrench, I piped the port engine fire pump into the bilge system and got underway to Bay Shore with the fire pump hose acting as the fire pump discharge.

The exhaust pipes were replaced with stainless steel. We thought they would last forever, but with years of use, they wear out on the bottom. We made them last a long time by rotating them a few degrees every few years. The stainless steel pipes were later replaced with Hetron resin fiberglass pipes that seem like they will last forever if you don't lose exhaust cooling water. The pipes fail and burn or melt if not cooled with water; a water flow alarm and high temperature alarm are in the water supply system to warn of lack of water flow with the exhaust.

Lost in Fog on Belle

One thick foggy morning going to Ocean Beach with the *Belle* on the "workmen" boat trip (always before 7:45 A.M.), I passed mid-channel buoy, clicked my stopwatch, ran my course and time of three and a half minutes, and didn't see buoy number eight. I could stop and circle around and try to find it, or I could go on my next course to buoy number seven, which I did. Thinking that I might have been to the west side of eight, I subtracted a degree from my course to number seven, but at the end of my time of one and a quarter minutes, I didn't find seven. I went on to the new course to five, ran the time out, nothing, click, click of the stopwatch, now on to the next course to then-number three. After about two minutes, on the northeast side of buoy number four that marked the channel to the east side of West Island, the stakes appeared dead ahead. I turned hard to starboard, passed number four on the deep water side, came back on my course to number three, and went on to Ocean Beach, arriving on time as if nothing had happened. I was lucky, the tide was high, and I saw the stakes before I ran into West Island. I think only my deckhand and I knew we were lost for half the trip!

Belle First Trip in Fog with Radar

The first use of radar by the ferries in Great South Bay started with Joe Pokorny at Cherry Grove Ferry. He mounted a radar dome on top of his office and had the display in his office by his marine radio. From there he watched and tracked his two ferries and directed them along their route. This worked well until the Federal Communications Commission (FCC) stopped them because it was against regulations. Joe put that set on one ferry and bought another set for the other ferry. In 1966, the size, price, and power requirements of radar became lower, and Patterson put a set on the *Belle* made by Canadian Marconi. It was one of the better sets available at that time, but required constant tuning and service.

Just after it was installed in early May, we had a thick fog on a Friday, and it got thicker as the day went on. By the time Zee Line made their afternoon trip off the beach, they decided it was too dense to continue to operate, plus it would soon be dark. Operating in the fog at night would be the same as having a blind captain; you cannot see beyond your bow. Zee Line sent their passengers over to travel to Ocean Beach on the *Belle.* We had two trips to make, both in the dark, but it was calm, and there would be no other traffic.

I was captain of the *Belle,* and Captain Roy Stoecker agreed to be the radar operator. We left with a good set of fog courses and a new radar. As we got close to a buoy, Roy would say, "You should see it now," and I would say, "I can't see it." He would not believe me, and he would look up from the radar hood that was needed on the old sets, but since he could not see it either, he put his head down again to the radar hood and directed me past the buoy.

When we slowed down off Ocean Beach, I needed help to find the entrance to the ferry basin. Again Roy said I should see it, and again he looked up, but then put his head down to the radar to help find the entrance. (The early radar sets did not have the close in scale that new sets now have.) The return trip to Bay Shore went fine, and we found the marina entrance. I told Roy that I needed a course up the creek, which again he could not believe that I could not see the nearby bulkhead. He looked up and put his head back down to the radar hood and directed me up the creek to the dock where we loaded up again for another trip. After making one trip in the fog at night, we had full confidence in the radar and now could sail in fog at night.

After learning how well we did that night, Zee Line quickly installed radar on their boats, and Patterson installed them on the rest of the fleet, except the *Maid* and *Turtle,* which only sailed during the day. In fact, Captain Tom Lenehan could sail the *Maid* to the beach with a bag over his head, and I don't ever remember Tom being lost in the fog. Tom also would make stops from Kismet to Point O'Woods with the difficult channels of Fair Harbor, Dunewood, and Atlantique.

For the long 1,900 mile ferry delivery trip from Patterson, Louisiana (100 miles west of New Orleans) to Bay Shore, when we picked up a ferry we had commissioned to be built, we installed Loran on the **Stranger, Voyager**, **Explorer**, and **Evening Star**. Loran could give a current accurate location and could be programmed in advance to give the course, distance, estimated time of arrival, speed made over the bottom as well as the distance off the intended track and the direction to steer to correct it. Loran is now being replaced by Global Positioning System (GPS), which uses satellite signals to do the same thing as Loran, but it's faster and more accurate. The GPS can be tied into the radar and circle the location of your next programmed buoy or dock on the radar screen

Belle Smoke from the Engine Room

POINT O'WOODS V, ZEE WHIZ, and police boat with BELLE (circa 1960s)   Luke Kaufman Collection

The three MWM German diesel engines in the **Belle** had dry exhaust manifolds. They ran hot, about 900°F, and were designed to deliver maximum heat energy to the turbocharger before the exhaust cooled. The manifolds did not stand up well and leaked after a few months of service. The new replacements were painted with a silver paint that burned off with a strong smell and smoke the first time they got hot, and after that they were fine.

On Wednesday, my day off, passengers were loaded onto the **Belle** after a manifold had been changed, but not run enough to burn off the paint. About halfway across the bay, Captain "Fireball" Fred had smoke coming out the engine room vents and thought he had an engine room fire. He called for assistance, and the Point O'Woods ferry changed course to come to his aid and took off his passengers. On opening the engine hatch, they only had a smoking exhaust manifold. When Fred got back to Bay Shore, Patterson chewed him out for calling for help without first determining what was burning or making smoke. I told Fred and all the other captains, "When you have smoke, the very first thing you must do is call for help. You can always call later and say everything is all right, but you can't call for assistance once a fire cuts off the power to your radio."

Belle Exhaust Hose Fire

When an engine is rebuilt, the ferry is taken out into the bay for a test run and to break in the piston rings and check for leaks. After rebuilding an engine in the **Belle** and taking her out in the bay on a winter day, the center engine alarm went off. The water temperature and oil pressure were fine so the mechanic went aft and checked to see if we had exhaust cooling water. He reported we had water coming out of the exhaust so the problem had to be that the alarm wire went to ground or the sending unit was on a hot spot on the exhaust pipe. When the mechanic checked again in a few minutes, he ran

43

back up to report that we had a fire aft over the center exhaust pipe. The center exhaust did not have water (he had originally looked at the wrong pipe), but the five-inch rubber exhaust hose was on fire as well as the wood seat over it. A CO_2 fire extinguisher stopped the fire, but didn't put out the smoldering wood so we had to use the fire pump and hose to get it out completely. While we were dead in the water with smoke pouring out of the boat, a clammer pulled alongside and asked if we needed help. The mechanic just replied, "No, we have everything under control," which was the same as saying that we do this often and it's okay.

Fire Island Queen Sinking at Captree

When passsenger traffic to Atlantique dropped below the level to require using the **Queen**, she became heavily engaged in all types of bay charters. Just about every charter trip had something unusual take place. One night, July 23, 1976, at the inlet side of the Captree Channel, the **Queen** turned at the buoy and ran aground and was stuck on a sand bar that comes out from shore to the buoy. In trying to get free, a plank was torn off the bottom in the port side propeller tunnel, and she started to take on water. The crew was not aware of the missing plank, and the aft compartment flooded, the stern went down, and the aft deck was just about water level while the bow was still aground.

I had just gone to bed when the phone woke me up. The first words I heard were "Emergency! Emergency! Emergency!" It was the captain of the last boat from the beach that had gotten the radio call that the **Queen** was aground and sinking. He received the call just before docking in Bay Shore. He was sent over to get the passengers off and bring them to Bay Shore while another ferry was made ready to take pumps and patching gear. All the passengers were safely in Bay Shore at about the time the sail would have ended. News of the grounding and sinking was on TV, radio, and in the morning newspaper. The only complaint I heard was from a woman in a wheelchair; she had trouble keeping her chair at the bar since it keep rolling aft, away from the bar that was at the forward end of the cabin.

Someone pointed out that the leak was in the middle of the engine room. The flooded seawater was at the top of the main engines, and they had been shut down, their black oil now on top of the water all over the engine room, the gen-set was underwater, and we were now on 32-volt backup lights. When I looked to where the water was boiling to the surface, I realized that the diesel bilge pump was still running underwater, its air intake was above water, and its large external flywheel was spinning water, making a disturbance that was mistaken for the leak.

By this time, after 1 A.M., we had a few pumps taking out water, but still did not know where it was coming in. The two forward void were dry, and I had the pumps concentrate on the engine room. I entered the engine room, water still to my waist, and the water was warm from the heat of the engines and black with oil. I shut down the bilge pump and as soon as the water was low enough in the engine room to drain the water out of the engine and refill it with oil, I cleaned the bilge strainer and started the pump. The steel bulkheads at each end of the engine room leaked water where they joined the sides of the hull, and where I could, I stopped the leaks with rags (the leaks were slowing down as the dry wood was now wet and swelling).

During this time, a deckhand mentioned that when he was looking for the leak, he noticed sand in the stern over the tunnel compartment. (It would have helped if he had told me this when I first arrived.) Now we knew where the water was coming in. Frank Mina brought his scuba gear with him and quickly located the area of the missing plank. It was about eight inches wide and four feet long. Frank had problems under the stern since it was only two feet off the bottom, giving him little room to put on a patch. The patch almost stopped the flooding and with one portable pump from the Coast

44

Guard, one great portable pump from the Saltaire fire department, one FIFI portable pump, plus the *Queen's* own bilge pump, the *Queen* was soon afloat.

The ferry that took the passengers to Bay Shore returned and towed the *Queen* to her dock, arriving before daybreak. We cleaned her up and had her looking like nothing had happened when the news media peopled showed up, after they had first gone to Captree looking for this sunken ferry. They had no story since all the passengers were safely home, the *Queen* was at her dock all clean and clear of the pumps and hoses, and no visible pumps were running (we did have a small, quiet pump in the boat to stay ahead of the small amount of water getting past the patch). Shortly after the media people left, our maintenance crew changed the oil, removed the starters, alternators, batteries, and washed everything with lots of fresh water, and had the engine room ready to operate again. Bill Brewster from the shipyard, who had been called and came out to the *Queen* during the night, hauled the boat a day later, and his yard installed a new plank, getting the *Queen* back in service in just a few days.

The *Queen* had run aground when the buoy at the entrance to the channel remained in its old location, well after a sand bar had built out from shore. The buoy was quickly moved to deeper water by the USCG, and they admitted it was in the wrong location.

Queen Aground

Another time the *Queen* ran aground was coming back with a charter from the lighthouse area at night with a deckhand at the wheel who was not used to coming from that far west. He turned towards Bay Shore after passing the second black buoy, like he would do when coming out of Kismet. He failed to go past the third black buoy and ran aground on Farm Shoal with an outgoing tide. The *Queen* was hard aground and called for help. She was too far into the shoal to get to her with a ferry, and the passengers were removed a few at a time with a Boston Whaler to a nearby ferry waiting in deeper water. This time the only thing hurt was the captain's pride and reputation because even though he was not at the helm, he bore responsibility for the safe navigation of the vessel. The *Queen* was pulled off after the passengers were unloaded, and the tide started to come in.

Queen Out of Fuel

All too often we would hear the dreaded call, "*Queen* to base," or if the phone rang during the night, you knew the *Queen* had a problem. Just after going to sleep, the phone rang one warm, calm summer night with the words, "The *Queen* is at anchor in the middle of the bay out of fuel." Like a fireman, I always had my work clothes ready to go, and I lived only five minutes from the dock where I always had my toolbox waiting. The late passenger boat had just pulled in from their last trip, and they had loaded my tools, extra fuel, and a long tow line, and they were ready to go when I drove in. Everything was on the *Patterson*, which was the wrong boat to tow with because of the difficult location to handle the towline. I told the *Patterson* crew to tow the *Queen* to the dock while I went on board, but not to set up until the *Queen's* anchor was pulled up and out of the way.

The *Queen's* crew said they had checked only one tank, and it was empty. After quickly finding the other tank full, I turned it on and turned off the empty tank, I checked the fuel filters on the main engines, and they were empty. I filled them all and then checked for a plugged fuel line from the tanks. Fuel flowed freely out of the fuel line to the engine so I tried both engines, which started and ran fine.

45

While getting the engines and generator restarted, I was told the **Patterson** had run over the **Queen's** anchor line and managed to get it into all of her three props, stalling all three engines. The **Queen** was now running, but her anchor line went off her bow under the **Patterson** to her props. From there it went to the anchor that was still embedded in the bottom (the line was underwater so we couldn't get to it). We pulled in enough anchor line to get the **Patterson** alongside the **Queen**, and then we headed for Bay Shore. After running hard, the anchor line broke at the **Patterson's** props, and we towed her to Bay Shore. While on our way, the Coast Guard called to ask who was towing who (after the **Queen's** call to the **Patterson** on Channel 16, the Coast Guard switched over to our working frequency, Channel 80, and listened in). Again, we were lucky, no wind, no one hurt, and no bad press. The **Queen** was back at the dock as if nothing had happened, but we did haul the **Patterson** and had to cut off the **Queen's** anchor line on all three props and shafts.

What made the engines run out of fuel with one full tank and a good flow of fuel out of the full tanks? It's always hard to get the true story, but if you interview everyone involved, someone always adds the key to the unplanned event. A new crew member was sent to the engine room to turn off the diesel bilge pump that had been running for a few minutes to take some water out of a compartment. He did not know how to turn off the pump engine; instead he turned off the main fuel valve, a ball valve that only needs a quarter turn and it's off. When the pump did not stop, he realized he had turned the wrong valve and then turned off the pump. He turned the fuel valve back on, but not before the main engines ran out of the fuel in the filters and stopped before getting fuel from the main tank again (that's why the filters were dry, but the main valve was on). If someone had told me this at any time before they got ready to tow, all I would have had to do was prime the filters and bleed the air out of the injector lines!

Queen Bent Rudder

Traveling along in the dark Captree Channel at night, the **Queen** went on the wrong side of the narrow channel and ran the bow aground. There was a very strong current that turned the boat, and when they backed off, her stern ran aground on the other side of the channel, bending the large center rudder. They had a difficult, but manageable time getting back to Bay Shore. Again, we hauled the boat, dropped the rudder, made the repair, and got her back in service.

Queen at Atlantique

Again, the radio call we hated to hear, "**Queen** to base." This time the captain was in a panic, stating he'd lost control after backing away from the Atlantique dock and run into some boats and broken a few mooring poles. The panic call made it sound like he might have sunk a boat. We loaded a pump and toolbox on a ferry and hurried to Atlantique, expecting to see damaged boats. The **Queen** was back at the Atlantique ferry dock undamaged. On entering the basin, we could see nothing wrong except two broken poles. When I went over to the one boat that had been hit, there was no damage; only the two stern cleats were pulled off, and a police officer was writing a report. He stated that no one was on board at the time of the incident, and I could get a copy of the report the next day.

The ferry that took me to Atlantique took the passengers that were to go on the **Queen** to Bay Shore and again I asked what had taken place and why. The captain thought his upper air-operated reverse gear control unit was leaking air because he heard air hissing from it on the trip to Atlantique. He took apart the unit to see if he could correct the leak, but he re-assembled it improperly, and the gear stayed in forward even when he moved the control handle to reverse. He gave it more throttle, thinking he was in reverse, and the **Queen** moved ahead faster to the east side of the marina, breaking a pole. The captain admitted he panicked; he did have reverse on one engine, but gave power to the engine in forward again and hit the boat even harder the second time. I re-assembled the control properly, and a few minutes later, we were on our way back to Bay Shore. The small air leak was in the engine room, but the air to make up the lost air was supplied through the upper control head, and that was the hissing he heard.

Queen Broken Steering Cable

The **Queen** used muscle power to turn the rudders to steer, using a large ship's wheel to get the leverage. In the aft steering compartment, a cable broke that wound on a drum that pulled the rudder quadrant. Since a USCG requirement called for a backup for steering failure, the **Queen** had an emergency tiller mounted inside the stern bulwarks. The tiller would be dropped over the top of the large center rudder stock that was covered by a deck plate, and we would steer the **Queen** like we would a sail boat with a tiller; move the tiller to port, and the bow would turn to starboard, move it to starboard, and the bow went to port.

The cable broke while the **Queen** was docking at the marina, and the captain decided to return to his dock at the Main Terminal and change boats. On the way up the creek to her dock, a deckhand was sent aft to man the tiller. At the same time, the captain was steering with the engines while the other two deckhands passed the word down to the deckhand on the tiller with directions to steer. I was on the **Belle** going past the **Queen** in the creek on my way to the beach and noticed that the captain had both engines almost wide open, trying to steer with the engines. When I looked on the stern, the deckhand at the tiller had his feet up against the bulwarks and was pushing with all his strength, in the wrong direction. When the word was sent down to go to port, he moved the tiller to port.

I turned the **Belle** around and over the sound of the **Queen's** engines had to get his attention to move the tiller the other way. As soon as he moved the tiller to mid-ship, the **Queen's** engines were put at idle, and they proceeded up the creek as if nothing was wrong. A new cable was quickly installed, and back in service she went.

It's interesting that when I first worked on the ferries, "<left rudder   right rudder>" was painted in two-inch letters above the forward-facing pilothouse windows. This was a Coast Guard requirement, a carryover needed when some early steam vessels' helms were turned the way they were on old sailing vessels.

Queen Breaks Cable at Brewster's Railway

QUEEN on Brewster's railway (circa 1978)   Ed Mooney photo

The displacement or actual weight of the *Queen* was well over 125 tons, a sizable vessel to drag out of the water onto dry land, which was done at Brewster's Shipyard on Ocean Avenue in Bay Shore. This was the most difficult boat they hauled because of her weight and her length and had to be done at least once a year for dry-dock inspection.

Marine railways are fairly steep. As the *Queen* started forward up out of the water, much of her weight would be on the forward marine railway car and put a great stain on the *Queen's* keel and hull. The rest of the cars didn't take any load until the boat was well up out of the water. Before hauling the *Queen*, the yard always installed new cable if the one in use was not in perfect condition. They also had to add another block in the cable pulling system to get the extra power or leverage, which meant double the pulling power at half the speed. All boats tied up across the creek were moved out of the way in case the cable broke, lines were in place from the *Queen's* bow down to the ground, and all water was pumped out of the *Queen* to make her as light as possible. Bill Brewster engaged the gear and started the haul-out. More than halfway up, the cable broke, and the *Queen* slid back down into the water. Fortunately, the water took away most of the speed, and the bowlines prevented her from hitting the bulkhead on the far side of the creek.

The yard continued to haul the *Queen* for a few more years for her annual dry dock, and then about 1972, they decided their railway was too old and weak to haul her any more. Bill Brewster made arrangements and sent blocking instructions to Muller Boat Works in Brooklyn, and that's where we had her hauled until 1989 when, in the process of hauling, the aft set of block gave way, and the *Queen* slid aft and fell over on the starboard chine blocks that were not yet in place. When Muller hauled a vessel, he wanted most of the weight to go on all the blocks soon after the boat started forward, which meant the stern railway car had to have blocking five or six feet high. These blocks were stacked, nailed, and braced in place. When the *Queen* fell, she was only part way out of the water and now could only go one way, which was back into the water, and the blocking reset. The problem now was that the damage to the starboard planks at the turn of the bilge had to be made watertight, and they were in the water. Doug Zegel and Jimmy Muller went into the cold water and made temporary repairs. The boat was then hauled and a careful inspection was made. The keel was distorted aft of the engine room, many of the frames were damaged and soft from age, plus there were a few broken planks.

It was decided that the seventy-year-old *Queen* would no longer pass a USCG dry dock inspection without major work on her frames and planks. Muller's yard in Brooklyn repaired the planks and made her watertight again, and she returned to Bay Shore under her own power. She was up for sale, but now at a lower price without a dry dock certificate.

Seaview Boat Aground

Before we had radar, sailing in thick fog was difficult, and sailing in thick fog at night was almost impossible so night trips would be canceled. But, of course, sometimes at night fog blew in while we were on a trip, and it was blind sailing; just slow down, trust our compass, stopwatch, and written courses. Fog courses were written and constantly checked every chance we had when it was calm, and when no boats were in our way on the course. All captains had their own stopwatch to record time between buoys on his compass course card. If done with great care, we could trust our compass and find each buoy on time. It helped to run our course to lighted buoys so we had a chance to find them in the dark. The schedule had few trips after dark, and if the fog was dense, with luck we would see the flash of a buoy if we were close enough. If we ran our engines at 1,000 rpm, we just doubled our normal running time between buoys. Time between buoys was written as part of our fog course at our normal speed, determined by our engine speed. A stopwatch was a navigation instrument needed to keep track of the (time) distance traveled. After our ferries had radios, we could talk to each other and slow down when close and could hear each other's foghorn and talk our way past each other.

On a busy spring Friday evening, fog blew in just after sunset as we got to the beach. We were now faced with a trip back to Bay Shore in the dark and fog. A Seaview ferry decided to go back west way (west way has more lighted buoys, and there is less distance from buoy to buoy). While I was underway to Bay Shore, I heard the Seaview boat call its base and report that it was aground. When base asked where they were aground, the captain replied, "If I knew where I was, I wouldn't be here!" As it sometimes happens with late evening fog, as the temperature changes, the fog lightens up a little. The captain could see he was east of East Island, and he was able to work his way to the channel. Before radar, it was the captain's skill against the fog, currents, and breeze; the fog won more times then I like to admit. All of Great South Bay bottom is sand or mud, and has more shallow areas then deep areas so we never damage the bottom of the boat - only the props and our pride.

Fire Island Maid Aground off Fair Harbor in Winter

Many trips have been made in the fog, heavy rainstorms, snow, ice, and dark nights. Another grounding I remember was the *Maid* on a bitter cold late December evening, with temperatures in the teens, the tide as low as it ever gets, the wind blowing out of the northwest, the sun about to set, and one of the most experienced skippers in the bay, Harold Garrett, at the wheel. We got stuck in the shallow water coming out of Fair Harbor, which was not a regular stop for us at that time. This was about 1950, before we had radios, so we were lucky that Carl Larson, a year-round bay front resident of Fair Harbor, saw that the *Maid* was not moving and rowed out in a small rowboat to see if we needed help. The wind was holding us on the shoal and preventing us from getting into deeper water. Carl rowed us one at a time to shore, and we stayed overnight at his house. It was so cold that crewman Joe McCue (a retired New York City policeman) had frostbitten fingers. The wind dropped out a little during the night and with a better tide, we got off the next morning.

Hole in Maid Caused by Ice When Leaving Bay Shore

During the building boom on Fire Island and before the bridge was built, the wooden *Fire Island Maid* made every effort to get to the beach in ice with much-needed supplies. Often she was loaded deep in the water. For winter service in ice, oak sheathing was fastened to the bottom and well above the loaded waterline. The oak was then covered with copper sheathing (so we could go through ice without damage to the planking and cotton chalking (without the cotton chalking, the boat sinks). At the bow, covering the stem and at the point where the boat breaks the ice, hanging by chains, was a 55-gallon barrel with the top and bottom removed, then cut down the side and folded to the shape of the bow. It worked well and protected the first few pieces of copper from folding back.

With heavy ice in the bay, the *Maid* left Bay Shore loaded with lumber for Saltaire and Dunewood. Just outside of Bay Shore, while passing through broken ice, the boat felt like she had hit a brick wall.

The bay ice is frozen salt water, which freezes below 28°F. Freshwater ice, which is clearer and bluer but hard as a rock, is what we hit leaving Bay Shore. We did not slow down and continued on. Halfway across the bay, we cleared out of the ice, and we were sailing along when Captain Dave Farrell thought the boat seemed down by the bow. To check the forepeak, we had to move the hot potbelly stove off the hatch. Dave was the first one down into the forepeak and found a foot and a half of water. By this time, we were past East Island and on our way to Saltaire. Dave had to cut away ceiling (inside planking to give a vessel added strength) to get to the hole and stuff it with pieces of a blanket. With the leak under control, we unloaded lumber at Saltaire and pumped out the rest of the water with a larger portable fire pump from the Saltaire Fire Department. The hole was now above water, and the bay ice was thin or broken with many open areas. With the extra pump on board, we went on to Dunewood, where we had to break heavy ice, and then unloaded the boat so we could go right to the shipyard, get a new plank, and start hauling again.

That was not the first time we had a hole in the *Maid* in the ice. There was no copper on the stern, just an extra oak plank, and when backing up into ice, the ice broke a hole in the stern, and the *Maid* started to take on a little water. By moving some of the load forward, the hole was above the water. When they got back to Bay Shore to haul out, both railways at Brewster's had boats that could not be put in the water since they had planks off. Barrels of fuel that had to go to the beach were filled and placed forward, getting the *Maid's* stern up out of the water, and the plank was repaired from a float. After years of working in ice, the copper had been damaged and patched to the point where it had to come off and planks caulked behind it. The clam dredges had replaced their copper with a white plastic called Kydex PVC, and that's what we put on the *Maid* (it worked better than copper).

Firebird Aground off Atlantique

It is extremely rare to have thick fog and a strong wind, but the (first) *Firebird* ran aground off Atlantique on a windy, foggy day with a very low tide. We had sailed over this area many times so the tide had to be very low, but the *Firebird* did draw ten inches more than the other boats. The shoal area was relatively small, and the captain was able to work his way off to deeper water.

Fireball Runs Aground Out of Kismet

The tide runs pretty fast past Kismet and Saltaire, and in heavy fog, traveling slowly and stopping when you hear another vessel ahead, you can get off course and drift with the tide, and when you resume course, it's a guess as to what the tide did to you. Before we had radar, the (first) *Fireball* came out of Kismet in fog as thick as it ever gets and had to go very slowly past anchored Captree fishing boats. When she came up on her course, she was on the wrong side of Farm Shoals, and she ran hard aground. The fog lightened up after a while, and the captain could see the buoy, but he was on the wrong side of it and had to go back the way he went in. When I got to Bay Shore from my return from Ocean Beach and reported the problem to Captain Patterson, he told me to fire the captain when he got back to Bay Shore. I informed Pat that he did not realize how thick the fog was at the beach, and that if he fired the captain, he would have to fire all of his captains since we all ran aground from time to time (and some still do even with radar). Pat quickly changed his mind.

Ball Aground on East Island and West Channel

There were other minor groundings in fog, and the *Belle, Flyer, Ball*, and *Queen* had many of them because they sailed most of the trips before we had radar. There were also clear weather groundings, some with full passenger loads on a Sunday afternoon with the captain trying to make a quick round-trip to get back for another load since we had long lines of passengers waiting at Ocean Beach.

Our ferries are semi-planing, riding somewhat on top of the water, not pushing through it like the *Queen, Maid*, and the older displacement boats. They gain speed and have less wake in shallow water, and captains can make better time by running in shallow water and taking shortcuts inside of buoys and running out of or alongside the channel. Some captains didn't always take into account the tide or added draft with a full load of passengers. Al Skinner once said "there's a lot of water in the bay, but it's spread out pretty thin."

The **Ball** came out of Ocean Beach with a full load, leaving many passengers behind; every boat was in a hurry to get back for another load. The captain went aground inside of buoy number eleven, the southeast end of East Island, badly bending the starboard prop and shaft, and ending the use of the boat for the rest of the day.

The following Sunday, again behind in getting people off the beach, the same captain on the **Ball** with a full load of passengers, trying to stay in shallow water, ran from buoy number one Dickinson Channel (not there now) to number seven. He was too far west at low tide and hit bottom, broke a strut off the bottom, bent the three props, and broke off the starboard rudder, which stuck through bottom planking. He proceeded to Bay Shore, unloaded the passengers, and told Patterson the **Ball** was shaking too badly to make another trip. We were so far behind at Ocean Beach that Patterson told him to get going back to the beach for another load of passengers. The captain actually went down the creek, but soon turned around and came back to the dock. He told Patterson she was shaking and could not make a trip; he was fired on the spot.

The next morning, Patterson told me to take the **Ball** to the shipyard to be hauled out. After backing out of the slip and putting an engine ahead, I called over to the dock to have the boat towed to the yard because the broken strut and prop were being whipped up against the bottom of the hull. Again, everything had to be repaired and back in service by late afternoon on Friday, which meant getting a strut, rudder, shaft, props, and a new plank over the rudder.

Roamer II Aground on East Island

A young, new captain running the **Roamer II** in fog ran aground near buoy number eleven, East Island. The grounding was not too bad since the props were in deep water and only the bow was aground. The captain put both engines in reverse, but not much happened. His deckhand told him that maybe it would work better if he shut off the center engine, which was direct drive without a clutch or gear and was still pushing him ahead. After shutting it down, they backed right off. (The captain told me the story himself; if he hadn't, his loyal deckhand would not have let on about what had taken place.)

Roamer II and Tow

Barge made from ASR (1958)   Ed Mooney photo

The ***Roamer II*** with the red 63-foot ASR barge set up as a side tow left Bay Shore for the beach. The barge was loaded with all types of building materials and a stack of plywood. Taking freight to the beach on a barge is always slow and weather-sensitive, requiring a greater skill level and care than on a freight boat. The ***Roamer*** was closed in with glass windows, making it difficult to handle the stern line to the barge. Before they had gone halfway across the bay, the wind picked up, and it got too rough to keep the barge alongside. The crew of the ***Roamer*** let go of the stern and spring lines, and they had the barge hanging off the bowline, keeping the ***Roamer*** stern into the wind. They called the office by radio and reported the problem and also stated the plywood was blowing off, one sheet at a time, they could not get on the barge and they could not tow with the wind and waves.

I was working on one of the ferries at Brewster's Shipyard and was told of the problem. The nearest boat was Brewster's ***Yardbird,*** which Bill Brewster said I could use. The ***Yardbird*** was only about three feet wide and sixteen feet long and had about twelve inches of freeboard mid-ship. She was a small tug with a gasoline engine, no pilothouse or shelter, with a steering tiller and throttle coming up out of the small deckhouse mid-ship that covered the engine. I put on my rain gear, and off I went, alone, deciding I could pick up crew from the ***Roamer***. The seas were big for the little ***Yardbird***, and she took on water over the bow. The engine started to sputter (the back end of the engine shelter was open), and the bilge water was splashing on the engine, getting the spark plugs wet. The boat had an inch and a half Jabsco pump with a long suction hose that was used to pump out other boats. I had to hang on and get the suction end of the hose from the bow deck and drop it into the engine room bilge and pull a lever to turn on the pump. Once the water was out, and no longer wetting the spark plugs, the engine ran fine. I had the ***Roamer'***s crew throw me the bowline that went to the barge, and I used it as a towline to tow the barge to Bay Shore.

Model A Ford into Ocean Beach Basin

Model A Ford, similar to the one off the MAID (circa 1950)   Luke Kaufman Collection

Before the Fire Island Bridge was built, all vehicles were taken to the beach on a barge or on the ***Maid***. Vehicles now go back to Bay Shore when they break down and can't be driven on the beach, but are loaded now on the ***Vagabond***. Bruce Kahler was to drive a Model A Ford, that did not have brakes, onto the ***Maid*** at the Ocean Beach ferry basin. A crew member was instructed to place a block in front of a tire when the vehicle was in place. The ***Maid's*** deck had an excessive amount of crown in the deck, like the back of a turtle. Bruce drove up one side of the crown, but the block was placed too late to stop him from going down the other side, knocking out the removable waist on the starboard side, and he ended up in the water with the Model A. Luckily for Bruce, there was no top on the Model A (the tops were always cut off to make the car into a flatbed truck), and he was easily able to get out of the car.

Until four-wheel drive became affordable, the Model A Ford was the most popular truck on the beach. The most desirable tires for them were bald and soft, taken from big cars. The tires were run with a minimum amount of air. A large air compressor was in the freight house to add air for heavy loads, and drivers were always taking air out when they had to go into soft sand; most of the time, they let air out of the tires after they were stuck.

Isle of Fire Shaft Log Tube Backs Out

Things seem to go wrong when you need a boat the most, especially when every boat is in service and running hard. On a busy Sunday afternoon, the *Isle* pulled into Bay Shore with a load of water in her bilge. A quick look discovered the starboard shaft tube (a threaded brass pipe) had unthreaded out of its shaft log. This can happen when the shaft packing is tightened, and the threads on the pipe and inside the shaft log are old and loose. After putting a sealer on the thread, threading it back in place, and installing a clamp on the pipe so it could not turn, the *Isle* was ready to hurry back into service, but the captain was reluctant to go after having water in the bilge, even though the boat was now dry. I had to show him that it was not leaking, and that he could not back out the tube even with a pipe wrench. It was safe, and he went back in service. In fact, it was a few years before we had to replace the tube.

False Reports of Grounding or Being Stuck off Atlantique in the Channel

When the eelgrass builds up in the bay and floats on the surface, there are times we can't move around it without getting it on the props, causing the boat to shake. It will stay on until we reverse the prop to wash it off. This means slowing down and backing on all engines, which can result in passengers reporting that we went aground. We also would get phone calls that a ferry was aground west of Ocean Beach because people weren't used to seeing a ferry stopped out in the bay.

In the 1950s and 1960s on a busy Sunday afternoon when the *Queen* was loading at Ocean Beach, other ferries had to stay out of sight or people would not get on the slow *Queen* and would wait for the faster backup boat that would get to Bay Shore ahead of the *Queen*. In good weather on a Sunday or holiday in the summer after 5 P.M., it was hard to get ahead of the long line of passengers waiting to return to Bay Shore. The big, 300-passenger *Queen* loaded first on the 5:30 P.M. run and was backed up by the *Belle*, *Flyer*, and whatever boat we could get, but generally we handled that trip. The next trip, 6:40 P.M., had to be handled without the *Queen* since she could not get back until 7:20 P.M. *The Belle*, *Flyer*, (first) *Fire Island Miss*, *XL*, *Saltaire III*, *Captain Joseph* (Captree fishing boat), and whatever boat Patterson could charter at that time of day tried to handle the trip, but often left some passengers on the dock, telling them we would have a boat there shortly. Often that would be the *Queen* at 7:20 P.M. or so, taking on a full load of passengers from the last trip plus people who were early for the 7:50 P.M. trip. (Most people waited without complaining.) As Patterson rebuilt and acquired more boats, we still had this problem. Ocean Beach and its surroundings continued to grow plus we now had Saltaire, Kismet, and Dunewood communities, and they were growing as well. A few of the other boats used as backup over the years were: *Running Wild*, a Davis Park ferry, a Point O'Woods ferry after his last trip of the day, and the *Islander* from Saltaire after his last trip.

Fire Island Flyer Hits Boat

On a busy Sunday afternoon (when else?), with every boat running as hard as they could, the *Flyer* was about five minutes behind the *Belle* in the west channel on a clear, sunny day with a strong southwest wind. I had the *Belle*, and about buoy number seven, I had to pass a slow moving boat, which was about twenty-four feet long, that had two kids sitting with their feet over the bow. The boat went to the east, then to the west, then to the east again. The operator was having trouble steering with a sea at his stern, and the weight of the kids on the bow had the bow lower in the water than the rudders. When a sea lifted his stern, whatever way the bow was facing at that time was the direction the boat went. I gave the boat lots of room when I passed and continued on to Bay Shore. I looked back a few minutes later and saw black exhaust smoke come from the *Flyer*. I was too far away to see what took place (this was before we had radios), but it appeared that the *Flyer* was under way again. A short while later, I found out that the *Flyer* had started to pass the wandering boat when it appeared it was going east and then it turned and went west. The *Flyer* had to go wide open in reverse and just made contact with the boat. No damage was done, and the *Flyer* continued on to Bay Shore.

The small boat owner reported the accident to the Coast Guard, and the *Flyer's* captain had to go to New York City USCG headquarters for a formal hearing on the accident. The boat owner was a recently retired Army colonel, and the Coast Guard officer was only a lieutenant, who had to call in a higher-ranking officer to control the meeting after the colonel tried to take charge. The facts of the case were that it was the colonel's first day out on his brand new boat, he did not have the boat under control, and he should have maintained course and speed. The findings of the case stated that the ferry did not blow a passing signal, the ferry captain, when seeing the erratic course of the vessel he was going to overtake, should have taken extra caution, and the ferry captain was licensed and had a greater duty to safety. A Letter of Findings was then put into the ferry captain's permanent file.

Complaints of Overloading

Full load on the BELLE, all on the upper deck (circa 1956)   Ed Mooney photo

With the rapid building of new homes on Fire Island during the 1950s and 1960s, more passengers arrived on Friday nights, Saturday mornings, and Sunday mornings, just like rush hour. Using boats that held 59 passengers on the *Courier*, 99 on the *Roamer*, 117 on the *Flyer*, 150 on the (first) *Fireball,* 150 on the (first) *Firebird*, 188 on the *Belle*, and 315 on the *Queen* (she could only

make one trip every two hours), we were hard-pressed to stay ahead of the arriving crowd. Most of these trips had to be backed up with a second and third boat. There were many trips that had so much luggage that the passenger load was less than capacity. Sometimes a passenger's luggage was on the boat, and the passenger could not get on and had to take the backup boat. Sometimes part of a family would get on and others would be left behind for the next boat; there were many angry passengers who did not listen when told not to get on the boat unless the family was all together. Boats would pull in and have more than a full load waiting at the dock. A careful passenger count had to be kept to prevent
overloading. In rain, we took less than a full load. This condition was even harder to control on a Sunday afternoon exit from the beach, and each boat would take almost a full load. In good weather, most people wanted to sit on the upper deck, and in the rain, they all wanted to be inside. It was crowded!

Letters and calls were made to the Coast Guard complaining of our unsafe, overloaded boats, and every summer inspectors from Coast Guard headquarters in New York City would count the passengers getting off in Bay Shore. Their count always matched the logbook count. Loading at the beach, we double-checked our count, first at the ticket gate, and again at the boat's gangway.

Patterson converted boats into ferries, but was limited to 150 passengers on a wooden boat built or converted after 1958. Boats built before 1958 (such as the **Belle**, **Queen**, and *Isle*) were grandfathered to a different set of rules, allowing the vessel to carry one passenger for each eighteen inches of seating and pass a stability test to safely handle that number of passengers.

Fireball (second) Hits Sunken Buoy

Years ago, a buoy on the east way route started to ride lower in the water, and the ferry company notified Fire Island Coast Guard Station that it was sinking. Because the local buoy boat was out east, they could not replace it before it sank. On the Friday night of a Fourth of July weekend, a ferry ran over the sunken buoy and bent two props and a shaft on her last trip to the beach. The boat could not carry passengers in that condition, and we could not handle the traffic over the Fourth of July weekend without the boat. When the boat returned after midnight, Doug Zegel and crew hauled her out of the water on our travel lift and started the difficult task of replacing a shaft and two props. Nothing comes apart easily at night in the heat of the engine room when you are in a hurry, especially the prop shaft out of the coupling. They had the boat back in the water, cleaned up and ready for service less than seven hours later at 7 A.M.

To accomplish this and many other overnight jobs to keep the fleet in service for big weekends requires a dedicated, skilled staff with the foresight to have in stock spare props, key-stock, shafts, shaft bearings etc., and, of course, our own travel lift to haul out. A summer breakdown requires mechanics to work well into the night or arrive early in the morning to get a vessel back in service. Without dedication, skill, and spare parts, many boats would have been out of service when they were most needed.

At the beginning of winter, the lighted bay buoys are replaced with can or nun buoys. There have been times when the ice gets so thick that it can run over the top of a buoy and keep it out of sight. The ice can also drag a buoy off station or break them free of their anchor, making it difficult to provide or guaranty winter service if we have ice. The bay at night in winter with any ice is dangerous. Running anytime into the wind in a snowstorm can be interesting, with visibility not much better than fog, snow difficult to clear off the windshield, and the radar giving a return from the snow and wave tops. Also, you are the only boat out there if you have a problem. Whenever a ferry is making a trip off-season, and the office isn't open, the parking attendant stands by the radio or the captain has a company cell phone. A boat doesn't sail without another boat made ready at the dock to switch to, or for a crew to come in and use in an emergency.

Stiff Leg Crane

Stiff leg crane (1974)   Ed Mooney Collection

It was probably in the early 1960s that Cap Patterson bought an old stationary stiff leg crane, rated about five tons. The crane was mounted in the corner by the lift slip and the *Queen's* dock. The ground was so soft that we drove nine 25-foot poles through bog and mud before we hit solid sand. On top of the nine poles we poured more than a foot of concrete over re-bar and steel fastened to the top of the poles. The crane had about a thirty-five foot boom, powered by a hand-cranked, air-cooled, single cylinder gas engine. It could boom up and down and rotate 360°. It required complete concentration when booming up or down, picking up or lowering a load.

To lower a load at the end of the cable and swing out over a boat, you pulled a large lever and lifted the load to take the weight off a paw or ratchet that had to be lifted out of place to release the cable drum to lower the load. All this time you had to press down with your foot on the brake that held the cable drum from turning, and you lowered the load by letting pressure off the brake. If you let off too much pressure, the load would fall. If the drum brake was wet, you could not hold the load. The most difficult and dangerous task was to lower the boom with a load, which took more pressure on the brake to control the boom. We had a policy never to lower the boom when we had a load on the lifting cable. If we had to raise or lower the boom, we set the load down first. Lifting a load with cable used another drum, brake, and lever like the boom. Again, power up, gravity down. Only a few of us operated the crane, and only a few wanted to.

We used it to lift engines and gears in and out of engine rooms. The boats originally weren't designed to have an engine lifted directly off the engine bed and off the boat. With some boats, we made a hatch through the overhead and lifted the engine straight up and off the boat in one lift. On others, we made a small opening through the top to drop down a cable and lifted the engine to the main deck onto an engine frame, and rolled it out the door or on the (first) *Ball*, and *Bird* rolled it aft out from under the overhead and lifted it off the boat. When setting an engine down onto the engine bed, a hand-ratchet hoist was used between the crane hook and engine. The engine was lowered near the bed, and the crane was turned off, lowering the rest of the way by hand, which was the only safe way.

One time, while I was standing on the overhead of the *South Bay Courier* guiding a reverse gear onto its engine bed and directing the crane operator, I had to step back quickly when the load started to drop too fast. The boom came crashing down on the cabin of the *Courier*. The paw that held the boom up was not fully in place when the brake was released, allowing the boom to free-fall. (I never did like that crane.)

We continued to use the crane for a few more years, lifting engines in and out of boats, and heavy items on and off the *Maid* and *Turtle*. Around 1974, one of the mechanics reported that the boom had bent while lifting a heavy load. When he asked who should repair it, he was not all that surprised when I told him, "That's the end of the crane." It was quickly cut up and sold for scrap.

Passenger Jumps Overboard On 1 A.M. Trip

In the 1990s, the makeup of the village board shifted from homeowners to business owners; that changed everything. The board now wanted a later boat. We agreed on a 1 A.M. off on Sunday morning. It's a big trip, and in good weather and holiday weekends, we need three boats. We take about two-thirds of a load on each boat for better control of people who have been drinking. We also have two security officers on each boat. The fare is higher and tickets are collected at the gate. The crew is paid extra because of the time of day, plus all the difficult people they have to deal with.

On a hot Saturday night on the 1 A.M. trip with a good load of passengers out of Ocean Beach, a crew member overheard a passenger make a bet with his friend that he would jump overboard, and he won when he jumped over the top rail while the boat was going east way off Seaview. The boat was quickly stopped and turned around, and a radio call was made to all concerned of the situation. The ferries, police, Coast Guard, and others looked for the jumper to no avail. Each time a searchlight would get near him, he would swim underwater. He swam to the Seaview bulkhead and climbed out. The police picked him up while he was walking on Bay Walk dripping wet. He claimed he went for a swim and did not jump off the ferry. He was taken to the ferry basin and identified as the jumper and arrested. The police would not let the ferry take her load of passengers to Bay Shore (I never got a good reason why; maybe they held her for evidence). Another ferry had to come from Bay Shore and take the passengers over to Bay Shore, and sometime later, they released the empty ferry. From the little we could learn about the jumper, he was in jail, could not make bail, was about thirty-five years old, a great swimmer, paid a fine of about $250, and not worth going after financially to recover our cost for overtime and fuel. At that time, there was no law about jumping off a ferry or a ship; now there is.

As part of that same law, you cannot chase after a vessel in a speedboat and jump the wake and bring action against the vessel for its wake if you are injured. Many years before this law was passed, a speedboat jumped the wake of a Sayville ferry and flipped over, almost killing the two people on the speedboat; they sued and won.

Fire Islander 110 Engine Would Not Start

The first Detroit 6-110 diesels had a gear-driven centrifugal blower on the back end of the bell housing that forced new air into the cylinder and blew the exhaust out (a two-cycle engine). Just before quitting time on a really windy day, Al Skinner called from the *Islander* while he was still tied up at Saltaire and reported that he could not start the port engine. It cranked over fast enough, but all he got was a pop-pop and it would not run. He reported that the northwest wind was too strong and if he tried to leave with one engine, he would end up on the beach. Bill Madsen and I grabbed our toolboxes, a jug of fuel, and a battery, and off we went with the *Flyer*. Al and his deckhand took the passengers to Bay Shore on the *Flyer* while Bill and I did all the standard things to get the engine started. When all failed, I decided to go on one engine by letting the stern swing away and holding the bow with a line into the wind toward the entrance. As Bill flipped off the bowline, a strong gust of wind blew the bow towards the west jetty. I put the starboard engine wide open ahead and just cleared the west jetty by inches. Bill was still on the bow and never thought we would clear. Bill then went to the engine room to close the doors and hatches. The tide was low, and I slowed down to cross the Saltaire bar. Just for the heck of it, I pushed the port starter button, and the engine roared to life instantly. Bill was surprised and figured that the engine could not blow the exhaust out of the exhaust pipe against the wind (the other engine had been converted to a side-mounted roots blower, which moved more air at starting).

A few years later, we ran into a similar problem on the *Islander* 6-110 diesels, now with roots blower, no wind, plenty of fuel to injectors, air intake clear, and turned over fast enough so the only thing left was to drop the exhaust elbow and try it without the water-cooled exhaust hose. It started right up and that's when Al explained that a passenger had told him he had seen black smoke coming out the exhaust. Al shut down the engine and finished the trip to Bay Shore on the starboard engine. He replaced the belt that had come off the water pump for cooling the exhaust hose, but did not tell us until after we disconnected the hose. The inside of the hose had burned and developed blisters that prevented the exit of exhaust gases.

We had a similar problem on the *Flyer* center engine. Artie Weis used her for the Point O'Woods run while his boat was out of service, and he had to tie up on the outside of the Point O'Woods boat basin. The wind was strong, and the stern of the *Flyer* faced the wind. The wing engines started without a problem, and the center engine was direct drive so he waited to start it until underway, but it would not start. After he arrived at Bay Shore, several crew members tried all the standard things to start it. When they called me to look at it, I told them to pull apart the rubber exhaust hose under the stern deck and try to start the engine with the hose off. Water poured out of the hose, and the engine started. Wind and waves had driven water into the hose, which could not drain or be forced out when starting, thus blocking the exhaust gas that must come out for the engine to start and run.

Refusal to Pay Fares

On a Sunday afternoon in 1979 on a good weekend, a thick fog rolled in, and people left the cool fog-darkened beach to get the ferry back to Bay Shore. The fog was so thick and the bay so crowded with boats that all the ferries had to run at reduced speed, even the ferries with good working radar. All of the scheduled trips were running late, each trip falling further behind, and we had overflow crowds waiting at Ocean Beach. The passengers left behind when we didn't handle the scheduled 6:35 P.M. trip left Ocean Beach at 7:30 P.M. and took 45 minutes to get to Bay shore, about one hour late.

Four women out of the boatload of about 150 passengers refused to pay because we were late. Even though we were late because of the fog, they didn't want to hear that, and the police were called. After spending one hour talking to the police, they were given a bench ticket requiring them to appear before a judge in Hauppauge County Court for theft of fare. One of the women was a lawyer, and she defended the other three. The following spring, the case was heard, and the three women paid after much protesting. The lawyer wanted a trial for herself, which the judge was going to give her, but she had a client to represent on the date given to her by the judge so she decided to pay.

Court Case of Bob Federico vs. Village of Ocean Beach, July 27, 1978

In the 1970s, the village of Ocean Beach had passed a very restrictive law to prevent any vessel other than the scheduled ferry from bringing people to Ocean Beach. This was during the same period of time the village had restrictions on the ferry schedule because the village board, made up of homeowners, did not want more people coming to Ocean Beach.

Captain Federico, owner of the **Captree Spray** dinner boat from Captree, landed a large group of people for lunch at Bay View Restaurant dock. After unloading the passengers, a village policeman went on board to issue Bob a ticket. While writing the ticket, Bob pulled out to return to Captree and would not return the officer to the dock. When he arrived at his Captree dock, local and state police were waiting to arrest him for kidnapping the officer. Bob was able to convince the police that the officer had no legal rights on a documented vessel, but for the docking at Ocean Beach, he received a ticket and would have to go to court. Bob won this case as the village law was found to be too restrictive.

The village passed a new code in March 1979 that required charters and water taxis to pay a fee, have insurance, a place and time to land, and to grant permission for village police to board the vessel.

Meeting a Mate

Fire Island Ferries may be the place for "meeting a mate." These situations were unplanned, I believe.

I met my wife, Pat Brown, when I was a new deckhand; her brother, Tom Brown, was also a deckhand for FIFI. Pat arrived at Maple Avenue dock a few minutes after I had just hit my head on a half-opened sliding hatch on the **Belle**. We dated for about a year until she went off to college in upstate New York. About a year after that, we got together again and married less then a year later.

Ernie Villing, a captain, met and married Dianne Magee, a ticket girl, now on our office staff.
Captain George Hafele met Gaye, the sister of co-worker Rick Moulton.
Captain Augie Giarratano married Jeanne the sister of deckhand Joe DeCamp.
Captain Kevin Colgan married Captain John Allen's sister.
Captain John Kettner married deckhand Nancy Lycke.
Deckhand Kevin Romeyk married ticket girl and office worker Jennifer Lynch.
Captain Louis Seeley married one of our first female captains, Katherine Eastman.
Captain Brian Magee married ticket girl Mary Hafele.
Captain John Healy married ticket girl Sharon Mulray.
Long-time freight crew member Mike Killien married ticket girl Margaret Rilley.
Captain Mike Miller married Liz Marx, who had been a deckhand and went on to become a
      New York Harbor Pilot.
Captain Dave Farrell married ticket girl Gail Selleck.
Captain Will Brogan married the sister of Captain Mike Eagan.
Dave Hait married ticket girl Mary Coonerty.
Breeze Vannoni married Kelly Jardin of the Evening Star crew.
Freight crew manager Tom Killeen married ticket girl Cindie Woppel.

Terrorists Crash Planes into World Trade Center Towers

September 11, 2001 was a beautiful, bright, clear morning. Two Detroit Diesel sales reps had just shown up from New Jersey, and Jim Barker and his marine architect had arrived from Rhode Island. We were all meeting to work on plans and specifications to build a new freight boat. We were on the dock after returning from the freight boat **Vagabond** when someone on the dock told us a plane had crashed into the World Trade Center. The TV at the dock was tuned to CNN, and we saw the airplane crash into the second tower.

The meeting quickly ended while I tried to make arrangements to send three boats into the city to transport people across the river since all bridges and tunnels were shut down. Three boats were fueled and made ready to go, crew was standing by; it would take us about two and a half hours to be at a city dock, but the port had been shut down, and we had to have clearance and docks to operate from. The Coast Guard was of no help, Suffolk County Emergency was of no help, the ferry operator New York Waterways was so busy they could not communicate with us, and telephones were down. All the ferries in the city, tugs, dinner boats, and sightseeing boats moved commuters across the rivers and finished by about 10 P.M.

New York Waterways called the next morning to thank us for our offer, which they had found on their answering machine. A few days later, as people returned to work and there were many travel restrictions on bridges and tunnels, ferry traffic was greater than New York Waterways could handle. They called for as many ferries as we could send. Our main season was over so we sent three vessels, the *Explorer*, *Voyager*, and *Fireball*; the others were still in service or winter work had already begun or needed to be completed before we could send them to New York City. The boats ran service for eight weeks from Weehawken and Jersey City, New Jersey, to Pier 11 at the South Street Seaport, not far from Lower Manhattan. Each vessel always had a FIFI captain and a New York Waterways crew. The captains stayed in the city area in quarters supplied by New York Waterways.

Thanks to George Hafele, Dave Anderson, and our captains Rory Allen, Scott Fogget, Mike Mills, Brian Gardiner, Matt Magee, and a few others who worked on the Hudson River operation, things worked smoothly for Fire Island Ferries.

STABILITY TESTING

BELLE inclining test (1958)   Ed Mooney photo

USCG regulations changed greatly in 1958, seven years after two un-inspected party fishing boats sank with the loss of life. One boat was the *Pelican* at Montauk Point in 1951, which sank with a loss of forty-five lives, deemed to have been caused by overloading. It was also found that the northeast winds forecast for Sunday arrived twenty-four hours early and that changed forecast arrived after the *Pelican* sailed around to the south side of Montauk Point and had to fight her way back into the wind and waves. The other party fishing boat, *Jack*, also sank in 1951 when she sprung a plank and eleven people died and three were saved.

Prior to 1958, if a vessel was under fifteen gross tons and under sixty-five feet in length, it was unregulated and not inspected. (It is interesting to see how many ferries were built under sixty-five feet and under fifteen tons.) The vessel could carry one passenger for each life jacket on board, and in many cases, that was unsafe. It's also been noted that before 1958 and for a few years afterward, vessels over sixty-five feet required a licensed first-class pilot and a licensed engineer. The engineer was dropped when pilothouse controls were used, and then the licensed pilot was dropped on vessels under one hundred gross tons, so today vessels are built under one hundred tons to avoid having tougher regulations and manning requirements. The captain's license of over one hundred tons is a more difficult, five-day written test plus time is required to be served on large vessels.

In the spring of 1958, new USCG regulations required all vessels for hire carrying more than six persons had to undergo a stability test, also called an inclining test. The test used weight, equal to the average weight of a passenger. In our case of men, women, and children, the USCG used 140 pounds per person multiplied by the number of passengers to be carried. This amount of weight was loaded down the center of the vessel. In our tests, we used cement blocks with an average weight of forty-two pounds each. When the vessel was loaded with blocks down the center aisles, marks were made on the hull, and then blocks were moved to one side of the vessel with careful measurements being kept in foot pounds moved (weight times distance moved). A vessel that leaned or listed too much before the required blocks were moved had the requested number of passengers reduced. (This occurred on a Captree ferry that carried many passengers on a high upper deck, and the number of passengers was lowered.) Blocks to equal their weight would be removed, the remaining blocks moved back on the centerline, new marks made on the hull, and the test would start over.

Most of the boats in the area conducted their test at our Main Terminal. The blocks were all loaded and unloaded by hand, and the last boat to be tested kept the blocks on and took them to Ocean Beach as freight. You also were required to have eighteen inches of seating for each passenger to be carried, and you could get one passenger for each ten square feet of standing room. Other regulations were also put into effect in 1958: the 15-gross ton exemption rule ended, all vessels carrying over six passengers had to have annual equipment and dry dock inspections, and radios were now required as well.

BELLE inclining test (1958)   Ed Mooney photo

FERRY OPERATORS TO WESTERN FIRE ISLAND

Looking back over almost 150 years of ferry service to Fire Island, you can see that only a few companies operated, and they lasted a long time and most were family-owned and run:

David S. Sammis to the Surf Hotel, about thirty-six years, circa 1856 to 1892.

Weis Brothers to Kismet, maybe twenty-five years from 1925 until 1950.

Herbert Patterson to Saltaire, 1922 to 1940s, and later his son Elmer to Seaview, Ocean Beach Park, 1936 to 1942. Elmer then ran Ocean Beach, Kismet, Dunewood, and Atlantique over a period of about twenty-four years from 1948 to 1972.

Cap Robinson to Ocean Beach, twenty-one years plus a few years before he had a contract with the village of Ocean Beach, from about 1922 to 1948.

Gus Pagels to Cherry Grove and Fair Harbor, and Fire Island State Park, for forty-seven years from 1925 to 1972.

The Zegel family, father and sons, to Seaview and Ocean Bay Park, may go back fifty-five years from 1929 to 1984.

Ed Mooney with Fire Island Ferries to Ocean Beach and other western Fire Island stops for fifty-six years from 1948 to 2004.

Bay Point Navigation Corporation, owned and operated by Point O'Woods Association, over 105 years and still in operation, from 1899 to 2004.

Village of Saltaire operated their ferry service for twenty-eight years from 1922 to 1950. Clyde Best and his son-in-law Ed Gangloff operated from Babylon and later from Captree to Fire Island State Park for about twenty years, 1944 to 1964.

Fair Harbor Ferry Company, Dick Block and Bill Leyrer, that went to Dunewood, lasted only two years, 1968 and 1969.

FERRY VESSELS TO WESTERN FIRE ISLAND

Much of the data about older ferry vessels came from books printed by the US Government under an Act of Congress of July 5, 1884. Titled *Merchant Vessels of the United States,* a new book was printed each year, beginning in 1884, listing all documented vessels, when and where they were built, size, tonnage, owner, home port, power, hull material, and its official number. Many vessels had the same name, but each vessel was given an Official Number or "ON" when it was built. That number stayed with the vessel, even if the owner, boat name, engines, deck arrangement, or home port changed.

Merchant Vessels of the United States, United States Printing Office, Washington, DC
Data was found in the books of 1892, 1893, 1894, 1895, 1900, 1902, 1914, 1923, 1924, 1925, 1927, 1929, 1930, 1935, 1937, 1941, 1942, 1946, 1947, 1949, 1951, 1952, 1960, and 1968.

Many of the old boats built before 1920 may be registered and listed in MVUS shorter in length than they actually were. At one time, they were measured to the rudder post; this may account for the length difference that I often found, many much shorter than I have reported.

Boats may have taken people to the Dominy Hotel at Kismet before the Surf Hotel was built, but I found no records of this other than Felix Dominy's logbook stating the arrival of guest by a sloop.

Over its fifty-seven years in service, Fire Island Ferries Inc. has owned thirty-five of the ninety-two vessels found listed below, as indicated by ✦.

There were ten early <u>ferries to the Surf Hotel on Fire Island</u> from the Babylon steamboat dock operated by Sammis, but others may have operated to his dock:

-1-   **Bonita**
Built before 1854 and owned by John D. Johnson. Another source has her owned by William K. Vanderbilt. She was leased or sold to David Sammis for service from Babylon to the Surf Hotel and was a steam powered, side paddlewheel, reported to have been crushed by ice at her mooring and sank.

-2-   **Wave** 1859
Served Surf Hotel.

-3-   **Francis C. Speight** 1862

-4-   **Wilmington** 1863-1872

-5-   **Minnie Warren** 1870-1872

-6-   **Surf** ON 115322
Built in 1872, Brooklyn, New York. Used by Sammis to the Surf Hotel from 1872 to 1877. Steam powered, side paddlewheel. 91.3' long, 15.4' beam, Gross Tonnage (GT) 64, Net Tonnage (NT) 41. *(Listed in 1884 and 1892 MVUS.)*

SURF (circa 1875)   This picture was found in many publications

-7-   **John A. Dix** ON 75440
Built in 1865 in Tonawanda, New York. Named for John A. Dix, who was the president of the M&M Railroad Company in 1856. Service to the Surf Hotel from 1873-1876.

-8-   **Zingara** ON 28107
Built in 1884 in Red Bank, New Jersey. Service to the Surf Hotel from 1886-1892. 56' x 10.5', GT 24.6, NT 16.

-9-   **Ripple** ON 110422   *James W. Wodsworth*

RIPPLE (circa 1888)   Ed Mooney Collection

Built in Northport, New York in 1880 as a side-wheeler steamboat yacht. Owned and operated by David Sammis to the Surf Hotel from 1888-1893. 70 hp steam yacht. New York State later bought and renamed her *James W. Wodsworth*. I found her also called *Cripple* because she broke down so often.

-10-   **Sylph** ON 116510

SYLPH at Babylon dock (circa 1892)   Ed Mooney Collection

Built in 1892 in Peekskill, New York. Steamboat side-wheeler, smokestack mid-ship, two masts. Ferry to the Surf Hotel 1892. 51.6' long, 12.6' beam, GT 22, NT 17. *(Listed in 1892 MVUS.)*

-11- **Connetquot** ON 12666

Side-wheeler, steamer CONNETQUOT (circa 1894) (post card)   Luke Kaufman Collection

Built in 1890 in City Island, New York for W. K. Vanderbilt as a steam yacht for use in Great South Bay. Registered home port was Patchogue, New York. 78' x 14.6', 27.6' overall outside the side paddlewheel guards, GT 42, NT 31. She had two inclined steam engines built by Peagrass of Cross Island, New York. Her cylinders measured 10" x 20", steel hull.

Purchased by Sayville Steamboat Company for $4,000 at the end of 1894 for service from Sayville to Point O'Woods (in those days, Point O'Woods was called Chatauqua Grounds). A group of people formed the Sayville Steamboat Company, sold stock, and purchased the vessel within two weeks after looking at her.

Their first test ride ended after pulling away from the dock and the steering cable broke. The boat had lain at the dock for two years out of service and was in great condition other than the cables. The next trial trip from Vanderbilt's Idle Hour Farm, now Dowling College, to Point O'Woods and back showed the vessel to be the finest and fastest boat on the bay. After a careful inspection of the vessel, and the fast trip to Point O'Woods and back, President Nunns of the steamboat company went immediately to Vanderbilt's place and signed the papers, transferring the boat to the Sayville Steamboat Company, and they set her up to carry 150 passengers as a ferry.

One written story of this vessel claims she was renamed *Mosquito*. My search of records shows an official number of 91243 for the *Mosquito* and an official number of 126661 for the *Connetquot*.

-12- **Mosquito** ON 91243
Built in 1880 in Greenpoint, New York for W. K. Vanderbilt and later used for service from Sayville to Chautauqua Assembly (Point O'Woods). Wood hull, 71.4' x 14', GT 24, NT 19, side-wheeler, 70 hp steam.

-13-   **Bay Shore** ON 3658   *Penataquit*

BAY SHORE, later renamed PENATAQUIT (circa 1897)   Ed Mooney Collection

Built in 1895 in Bay Shore, New York. Reported to be one of the first ferries to leave from Bay Shore in 1895. Served the Surf Hotel and Chautauqua Assembly at Point O'Woods. 88.4' x 20.6', GT 4, NT 62, 75 hp steam, screw propeller, wood hull. Had to be a large ferry at that time. Also reported to be 102' long.

-14- ★**Turtle** ON 145776   Radio call sign WYZ5091

TURTLE at Saltaire (circa 1970)   Ed Mooney photo

TURTLE taking sand and gravel to Ocean Beach for a new sewer plant (1977)   Ed Mooney photo

Built in 1898 in Patchogue, New York as a flat deck, steam powered, stern wheel, self-propelled barge with a flat bottom. Length 64.9', beam 16.2', draft 4', GT 36, NT 24. The *Turtle* was constructed of slow growth, long leaf yellow pine with planks 3.25" thick x 14" wide, and some as long as 42 feet. Most of the planks and inside longitudinal bulkheads are in great shape 100 years after her construction. This type of pine tree was so widely cut down that there are only a few forests of old growth left standing. The planks had three-quarter inch iron rods tightly driven through drilled holes from the top plank down to the chine as dowels. These were spaced about three feet apart, joining the side planks together along with heavy frames. Inside the hull there were two longitudinal bulkheads or walls made of the same pine material to support the deck and to make the boat rigid.

The *Turtle* has been reported to have carried most of the lumber and building material to Point O'Woods in the early 1900s. She was later owned by White Cap Fish Company to set and maintain the poles and fishnets along Fire Island beach. After that, she was used as a dock builder's barge.

The *Turtle* was bought by Elmer Patterson for FIFI in January 1968 from Raymond E. Phelps Company Inc., Brooklyn, New York, where she was being used in the dock building trade. Patterson made a flat deck, self-propelled barge out of her again, fixing one gas engine and replacing another. The engines were replaced in 1972 with 6-71 diesels of 175 hp each. The *Turtle* was used as a much-needed freight boat, taking most of the material to build the new Ocean Beach sewer plant in 1972, the Ocean Beach telephone building, pre-fab houses, Saltaire's boardwalks, bottled gas, etc. Because of her age and many years of hard use, she leaked around the shaft logs, and if run in heavy seas, she leaked in a few other places. The *Turtle* sank at the dock after a rough return crossing from Ocean Beach on a winter weekend. We pumped her out, changed the oil, starters, alternators, and batteries, started the engines, caulked the leaks, and we were back in service a day later. She sank at the dock twice more and was near sinking a few other times so we had plenty of practice pumping her out. She was removed from active service August 15, 1981, and in February 1983 sold to K and R Marine Construction. After removing the engines, they cut off the stern aft of the leaking shaft logs and shortened the boat since it was too long for dock building. They later sold her, and in 2003 she was still in use by another dock building company. You can still see her working along the south shore in the Bay Shore area.

The *Turtle's* original ship's steering wheel, mount, and compass are in the hall outside the Fire Island Ferries' office. The wheel and mount were removed when the rope and chain steering was changed to gearbox and pipe (from an old car). Joe Tomma, one of the owners of White Cap Fishing

Company, saw the wheel in the hall and brought in the compass to go with it. It had been under his workbench for many, many years.

*(1937 and 1942 MVUS listed the **Turtle** with 80 hp, owned by Peter De Roo, 1927 through 1935. Owned by John Griek, registered for fishing. 1949 MVUS listed Long Island Fish Company as the owner.)*

-15-   **Patchogue** ON 110596

Ferry PATCHOGUE (circa 1895)   Ed Mooney Collection

She may have run to Point O'Woods from Patchogue about 1895.

-16-   **Point O'Woods** ON 150811

Ferry POINT O'WOODS   Picture from Point O'Woods Yacht Club

Actually built in 1899 in Patchogue, New York for Arundel Corporation, Baltimore, Maryland; reregistered at home port Patchogue, New York. Owner Captain Karl Kahler. Built for passenger service to Point O'Woods. Wood hull, 52.2' x 14.8', GT 27, NT 23, gas screw, 62 hp. *(Listed in 1929 MVUS.)*

Circa 1900 - The Point O'Woods Ferry (the first so named). Captain Karl Kahler is on the right.

Ferry POINT O'WOODS (circa 1900)   Ed Mooney Collection

-17-   **Point O'Woods II** ON 201945

6361   THE LANDING, POINT O'WOODS, L. I.   ILLUSTRATED POST CARD CO., N.

Having lovely time with you were here. M. B.

POINT O'WOODS II at Fire Island   Copy of 1908 postcard from Jen Kahler

POINT O'WOODS II (circa 1905)   Point O'Woods Yacht Club photo

Built in 1905 in Bay Shore, New York for Bay Point Navigation Corporation. Registered home port Patchogue, New York. Wood hull, 91' x 16', GT 45, NT 32, steam screw. There is a picture and small plan drawing of *Point O'Woods II* at the Point O'Woods Yacht Club, which shows the boat as being 91' x 16', steam, screw with a draft of 3' 3", and a second picture with a caption stating that she was converted to an internal combustion engine about 1920. The plans show this as a long, narrow hull with a shallow draft; she looked like a large canoe. *(Listed in 1929 MVUS with a 62 hp gas screw owned by Arundel Corporation of Baltimore, Maryland.)*

-18- ✦**Point O'Woods III** ON 219589   See *Fire Island Queen*

POINT O'WOODS III (circa 1939)   Ed Mooney Collection

POINT O'WOODS III unloading onto train at POW dock (circa 1947)   Ed Mooney Collection

There is a 1947 picture of **Point O'Woods III** at Point O'Woods dock, unloading freight for the store and club off the well deck forward of the main cabin onto the train. If the date is correct, then Patterson bought her at the end of 1947 and only had the winter of 1947/1948 to convert her into the **Queen**. Point O'Woods must have expected delivery of their new **Point O'Woods IV** in the spring of 1948, and she arrived about Labor Day of 1948.

-19-   **Seatra** ON 226414

The **Seatra** is reported to have been a ferry to Point O'Woods and may have served in 1948 while the association waited for their new boat.

SEATRA (circa 1947)   Photo from Dave Kahler

The **Seatra** was built in 1927 in East Booth Bay, Maine, 800 hp, gas screw, 32 GT, 22 NT, 62.5' long, 12.1' beam, 2.3' draft (*1947 MVUS owner Horace D. Newins.*)

POINT O'WOODS IV (1948)   Ed Mooney photo

Built in 1948 for Bay Point Navigation Corporation to replace *Point O'Woods III*. Wood hull, 65' x 16.4', GT 64, NT 51, three decks, 118-passengers, two powerful Cummins engines, 225 hp, 6-cylinder diesels. Designed by a committee that wanted to keep the style of the old *Point O'Woods III*, I was told that she was built by a Jamestown, Rhode Island shipyard that built tug boats, and the hull looked like it.

It was my first summer at FIFI, and all summer long, we waited for this new Point O'Woods ferry. As I remember, she arrived at the end of the season. My first sight of her, she was pushing lots of water and making about ten knots in deep water and less in shallow water. She always had to stay in deep water as a displacement boat.

Displacement hulls hate shallow water. They are too heavy to plane, and the water has to flow around and under the hull; they push water out of the way. Water also has to flow under the hull at a greater speed between the hull and the bay bottom; this causes a decrease in pressure under the hull, and the hull drops lower in the water and slows down while its wake gets much bigger, creating a wave off the stern. If all of Great South Bay or at least the ferry route were more than twenty-five feet deep, maybe we would still be using fine line displacement hulls. They require less horsepower, but their speed is limited to the square root of their water line multiplied by 1.3. After that speed, they just pull a big wake or try to plane off.

Point O'Woods IV was given to Fred Scopinich of Hampton Boat as partial payment for the conversion of the 63' air/sea rescue boat into *Point O'Woods V*. In 1964, Bob Federico bought *Point O'Woods IV* from Hampton Boat and used her from Captree Boat Basin, doing sightseeing and moonlight sails and any type of charter. Bob continued to use the boat name against the wishes of Point O'Woods, but they had failed to make it part of the contract of sale with Fred Scopinich. Bob sold the *Point O'Woods IV* in 1968, with the payment being made at a local bank, paid for in cash that was taped to the buyer's skin under his shirt. The bank had trouble counting the bills as they stuck together from the tape residue. She went to Clearwater, Florida. Captain Bob said that selling it was like selling one of his children.

POINT O'WOODS V (circa 1965)   Ed Mooney photo

Built in 1943 in Miami, Florida for the US Navy as an air/sea rescue boat. Wood hull, 63' x 15.6', light framing. When in Navy service, it had two large V-12 Hall Scott gas engines of 640 hp each, 2" shafts. Converted in 1964 by Fred Scopinich, Hampton Boat, East Quogue, New York into a ferry for Bay Point Navigation Corporation (Point O'Woods ferry). The manager of Point O'Woods Association at that time was Mr. Elserode, and board member Charles Lowly was Point O'Woods ferry director. Scopinich sold Point O'Woods the completed vessel, hull, engines, conversion plans for the USCG, fuel lines, tanks, fire mains, bilge, pump, lighting, steering, and everything ready to carry passengers, all for $52,254 plus the trade-in of *Point O'Woods IV*.

Captain Patterson assisted in the design and the following changes were made: two Detroit 6-110 diesels with Allison 1.5-to-1 gears, two decks, freight deck and freight doors aft, USCG certificate for seating of 102 passengers, licensed for 119. Scopinich and Patterson delivered a nice looking boat to Point O'Woods. She needed more power when carrying a full load of passengers and luggage, which only happened on holidays and at midsummer change-of-renters on July 31 and August 1. The rest of the time, she was fine with an average load of less than forty.

Artie Weis was her captain during her use as the Point O'Woods ferry. She was sold and replaced in 1985 by *Point O'Woods VI*.

POINT O'WOODS VI (circa 1995)   Ed Mooney photo

Built in 1969 at Escanaba, Michigan by T. D. Vinette as a ferry for Shepler's Marine, Mackinaw City, Michigan, for lakes, bays, and sounds. Semi-planing, steel hull, and steel cabin, 62' x 17.5', GT 70, NT 49. Two V-12 Cummins diesels, 525 hp each, Twin Disc 2-to-1 gears, 2-fi" shafting, 700 gallons fuel, 106 passengers. Reported to have been built by a metal tank builder, hull plating 3/16" on the bottom and 5/32" on the side (that's light steel). Davis Park Ferry (the Sherman brothers) bought *Patricia* from Shepler Marine and renamed her *Mackinac*. They added a second deck and raised the certificate from 106 to 150 passengers. Davis Park Ferry had a major breakdown of one of the Cummins diesels and replaced it with a Detroit 12v71N.

Around 1985, Point O'Woods bought the *Macinac* from the Shermans and renamed her *Point O'Woods VI*. Point O'Woods raised the lower deck aft to the same level as the engine room hatch deck and used it as a freight area. They removed the upper deck aft, leaving two decks forward and one deck aft. *Point O'Woods VI* is heavy and under-powered, requiring the engines to be run hard, bringing about frequent engine overhauls. At 1,900 rpm, she makes only about seventeen knots. Point O'Woods removed the fixed trim tabs because they put the bow down enough to throw spray on windy days, and they ran her that way for a few years. One of Fire Island Ferries' captains, Billy Tossoro, left FIFI to become the Point O'Woods captain (they give the captain a house at the beach for the summer). Billy T. had controllable trim tabs installed at the beginning of the 1999 summer season. The tabs made a big improvement to the ride and wake and took some of the strain off the engines. She was sold to Sayville Ferry in 2004 to be converted into a freight boat.

-23-   **Point O'Woods VII** ON 1139591   Radio call sign WDB3896

POINT O'WOODS VII (August 2003)   Ed Mooney photo

Built in Freeport, Florida in 2003 by Freeport Shipbuilding for Bay Point Navigation Corp. GT 65, NT 52, 70' long, 19' beam, all aluminum, two 6-cylinder Cummins, 760 hp, QTA 19 diesels, keel cooled, 2-to-1 Twin Disc gears, 34" props, 23.5 knots maximum, 19 to 20 knots cruise, two decks, 150 passengers.

Ocean Beach Ferries

-24- **Goodenough**

An early ferry to Ocean Beach. Open boat with a canopy top. From a picture too poor to print (circa 1910), she looks to be about thirty-five feet long and slow moving. Reported to have been used by John Wilbur to take prospective lot buyers to Ocean Beach. (The only information I have on this boat is a picture.)

-25- **Berkeley** ON 204920 (NOTE: This ON looks too high for the date built.)

BERKELEY at Ocean Beach (circa 1910) (note the pole dock) Courtesy of Ocean Beach Historical Society

Built in 1887 in Patchogue, New York, and owned by Captain Albert C. Kahler. 35' long, 13.7' beam, GT 10, NT 8, 12 hp, gas engine, one deck, low freeboard, round bottom. Used by John Wilbur to bring potential property buyers to Ocean Beach.

-26- **Storm King**

STORM KING at Ocean Beach (circa 1915)   Courtesy of Walter Thornberg

This picture and Walter Thornberg telling me he rode on her as a child are all I have on this vessel. Note Ocean Beach sign on building over stern.

-27- **Traveler II** ON 92592 *Maspeth Golden Fleece*

TRAVELER II long, slender, and faster than other ferries of her time (circa 1935)   Luke Kaufman Collection

TRAVELER II, Bay Shore (circa 1935)   Luke Kaufman Collection

Built in 1894 in Morris Heights, New York. Home port Bay Shore, New York. Owner Azariah Robinson, Ocean Beach Ferry Corporation. Wood hull, length 75', beam 13.5', GT 45, NT 35, two gas engines, total 100 hp, screw props. Long and narrow, she was faster than other ferries in use at that time and was a popular ferry. The *Traveler II* required a three-man crew because she was over sixty-five feet long; she had to have a licensed pilot, a chief engineer, and a deckhand. She has been reported to have served Ocean Beach from 1920 through 1941.

The Islip Press of December 1928 has the *Traveler* at length 85', 14' beam, powered by a 60 hp Fairbanks Morse diesel, about 175 passengers, purchased by Robinson in 1920 for Ocean Beach service.

-28- **Mildred** ON 93183
Built in 1901 in Patchogue, New York. Home port Patchogue. Wood hull, length 41', beam 13.6', GT 14, NT 12, gas engine, screw prop. Reported to have also served Point O'Woods. May have been part of John Wilbur's Ocean Beach boats. It's been reported that he had three boats and named them after his daughters.

76

-29-   **Phyllis** ON 207817

Built in 1905 in New Rochelle, New York for the Babylon Bay Men's Association. Used by John Wilbur for two years (1905 and 1906). Reported to have been a sailboat with the mast removed and a gas engine installed. 40' long, 11.3' wide, GT 12, NT 11, 20 hp gas engine. (*1927 MVUS has Susie T. Barthelms as the owner, and 1937 MVUS with T. B. Bland as owner with a 20 hp gas engine. 1942 MVUS and 1949 MVUS have the owner as James E. Zegel with a 60 hp gas engine.*)

-30-   ✦**Chesapeake** *ON 204908*

CHESAPEAKE (circa 1929)   Ed Mooney Collection

CHESAPEAKE (circa 1958)   Ed Mooney photo

Built in 1906 in Havre de Grace, Maryland. Wood hull, 45.8' x 14.4', GT 14, NT 10, 75 hp, gas engine, single prop, two decks. In her early years, *Chesapeake* was owned by Cap Robinson (Ocean Beach Ferry Company), and used as a passenger ferry to Ocean Beach from 1922 to 1929. After 1929, she was Robinson's daily freight boat and backup passenger boat on Sunday afternoons until 1947. (*Owned by Ocean Beach Ferry Corporation in 1949 MVUS.*) Pat Patterson (FIFI) had Al Olson buy her from Robinson for him in 1954 and used her for passengers and freight. The old gasoline engine was replaced with a GM 4-71 of 165 hp. FIFI sold the *Chesapeake* in 1960 to Ed Lapinski to use as his freight boat for his Fair Harbor grocery store. The *Chesapeake* was also the Fair Harbor garbage boat to Bay Shore until the Suffolk County Health Department prevented Lipinski from carrying groceries on the same boat.

When Ed passed away, the boat and store were sold separately; the boat went east, and the store was sold to the Whitneys of Fire Island Markets.

In the 1950s and early 1960s, three FIFI captains lived on Fire Island - Terry Horton, Bruce Kahler, and Harold Wilder - and they brought the schoolchildren to Bay Shore in the morning on the *Chessy* under a contract with the Fire Island School District. The *Chessy* had copper over oak on her bottom to protect the hull in ice. Construction on Fire Island was booming at that time, and the *Chessy* would take a load of building material to the beach and after unloading stay at the beach overnight. Most of the material they brought over was delivered by the crew to the job site. The old *Fire Island Miss* brought the kids back to the beach in the afternoon, and then took the workmen off at 4:30 P.M. The *Chessy* was slow (about fifty minutes one-way). *(Listed in 1929 MVUS as owned by Azariah Robinson and in 1960 MVUS as owned by Eddie Lapinski.)*

-31-   **Winifred** ON 206380

WINIFRED (circa 1910) (postcard)   Ed Mooney Collection

Built in 1909 in Islip, New York. Wood hull, 44.9' x 13', GT 14, NT 9, gas screw, 25 hp, four-cylinder, hard starting engine. A ferry trip could take as long as an hour and a half. Ran passenger service to Ocean Beach from 1909 to 1912. *Winifred* was part of at least a three-boat fleet used by John Wilbur to transport prospective property buyers to Ocean Beach, free of charge. Reported to have ended her Ocean Beach service in 1914. Reported to have been dismantled in Massachusetts in 1954. *(1927 MVUS owner New York, New Haven, and Hartford Railroad with its home port of New Haven, Connecticut. 1929 MVUS owner James H. Ellis, fishing, 40 hp, home port of New Bedford, Massachusetts. 1937 to 1949 MVUS, fishing, 40 hp, owned by Sarah Smith.)*

-32-   **Evelyn** ON 211449

EVELYN at Ocean Beach (circa 1916)   Wally Pickard photo

78

Built in 1913 in Brooklyn, New York. Home port Patchogue. Wood hull, length 80', beam 18.4', GT 69, NT 54, (twin 50 hp kerosene engines reported to have been in her), screw props, two passenger decks. Service to Ocean Beach from 1913 to 1917. Reported to have burned in 1917 after only a few years of running to Ocean Beach. In this picture, she appears to have a smokestack for steam, although early gas engines ran their exhaust out of a false stack and looked like a steamer.

-33-   **Pathfinder** ON 211343

PATHFINDER (circa 1925)   Ed Mooney Collection

Built in 1913 in Sayville, New York. Wood hull, length 38.4', beam 13.8', GT 14, NT 12, 52 hp gas engine, screw prop. Ocean Beach passenger ferry from 1925 to 1928. Shows up in Gus Pagel's 1943 ledger as chartered for service to Fire Island State Park a few times in July and August. She is reported to have run from Point O'Woods to Ocean Beach on Sundays to bring people to church. (*In 1929 and 1937 MVUS, owned by Albert C. Kalher of 45 Maple Avenue, Bay Shore, with a 48 hp gas engine and was the Point O Woods freight boat. Listed in 1949 MVUS, 100 hp diesel, owned by Bay Point Navigation (Point O'Woods.)*

-34-   **Ocean Beach** ON 228256   *Nautican*

OCEAN BEACH (circa 1948)   Ed Mooney Collection

OCEAN BEACH leaving Bay Shore (circa 1930) (postcard)   Ed Mooney Collection

Built in 1928 in Brookhaven-Patchogue, New York at Newey's Shipyard for Captain Azariah Robinson (Ocean Beach Ferry Corporation). Entered service in 1929 from Bay Shore to Ocean Beach. Wood hull and cabin, 78.4' x 22.5', GT 130, NT 80, single 140 hp Atlas medium speed diesel, gasoline-powered generator, 250 passengers, two passenger decks, and an elevator to a lower freight deck used for 300-pound blocks of ice. Fire Island did not have electricity until the late 1930s, and ice was still used in the late 1940s. The boat required a licensed chief engineer and first-class pilot. In some cases, the registered length is less than the actual length, and this seems to be true with the *Ocean Beach* since the boat was eighty-seven feet long.

In the summer, all the children in the village would be at the dock waiting for the Friday evening arrival of their fathers, who had gone to work in the city for during the week and would be returning on the *Ocean Beach*. The kids called her "The Daddy Boat."

Harold Garrett was the captain for many years and told me of his trip out of Ocean Beach to Bay Shore when the 1938 Hurricane hit. After backing out of the Ocean Beach basin at 3 P.M., the ferry *Ocean Beach* could not make headway to the west into the wind and incoming tide and storm surge. She was driven astern with the 140 hp diesel full ahead. Captain Garrett dropped two anchors and was still driven east. The tide was extremely high due to the storm surge, and the hurricane winds carried him past the Point O'Woods dock onto the flats to the east of Point O'Woods, leaving him hard aground when the storm surge rapidly went out. A dredge had to dig a channel past the Point O'Woods basin to get the boat to deeper water.

The boat was deeper in the stern than in the bow, allowing the wind to blow the bow off faster than the stern, and when entering the Ocean Beach basin in a northeaster, the captain would head for Houser's Hotel and let the bow fall off to the west, keeping up a good speed for control. After entering the basin, he had to ring down to the engineer for full-speed astern and hope to stop before hitting the south bulkhead.

Money to build the 250-passenger ferry *Ocean Beach* began being raised in 1927 by selling preferred stock shares in the Ocean Beach Ferry Corporation to a few Ocean Beach residents.

80

The Islip Press of December 13, 1928 stated that over one-half of the $25,000 issue of cumulative preferred stock had been sold. The shares were to pay 7% per year on the unpaid notes. If payments were not made to the stockholders, they could meet and have a voice in the running of the company. No payments were ever made, and meetings were never held. Nineteen years later, the boat went out of service while Robinson fought the village in court to regain the Ocean Beach run. The boat was sold about 1953 and sailed to Florida. The last heard of her was a Florida newspaper picture showing her in flames from bow to stern.

-35-   **Margaret** ON 230598   *South Bay Challenger*

MARGARET (circa 1950s)   Luke Kaufman Collection

Built in 1931 as one of seven rumrunners built by Wheeler Boatyard at Clausen Point, New York. 56.3' x 11.2', two 6-cylinder Hall Scott, 225 hp, gas engines, and she was reported to have a small third engine in the center when she was a rumrunner. The *Margaret* was an exact copy of the rumrunner *Vagabond* and was secretly built in an adjoining covered shed where a duplicate was made of each piece that was made for the *Vagabond*. Naval Architect Ralph Bitters drew the plans, and the builder did not want him to know they were using his drawings and plans to make a second boat. She was reported to have started service for Robinson in 1941.

The *Margaret* (wood hull and cabin, one deck, 85 passengers) and the *Lovebird* (later renamed *Miss Ocean Beach*) were Robinson's two speedboats and were held in his separate company, Ocean Beach Express. These two boats were used by Zee Line after 1948 to Seaview and Ocean Bay Park during the time Robinson was in court trying to get back the Ocean Beach run. Robinson sold the *Margaret* to Zee Line about 1951 after he lost his court case with the village. *(In 1941 and 1942 MVUS, owned by C. T. Morris (Babe) part owner of Ocean Beach Ferry; 1949 MVUS owned by Ocean Beach Ferry Corporation, 550 hp; 1951 MVUS owner Tonis M. Zegel; 1960 MVUS owned by Elwood S. Zegel.)* In 1967, Zee Line sold the *Margaret* to Dick Block and Billy Leyrer, owners of Fair Harbor Ferry Company that ran Dunewood service in 1968 and 1969. They renamed her *South Bay Challenger.*

-36-   **Miss Ocean Beach** ON 230858   *Lovebird   Fire Island Pines   Flying Hornet*
Built in 1931 in Brooklyn, New York by Wheeler Boatyard. 56.3' x 11.2', GT 14, NT 9, 1,100 hp. Built for Anthony Russo as a rumrunner and used by Vannie Higgins. The *Lovebird* was rebuilt about 1937 and used as a ferry by Ocean Beach Express Company. 75 passengers, two Hall Scott Invaders, 225 hp gas engines, much later replaced with two Gray Marine 6-71 Detroit Diesels of the same horsepower, draft 3', one deck, two props, wood hull and cabin, lightly built. Called *Missy*, she was one of two ex-rumrunners that Robinson bought and converted to match the speed of Patterson's two fast boats that ran out of nearby Seaview. While named *Lovebird*, she collided into Patterson's *Vagabond* on June 26, 1937 near East Island, but was not damaged. Her name may have been changed in 1938 to *Miss Ocean Beach.* Her service to Ocean Beach ended on April 30, 1948 when Robinson lost his contract. Zegel used her for service to Seaview and the Park while Robinson waited for the

MISS OCEAN BEACH pulling into Ocean Beach basin (circa 1940)   Shirley Patterson Collection

courts to decide the Robinson vs. Ocean Beach case. I was told that Cap Robinson was a part-time captain for Zegel while waiting for the case to end. Around 1958, she was sold to Ken Stein of Sayville Ferry for service to the Pines and the Grove. He renamed her *Fire Island Pines (1960 MVUS)*, and shortly afterward changed her name to *Flying Hornet*.

MISS OCEAN BEACH (circa 1940)   Luke Kaufman Collection

Fire Island Ferries Inc. Vessels

-37- ✦ **Fire Island Queen** ON 219589   Radio WB7119   *Sarita   Edithia   Mousquetaire Point O'Woods III*

Built in 1920 at a reported cost of $200,000 at East Booth Bay, Maine by Adams Shipbuilding Company as *Sarita*, a cruising houseboat yacht, for John H. Hanan. At one time while she was named *Sarita,* she was owned by John R. Fell. Also owned at one time by the Paul Defere family of the Bay Shore area. In 1934, she was bought by Bay Point Navigation, the ferry operating subsidiary of Point O'Woods. Length 98', beam 22' 10", draft 5', wood hull and cabin, original engines were twin 125 hp Winton gasoline, next were 200 hp Winton diesels, then in 1947-48 were 200 hp General Motors 6-71

FIRE ISLAND QUEEN at Ocean Beach (1948)   Ed Mooney photo

diesels, then in 1964 300 hp GM 6-110 diesels with the old mechanical 3-to-1 Twin Disc gears from the first GM 110s, and in 1980, the engines were changed to late model 6-110 with hydraulic 3-to-1 gears. 3" bronze propeller shafts, props on the 6-71, 36" x 32", 3-blade and 36' x 36", 3-blade on the 6-110s. She was a ten to twelve knot boat and in deep water, when empty with good props and a clean bottom, she could make thirteen knots.

I found a letter dated March 27, 1934 to Point O'Woods' Captain Albert Kahler at 45 Maple Avenue, Bay Shore, from the USCG with the results of a stability test on the motor vessel **Mousquetaire**, 106 tons displacement, then being renamed **Point O'Woods III**. This letter allowed them to carry a reasonable amount of cargo on the well deck, but gave no calculation of passengers. Another letter shortly afterward gave a passenger capacity of 210 passengers. Her first Point O'Woods captain was Albert Kahler, son of Captain Karl Kahler. Captain Elmer Patterson helped install new Winton diesels and was her licensed engineer.

When she was put up for sale by Point O'Woods, Patterson told anyone interested in the boat that she had wood rot in the stem that would require major work and cost. When no one else showed interest in the boat, Patterson (FIFI) bought her, bad stem and all, from the Bay Point Navigation Company in October 1947. A year later, he had the shipyard drill small holes in the rotted area and filled it in with a product called Get Rot, which became hard as wood, and when painted over was as solid as oak. Patterson renamed her **Fire Island Queen** and began service to Ocean Beach in 1948. The stem and boat went on for another forty-four years. *(Listed in 1937 MVUS as Point O'Woods III, gas screw, 200 hp, and listed in 1949 MVUS as Fire Island Queen, 400 hp).*

FIRE ISLAND QUEEN (circa 1980)   Ed Mooney photo

The following (reprinted with permission of the *Fire Island Tide*) is part of a story written by Jay Weimar and published in the *Fire Island Tide* on August 25, 1978. At the time it was written, Jay worked on the freight boat ***Fire Island Maid***, and also managed the Ocean Beach freight house. He was in college, writing this story for school credit.

Built in 1920 for John H. Hanan by Adams Shipbuilding Company of East Booth Bay, Maine, the cruising house-type yacht was christened ***Sarita.*** The interior carefully designed to accommodate luxury furnishings; the exterior soundly constructed to withstand stormy weather. From bow to stern, the ***Sarita*** was intended to be the epitome of class and comfort for a yacht of its time. The boat consisted of three decks: the lower deck, enclosed with the stability of a large hall, housed the majority of the ship's facilities. Five elaborate staterooms and three full bathrooms occupied the forward half. The stern section included a galley (adjacent with pantry and walk-in freezer), crews' quarters, and engine room. An immense dining room, impressively decorated with handcrafted paneling and mirrors, lay at mid-ship.

On the promenade deck, the cabin featured a beautiful deck salon, considered the "living room of the ship." Forward was a master's stateroom, a small study, and another bathroom. The remainder of this deck was open, save the stern, which was protected by a canvas awning. The bridge deck consisted of a small cabin, serving as both a wheelhouse and the captain's quarters.

Throughout the yacht were numerous conveniences, which made life on the water as comfortable as possible. All rooms had hot-water heat and electric lights. The bathrooms were equipped with full-sized tubs or showers. A dumbwaiter ran to the deck salon, conveniently serving the promenade area. The engine room noise was muffled by thick insulation, so the dining in the next room was peaceful, even when running at full throttle. Paneling covered most of the walls, and all fixtures on board were brass. Beautiful aesthetic and pragmatic qualities combined to make one feel more a hotel guest than a boat guest.

Hanan owned the yacht for ten years, and eventually changed the name to ***Edithia*** (reason unknown). During this time, home port was New York harbor, and ***Sarita*** frequented the waters of the Hudson River and Long Island Sound. Hanan, a wealthy businessman, often entertained business acquaintances. He set weekends aside for leisurely cruises with his family. After the summer of 1930, Hanan, feeling the effects of the recent Depression, decided to sell the ***Edithia***. Unexpectedly, he didn't have to wait long.

Paul E. Defere of Bay Shore, an international lawyer and famed yachtsman, bought the boat in the fall of 1930 at Todd's Shipyard in Brooklyn. Defere was a longtime member of the elite New York and Columbia Yacht Clubs and previous owner of many large pleasure boats. Impressed with the character and distinction of his new yacht, he proudly named it ***Mousquetaire.***

The yellow-edged pages of the old logbook reveal much of the yacht and its travels under the direction of Paul Defere. It was a cold morning on November 12, 1931, when the ship left New York en route to Florida. On board were a crew of six and the Defere family. A captain, two engineers, two seamen, and a steward made sure the owner and family were comfortable. The ship handled well in open waters of the Atlantic and made frequent stops along the coast to obtain supplies and visit select communities. Guests were often invited aboard for dinner and sometimes the yacht lay at anchor for days at a time.

On December 2, the ***Mousquetaire*** reached Mayport, Florida. From there it proceeded to stop at all the major resorts on the Eastern Coast: St. Augustine, Daytona, New Smyrna, Melborne, West

Palm, and finally Miami. Traveling the Intercoastal Waterway south through Florida, the *Mousquetaire* utilized its two speedway motor launches and Lawley dinghy to transport supplies and passengers to and from the yacht. In fact, the only time the boat actually docked was when it refueled or needed repairs.

The *Mousquetaire* lay at anchor in Miami for the entire month of January 1932. Then on February 4, it was chartered by three New York doctors and their wives to cruise the Florida Keys. The cruise lasted almost three weeks, during which the party spent many hours angle fishing. When the boat returned, it was immediately chartered again by more wealthy New Yorkers to Key West. It was during the charter that liquor was found on board in a guest chambers by federal officers and promptly removed.

The *Mousquetaire* returned to Miami in March, but it wasn't until May that the yacht slowly began its long journey back to New York with Defere. Once home, the boat would never leave the waters of Great South Bay.

In 1934 Defere decided to sell the *Mousquetaire,* retiring as one of the most reputable yachts-men this area has ever known. The boat lay idle at Bishop's Shipyard in Patchogue until the fall of 1935 (Mooney Note: actually, it was 1934) when plans were suddenly drawn to convert the yacht into a ferryboat.

Captain Albert Kahler of Bay Point Navigation (an old subsidiary of Point O'Woods Association) was looking for a respectable boat to replace his dilapidated ferry *Point O'Woods II.* Captain Elmer Patterson (who would later originate Fire Island Ferries) suggested the *Mousquetaire* as a capable successor. Kahler was impressed by the yacht, but bewildered to its worth as a ferry. Patterson said the solution was simple: "Strip her."

During the winter of 1934-1935, the boat was stripped and prepared for commercial use. Only the master stateroom and crews' quarters were preserved from the initial yacht. The original twin 125 hp Winton gasoline engines were replaced with twin 200 hp Winton diesel engines. Seating was installed to accommodate 100 passengers and a luggage compartment was added to the bow. The ferry was painted white and rightfully renamed *Point O'Woods III.*

During the summer months, the crew lived on board, with the captain enjoying the rights of the plush stateroom.

For over ten years, the ferry made daily trips to Point O'Woods. Eventually, time and weather began to take their toll on the wooden boat. Repairs and upkeep became frequent and expensive. The ferry had served its purpose well, but now Captain Kahler wanted a new boat. In 1947 the *Point O'Woods III* was put up for sale. Within minutes Captain Patterson (then getting the boats needed to form Fire Island Ferries Inc.) was ready to make a deal. Shortly after, the boat was named the *Fire Island Queen.*

A total overhaul began immediately. The wheelhouse was dropped to the promenade deck and the engines were replaced with twin 200 hp General Motors diesel engines. The remaining rooms on board were removed and a railing was erected around the upper deck to allow for additional seating. When completed the capacity increased from 100 to 315 passengers. The *Queen* then ran from the end of Maple Avenue dock on the west side, Bay Shore to Ocean Beach for approximately ten years before having to be remodeled again.

In 1957 Coast Guard regulations forced Patterson to change the structure of the ferry from three decks to only two. (Mooney Note: He lowered the main deck and removed the lowest deck that was down in the hull.) This resulted in an enclosed lower deck running the entire length of the boat and an open upper deck surrounded by a protective railing. Also at this time the engines were replaced with twin 6-110 300 hp General Motors diesels and the forward luggage compartment was removed. The new regulations no long required lifeboats or an engineer. (Mooney Note: Harry Wilson was the chief engineer from 1948 to 1952, then Bill Madsen took over. When the engineer was no longer needed on the *Queen*, Madsen became port engineer and mechanic, installing or changing engines in the *Queen*, *Turtle*, *Chesapeake*, (first) *Miss, Belle*, (first) *Flyer*, *Fireball*, (first) *Firebird*, and *Roamer*.)

The *Queen* today is a product of this renovation and can accommodate up to 285 passengers. The ferry makes daily trips to Islip town beach, Atlantique and is regularly chartered for moonlight sails. The charter sails have become increasingly popular over the last few years with numerous social and private groups throughout Long Island. Usually groups hire a band to play on board and a caterer to serve food and drinks to members and guests.

Ed Mooney, President of Fire Island Ferries Inc., feels that the *Queen* is a valuable part of the ferry company because of its size and accommodations.

"The *Queen* is unique in that it is the only large boat we have with enough facilities to handle such charters as we offer. The charters are very popular every summer," Mooney said.

Bill Ryan, present captain of the *Fire Island Queen*, feels the ferry maneuvers well for a 100-foot vessel.

"The *Queen* handles surprisingly well for a boat of its size and weight. She runs good, and is trustworthy and seaworthy," Ryan said.

Although the *Queen* cannot keep up with the newer and faster ferries on the bay, it still retains character that is unmatched by any boat in this area. This ship has experienced more changes, seen more ports, and cruised more miles of water than most boats could hope for in ten lifetimes. It deserves the respect that its royal name suggests. The *Fire Island Queen*, yes, old and slow, but still reliable, continues to cross Great South Bay.

***

In April of 1948, only two weeks before going into Ocean Beach service, Patterson was working with the USCG to get a Certificate of Inspection. He needed approval of a new exhaust system and fuel tank piping. Pat received all the needed paperwork just in time to sail on the start-up date of May 1, 1948.

In 1957, the *Queen* was changed from a three-deck boat to two decks. A few years later, the pilothouse was lowered enough to go under the bridges on the way to Jones Beach Marine Theater without needing the bridges to be raised. By doing this, Patterson led Pagels to believe he was not going to bid on the run to Atlantique, then submitted a bid and won.

The *Queen* was one of the few boats in the bay with a radio, but had no way to communicate with other ferries and the office, except through the marine operator. Once other ferries left the dock, they were on their own, many times going all the way back to Ocean Beach to back up the last trip, only to find that she was not needed. In 1958, as part of the major changes to regulations governing passenger vessels, radios would be required on all vessels for hire carrying more than twelve persons. Patterson, Pagels, and Zegel tried to obtain a waiver to this rule (the radios plus the other regulations were costly), but they were turned down by the FCC. They also had a need to increase the size of their fleets to accommodate the growing number of new homeowners, but profits were low. Captain Patterson bought cheap radios that required constant repairs and soon had to be replaced. Some of these new replacements, which were made by Motorola, were in service for over twenty-five years before having to be replaced.

As new ferries were built, the **Queen** was used less in passenger service, but continued to be used in charter service of all types. The passengers on the charters and maintenance of a sixty-nine-year-old boat were more trouble then the small profit made. We sent the **Queen** to Brooklyn to be hauled for her 18-month dry dock inspection because we wanted to renew her certificate and sell her; we did have an interested buyer from upstate New York. While hauling the **Queen** at Muller's Boat Works, Brooklyn, on a marine railway, the keel blocks on the hauling carriage gave way, and the **Queen** slid aft and rolled to the starboard before the chine blocks were in place. (The chine blocks can't be put in place until the boat is about halfway out of the water.) When she slid aft, she was unsupported from the engine room aft, and the keel bent. Falling to starboard, she landed on the mid ship chine block and broke planks and frames. Doug Zegel and Jimmy Muller went into the cold water and put a temporary patch on the hole, put her back in the water, fixed the collapsed blocking, and hauled her out again. On a more careful inspection, there were more frames and planks that were soft from age that would have to be replaced, and it would cost more than the vessel was worth. Muller fixed the broken planks and frames, and the boat returned to Bay Shore under her own power, but without a Certificate of Inspection. We lowered the asking price because there was not much value without a current Certificate of Inspection.

Bob Matherson of Oak Beach Inn fame (also known as OBI, which was a nightclub/bar) arrived at my office in November 1989 and asked if the **Queen** was for sale. I told him yes, for $20,000. He asked if I would take $19,000, and I quickly told him I would. I also told him the boat did not have a Certificate of Inspection and didn't think she could get one. Bob returned an hour later with a check and asked when he could have the boat. I told him that we could have her ready by 9 A.M. the next morning, and if he wanted, we could deliver her to his dock at OBI. Bob requested to accompany us on the trip.

The next morning, I told Captain Ernie Villing to take the **Queen** to the OBI dock and that when he got to the OBI dock to get out of there; don't have coffee or a beer, don't talk to anyone, just get in our waiting van and leave. To get to the OBI dock, you have to go almost to the inlet and come back close along the shore of Oak Beach. Bob asked if he could blow the ship's whistle that can be heard miles away, and Ernie agreed. Bob blew that whistle so that anyone who was home came outside to find out what was going on. When they did, he gave them an obscene gesture. (For years, local residents, the town of Babylon, and New York State were in court against him and OBI.) After docking, Bob insisted that the crew have a cup of coffee, but when Ernie saw the police cars out front, he quickly left.

Bob was in court for a few years about keeping the **Queen** and a barge larger than the **Queen** at his dock. He let the **Queen** go to ruin, and she sank at the dock. Bob lost his case and was ordered to remove the **Queen** and the barge. He hired a contractor to break up the **Queen** and take her away, but the contractor got nowhere and had to get Russ Rielly with his big excavator to do the job. It was a sad day for many to see this grand old lady end this way.

FIRE ISLAND MISS (first) (circa 1954)   Ed Mooney photo

Built in 1931 in Brooklyn, New York as a high-speed rumrunner, wood hull, length 55.2', beam 11.3', GT 14, NT 10, 75 passengers, twin 600 hp, converted Liberty airplane engines. Patterson introduced the *Vagabond* as the first high-speed ferry in the bay and ran her to Seaview from Bay Shore in 1936. Patterson was one year ahead of Robinson with a fast ferry. A year or so later, Patterson converted the ex-rumrunner *Artemis* for the Seaview run. A picture of the *Vagabond* at that time shows her with an upper deck forward. Prior to the new USCG regulations of 1958, a vessel under sixty-five feet in length could carry one person for each life jacket on board, which meant you carried as many passengers as you could. At peak travel times, passengers would push onto a crowded boat, or then have to wait an hour for the next ferry. A small boat like the *Vagabond* (*Fire Island Miss*) carried nearly 100 passengers when necessary. (Patterson did not want more than seventy-five carried and raised hell when a captain carried more.)

When Fire Island Ferries was incorporated in April 1947, Patterson put up the *Vagabond* as part of his investment into the corporation. The gas engines were replaced with two World War II surplus Gray Marine diesel engines (General Motors engine design) set up just the way they were in landing craft. They worked well, but needed constant attention because they were run too hard, often for twenty-five minutes at times, despite the military-rated battle speed that was to be run for no more that ten minutes at a stretch. Oak sheathing covered with copper flashing was added to the bottom and about eight inches above the water line, allowing her to operate in ice without the ice cutting into the planks or taking the cotton out of the seams.

The building boom of new homes at the beach that started in 1950 required workmen from the mainland, and before the Fire Island Bridge was completed in 1954, ferries were the only way over, often going through ice in the winter. There was a coal burning potbelly stove in the forward cabin just behind the pilothouse that, with proper care, burned all winter. There were times in the winters of the 1950s and 1960s when the bay froze over for weeks, and we could not break through to Fire Island. I was on the *Miss* one time with Captain Harold Garrett 300 yards to the west of the Ocean Beach basin entrance, and Garrett pushed the engines wide open, but we could not break through to the basin; many layers of ice had been run together by the tide and northwest wind.

FIFI had a contract from 1958 to 1964 to bring the Fire Island schoolchildren to Bay Shore. If the ice made it doubtful that we could continue that service, we made arrangements to sail from the Captree Boat Basin to the Coast Guard Station, a short run just inside the inlet with a strong current that kept ice from forming. One morning, the ice was too thick to get out of the Captree Basin. As soon as we got to Captree, we started the engines and put them in forward gear and ran them hard for over a half hour. Normally the prop wash would break and clear the ice astern, and we could back up, turn around, and get out to ice-free water. The ice did not open after running for one hour, and the inlet was frozen to the Coast Guard Station. The kids got a day off from school, and we worked the rest of the morning to clear the ice behind the *Miss.* After the bridge to Fire Island opened in 1964, schoolchildren were brought to the mainland on four-wheel drive school buses.

It takes more than one or two nights for the bay to freeze over. The bay water must first be chilled by recent cold temperatures, then the wind has to let up, and usually the tide is very low from high pressure stuck over our area and a northwest wind. The east bay freezes first because it's shallow and further from the warmer ocean water from the inlet.

In 1961, the *Fire Island Miss* was stripped of all usable equipment and engines and sold to Jim Gillan for one dollar. Captain Gillan sank her in the Atlantic Ocean as a fish wreck. She had many years of hard service and would have required a major rebuilding, but carrying only seventy-five passengers did not justify the expense. *(Listed in 1945 MVUS, owner Lt. Commander Patterson, Vagabond.)*

-39- ✦**Fire Island Maid** ON 231535 Radio WYZ5027 *Captain J. W. Parker Sr.* *Viking Sr.*

FIRE ISLAND MAID (circa 1960)   Ed Mooney photo

FIRE ISLAND MAID (circa 1956)   Ed Mooney photo

Built in 1932 in Tuckerton, New Jersey. Length 58', beam 18', GT 44, NT 40, one 6-cylinder Mack diesel, 125 hp, Twin Disc X8708, 3-to-1 mechanical shifting reduction gear, with a 36" prop. Later, the engine was replaced with a Detroit 6-71 diesel, a rebuilt Navy surplus that had such low oil pressure on start-up that it had to be corrected before it could be used in service, the pressure relief valve was fine, the oil pump was changed, the bearings were new, and the oil plugs in the block were installed properly.

Bill Madsen noticed that the stamp style of numbers on the main bearing caps did not match each other, but were in proper sequence. There is a product called plastic gauge, a strip of plastic with a known diameter that is set on the main cap and the bearing is tightened to its specified torque. When the bearing is removed, the plastic width is measured; the clearance is determined by the width of the flattened plastic. The opening between the crankshaft and bearing was so great that the oil just ran out and did not develop pressure. The bearing caps must stay with the same block they were line-bored with at the factory. They are not interchangeable from block to block and must be installed back at the same bearing location each time they are removed. The 6-71 block can be turned end-to-end to get the blower on the side you can work on in a tight engine room. If you turn the block around, you may end up with number seven main bearing in the front of the engine, and that's how you must re-install them. A replacement long block (a block with crankshaft, con rods, pistons, camshaft, and timing gears) had to be found and installed. The Navy engine was repaired by obtaining seven new un-bored bearing caps and getting the block line bored. The old reverse reduction gear was adapted to this engine.

The *Viking Sr.* was built as a fishing boat and used as a surf clam dredge out of Freeport, New York in the ocean off Jones Beach. Her bottom was too flat for ocean work. Patterson acquired her in 1947, renamed her *Fire Island Maid*, and had plans drawn to add a second deck for passengers, but he never carried out the plans. She never transported passengers, except before the bridge was built, and carried a few year-round residents who were desperate for transportation when the bay was frozen and we could not run passenger service. Oak sheathing covered with copper flashing was nailed to the bottom to protect the planks and caulking when going though ice.

The sixty-five foot Coast Guard icebreaker *AB 25* sank at Crazy Charlie (the buoy off Saltaire) by heavy ice about 1940 while breaking ice for a tanker on its way to Patchogue. The *Maid* was only a fair icebreaker and had to give up service when ice was over six inches thick. The tide and wind also piled ice into layers too deep for the *Maid* to get through. I remember one trip that took three hours to get to Ocean Beach, and by the time we unloaded, it was almost dark. We did not want to make the trip back to Bay Shore with the ice running over the buoys, keeping them out of sight. In the winter, lighted buoys are replaced with can and nun buoys. This was before we had radios and radar, and the *Maid* never had a searchlight or radar.

We spent the night at Harold Wilder's. That night, the wind blew hard from the east, and we had a good outgoing tide breaking and moving most of the ice. The next morning, we returned to Bay Shore, not hitting much ice until near Bay Shore.

Before the bridge from Captree to Fire Island was completed, the *Maid* was the vital link to the mainland for the island's few year-round residents. If ice prevented service for several days, when we resumed service, someone from just about every family would come by to pick up their supplies at Ocean Beach. The *Maid* was loaded and unloaded by hand, all the lumber was taken off a truck and loaded a board or two at a time, bags of cement loaded one bag at a time, sand was dumped on a barge and then shoveled off into a Model A truck, groceries were unloaded from a truck and rolled down a conveyer and stacked on the *Maid* by hand.

FIFI sold about forty-five newspapers by the honor system: The crew of the 7:30 A.M. work boat, after writing residents' names on the newspapers, left them spread out on the counter in the unlocked freight house.

During the boom years of the 1950s and 1960s, FIFI had four trucks at Ocean Beach: a Model A Ford flatbed, a V-8 Ford, a Model A made into a small, self-tipping dump truck, and a Chevy truck that had been the Point O'Woods' fire truck. The freight crew loaded lumber and other building material directly onto the trucks by hand, and the passenger crew delivered it to the job site on her layover from about 10:45 A.M. until 4:30 P.M., then the passenger boat crew made the worker trip to Bay Shore. While the trucks were making deliveries, the freight crew continued to unload and stack lumber on the dock for the trucks to deliver after the *Maid* left for Bay Shore. We trucked material to Ocean Bay Park, Seaview, Ocean Beach, and as far west as Fair Harbor; just about all the contractors used our service. In 1954, the year the new school was built, we delivered all the material to the site while we also transported material for twenty-seven new houses.

The *Maid's* last year of service to the western end of Fire Island was in 1983. She was sold to Sayville Ferry and used as their freight boat for a few years before they dismantled and burned her as a training drill for a local fire department.

-40-   ✦**Fire Island Belle** ON 255469   Radio WJ8546

FIRE ISLAND BELLE (circa 1960) Photo taken from stern of RUNNING WILD by Homer Baumgartner

Built in 1948 by Wheeler Boatyard at Clausen Point, New York for Fire Island Ferries, Inc. (Ed Davis, Elmer Patterson, and Bill White.) Length 65', beam 16' 6", single planked wood hull and cabin, two decks, 188 passengers, three 6-71 Gray Marine diesels, three 1.75" shafts. Later, when the MWM German engines were installed, the shafts were changed to 2", the prop size changed as engines changed, the 200 hp, 6-71s turned 24" x 22", the MWMs turned 26" x 24", and the 12-V 71s turned 26" x 26", 4-blade, first set of gears, Twin Disc X8708, 1.5-to-1 mechanical gears, Capital hydraulic HYC 25,000, 1.5-to-1 installed on the MWMs. She was the first ferry designed and built as a fast ferry, semi-planning hull for Great South Bay. Before that, all the fast ferries were converted rumrunners. She was also the first to have three props.

The *Belle* entered service to Ocean Beach in late June of 1948. Patterson also tried to run service to Ocean Bay Park in 1948, but could not handle both stops and gave up the Park about the Fourth of July.

91

Captain Jim Daly was hired to run the *Belle*, but after one trip, he quit; three engines were too much for him. Pat then hired Captain Howard Carlson, who ran the *Belle* for her first two summer seasons; he was the captain the first year I was a deckhand.

She was built of a high-grade of quarter-sawn fir, and the bottom design was that of an enlarged rumrunner. The three engines were military surplus Gray Marine, 6-71 diesels, rated 225 hp, at 2,100 rpm, a battle setting on the governor, meant to be run only for short periods of time. When run hard in deep water with a load of passengers, black smoke would pour out the exhaust, the engines would run hot and overheat, cylinder heads would crack, exhaust valves burned, timing gears broke, a hole could be blown through a piston, the reduction gear got hot and stuck in gear or the bearings failed. Not one of the three engines could run for more than two weeks without a breakdown.

I became captain of the *Belle* at the beginning of my third year with FIFI. Patterson informed me that I was given the *Belle*, even though I was junior to the other captains, because I was the only one who could keep the engines running. If the passenger load was under 125 and the engines were running well, I could go east way with a good chance of keeping it up and making a half hour trip. If I had a load over 125 passengers, I could get her up out of Bay Shore and make it to buoy number seven west way when I had to take her off plane and bring the engines back to about 1,300 rpm or hull speed and get into deeper water. The engines cooled down, and the trip took about eight minutes longer. This way, we kept the engines running and made round-trips in about one hour and ten minutes (when almost empty in one direction). With a full load out of Ocean Beach, I would run off-plane west way to buoy number eight and hope I could plane her off there. The shallow water from number eight to Bay Shore is where you lost most of the time if you did not get her up on plane.

The *Belle* was underpowered, and Patterson had the ferry company mechanic/engineer, Bill Madsen, remove the center reduction gear, install a V-drive with an input shaft on both its ends and mount it behind the center engine, and mount a fourth engine aft of the V-drive, driving into the V-drive; we now had more power and more problems. The major problem was we broke crankshafts in the rear engine. After the second broken crankshaft, Patterson decided to try something else. GM Detroit Diesel always had a research and development program to correct the problems and develop more horsepower with the 71 Series. They came out with a new head with four valves per cylinder, a better piston and rings, and increased the horsepower with a big turbocharger. We removed the fourth engine and V-drive, and rebuilt the engines as turbocharged with 90-millimeter injectors and new 4-valve head. The *Belle* now carried a full load east way without a problem, until mid-August, when the rings wore out and the compression got so low that we had to use ether to start an engine that cooled down overnight (this was after about 800 running hours). The turbo also created a high exhaust temperature that burned exhaust valves. After a few years of this, the turbos were removed and the roots blower were returned to normal speed, making it what Detroit later called an "M" engine. This worked well, put out horsepower, and had a longer life between overhauls. Patterson wanted more power and speed, and removed the center 6-71 and installed a German-built 400 hp MWM 232 V-12 with a power takeoff in place of a marine gear to save weight. It was a nice engine, and he replaced the port and starboard engines with the MWMs and new Capital hydraulic marine gears.

The *Belle* was the workhorse of the fleet for the first twenty-four years of her life, making over 1,000 round-trips a year and carrying about 100,000 passengers a year. With the arrival in 1972 of the new ferry *Captain Patterson*, the *Belle* was no longer the major carrier of the fleet. She continued to make about 1,000 trips a year, but now carried less than 100,000 passengers; those figures started to drop as the other new boats came on-line. The *Belle* was sold in November 2000 and went to Freeport, New York to be rebuilt as a private vessel.

92

FIRE ISLAND BELLE after conversion on the way to Connecticut (2003)   Ed Mooney Collection

-41-   ✦**Fire Island Flyer** (first) ON 232239   Radio WJ8549

FIRE ISLAND FLYER (first) at Ocean Beach Basin (1955)   Ed Mooney photo

Built in 1933 in Morris Heights, New Jersey by Consolidated to be one of the largest and fastest rumrunners, but Prohibition ended in 1933, and the boat was never finished to run rum. She was designed to have four V-12 400 hp aircraft engines, and a small, quiet gas engine in the center to sneak into landings at night without being heard (the aircraft engines could be heard for miles).

Bought and rebuilt by Patterson in 1954, we used the *Flyer* with just two engines in 1955 and added the center engine in 1956. The *Flyer* was used on all stops between Kismet and Ocean Beach. Length 65', beam 13', one deck, three engines, 6-71, props, 3-blade, 24" x 22" port and starboard, 1.5-to-1 gear, center prop 21" x 17", direct drive, shaft size 1.75". We used her thirty-six years for service from 1955 to 1991.

She was dismantled and sunk off Jones Beach as a fish wreck in 1991. Just after she was sunk, we had a severe storm and parts of the *Flyer* washed onto Jones Beach. The largest piece was the stern, with her name in big, bold letters. We had to send over a crew to clean up the parts that floated off the bottom and load the pieces into thirty-yard containers. We probably put too much concrete and broken-up sidewalks inside the hull, which made her sink so fast that she broke up when she hit bottom.

ROAMER II at Bay Shore dock (1975) - Captains Jack Romeyk, Richard Dean, and Dave Farrell   Ed Mooney photo

Built in 1940 in Algonac, Michigan by Chris Craft Yacht. Length 55.2', beam 13.3', draft 3.6', GT 14, NT 10, one deck, 98 passengers, 470 hp, wood hull and cabin. She was converted into a ferry after suffering a fire when she was a yacht. The first time I saw this boat was at the Babylon town dock, about 1948, when I went on her to the Fire Island State Park to visit my girlfriend, Pat Brown, later to be my wife. At that time, the *Roamer II* had two 6-71 diesels with 2-to-1 gears (28" props), and was operated by Captain Clyde Best and owned by his wife, Mattie Best. After the bridge to Captree was completed, Captain Best moved the operation there and sailed from Captree Boat Basin until the Fire Island Bridge opened to traffic. Then service ended from Captree, and they sold the *Roamer II* to FIFI on April 16, 1965. Captain Best's son-in-law, Edmund Gangloff, was operating the ninety-passenger *Roamer II* when she was sold to Patterson. In 1966, Patterson built a pilothouse on the foredeck and was able to add nine passenger seats to the old pilot station area.

Before Patterson bought the *Roamer II*, Bob Federico had a verbal deal with Gangloff to buy her, and Bob started to paint her prior to the deal being signed. Bob decided to save a lot of travel time from the mainland to Captree Boat Basin and moved the boat to Babylon, closer to his home. Gangloff had Bob arrested for stealing the boat, and the police took Bob to the Babylon police station. Bob grew up with the police lieutenant, who took him into a back room, talked to him alone, and then brought Gangloff alone into the back room and talked to him. There was no intent to steal the boat, and they released Bob. Before the sale to Bob closed, Patterson bought the *Roamer II* (Captain Best and Patterson were old friends going back to the 1950s).

Patterson changed the 2-to-1 gear to 1.5-to-1 to use a smaller diameter prop with more pitch in the mistaken idea that she would go faster. She did go faster empty, but did not carry a load well. A third 6-71 was added in the center and forward of the main engines, which improved performance, but she was not a good ferry. She had three engines, 600 hp, carried 98 passengers, and was not as fast as the other ferries. 1980 was the *Roamer's* last year of service for FIFI. While owned by FIFI, she was leased to George Henrich, President of National Seashore Ferry, Inc., and sailed from Forster Park, Sayville, and later from Brown's River to Barrett Beach for Sayville Ferry.

George died in the late 1970s, and Harry Schneph ran the service to Barrett Beach through 1980. Paperwork was completed for him to buy the *Roamer II*, but at the last minute, he backed out of the deal, ending eight years of service. No one wanted to take over the Barrett Beach run.

The *Roamer II* was sold to the town of Islip in June 1981 for $42,500, and was operated by Ken Stein of Sayville Ferry to Barrett Beach. The *Roamer II* was later owned by Sayville Ferry. Ken removed the three 6-71s and installed two 8V-71s. That arrangement worked out well for speed when carrying a full load of passengers. She was still in service in 2004.

-43- ✦**Fireball** (first) ON 253644 Radio WA5422 *Gloria Ann*

FIREBALL (first) in Virginia (1959)   Shirley Patterson Collection

FIREBALL (first) before the top was added (1960)   Ed Mooney photo

Built in 1941 in Miami, Florida as an air/sea rescue boat for the US Navy. 63' long, 15'4" beam, GT 44, NT 30, 450 hp. Measured for a Certificate of Tonnage at Newport News, Virginia in 1947 as the *Gloria Ann*.

Owned by Saltaire Ferry Company, Inc., a separate company at that time owned by Patterson, Bill White, and White's cousin, Dr. Eldridge Smith. Patterson found the boat as a stripped-out hull (1959) in Virginia and had it towed to Bay Shore by the *Fire Island Miss* with Captain Hoyt Rollinson, a retired Coast Guard officer, in command along with Charlie Byron as crew.

The boat was a mess, but as with all the other vessels Patterson converted, it worked out well: three 2" shafts, 6-71 Gray Marine diesels port and starboard, GM tank twins in the center driving

95

forward into a V-drive. She made her first trip to the beach in 1960. The port and starboard engines were replaced with 6-110 engines from the *Isle of Fire* in November 1972. She had two decks forward, one deck over and aft of the engines. She was used the first summer without a top over the upper deck and only had a small forward cabin down below for bad weather. The aft overhead was added in 1961.

The main captain (1963 -1969) on the *Ball* was "Fireball Fred" Freiermuth. Fred always kept the boat spotless, well painted, and the brass shining. Fred always seemed to be in the middle of action, rescuing people from burning and sinking boats, and even finding a dead body. There was never a dull moment when Fireball Fred was around. However, we had too many complaints about his foolish actions and sadly had to let him go.

The *Fireball* was acquired in 1967 by FIFI when the Saltaire Ferry Company merged with FIFI. FIFI sold her in 1978 to a former captain, who had worked for us for a few years, and she went to Lake Harris, Florida, just north of Disney World, where she sailed as a sightseeing boat.

-44-   ✸**Firebird** (first) ON 258328   Radio WK3979   *Seahawk*   Military #77458

FIREBIRD (first) (1964)   Ed Mooney photo

Built in 1944 by Herreshoff at Bristol, Rhode Island as an air/sea rescue boat for the US Navy. She was changed very little when she was first converted for ferry use for Bridgeport and Port Jefferson Steamboat Company in 1960. They named her *Seahawk*, and she was owned by Arthur Tooker. The major changes he made were to replace two large gas Hall Scott 12V, 630 hp, with Allis-Chalmers diesels, model 21000, 540 hp each. Length 63', beam 15', draft 5' (she drew a foot more than most of the other ferries), 44 GT, 30 NT, two decks, 49 passengers, wood hull and cabin. The lower cabin, forward of the engine room, had portholes up high, and you could not easily see out of them; this cabin was rarely used by passengers.

Port Jefferson Ferry sold her to Fire Island Ferries in 1962. FIFI added a Detroit Diesel tank twin (two 6-71 side-by-side driving into one gear, mounted in an aft engine room just behind the main engines driving a third shaft through a V-drive). She was our fastest ferry at that time. Patterson changed the boat completely and brought the seating and certificate up to 149 passengers; a new stability letter was issued in May 1963.

She was the only boat we ever had with the pilothouse mid-ship. She was a slow boat to load and unload; luggage had to be handed high up and over the forward waist. Most of her service was

FIREBIRD (first) (1963)   Ed Mooney photo

between Bay Shore and Ocean Beach. She was sold in January 1984 to Thomas Doss of Norfolk, Virginia. Jack Romeyk went with the new owners from our Bay Shore dock to the boat basin at Fire Island State Park, where he got off the *Bird*, she went out the inlet, and we have not heard of the *Firebird* since. She served us well and carried many passengers in her twenty-two years at FIFI, but I was glad to see her leave.

-45-   ✦**Captain Patterson** ON 539334   Radio WYZ7190

CAPTAIN PATTERSON sea trial (1972)   Blount photo

Built in 1972 by Blount Marine at Warren, Rhode Island for Fire Island Ferries (owners Ed Mooney, John Van Bree, and Frank Mina). Length 75', beam 18.3', draft 5.2', GT 58, NT 39, three 12V71TI turbocharged, inter-cooled Detroit Diesels, 595 hp each, three 2.25" shafts, Twin Disc MG 514, 2-to-1 gears on each engine, 34" x 32" 4-blade props, 300 passengers, steel hull, aluminum cabin, two decks. Captain Elmer Patterson had the right to name the first new boat we built after buying the company from him. He named her after his father, Captain Herbert Patterson. Richard Taubler was the naval architect, using the basic concept that Patterson had drawn. Plans were modified by Blount, adding 12" to the beam to keep her from drawing over six feet with a full load. Until the sea trials were run at Blount's, there was great concern as to her speed, wake, and how she would perform with 300 passengers.

Builders always take a new boat out on a builder's trial run without the owner. They then correct defects before they run the owner's sea trials. We got to know the workers building the **Patterson** during the six months it took building her since we went up to Rhode Island every ten to fourteen days. When we arrived for the owner's trial run, the workmen were all excited and giving us thumbs up. This was the fastest boat they had ever built, which they knew from the builder's trial that had occurred two days earlier.

She was the first of the big 300-passenger fast ferries (before this, all big ferries in the bay were slow). The boat performed so well that we built three more like her: **Miss, Traveler**, and **Ball**. In 1976, the **Patterson** went into New York City to provide service across the East River during a subway strike, but the strike was settled and the boat wasn't needed. Beginning in 1991, the **Patterson** was used to make more freight trips than passenger trips since she was used for passenger service only Friday nights, Saturdays, and Sundays.

-46- ✦**Fire Island Miss** (second) ON 573136 Radio WJ8547

FIRE ISLAND MISS (second) (1976)   Ed Mooney photo

Built in 1976 by Blount Marine at Warren, Rhode Island for Fire Island Ferries (Ed Mooney and Frank Mina). (We gave Luther Blount a deposit on October 31, 1975.) The **Miss** is a copy of the **Captain Patterson** that had by then operated with great success for four years. The few changes that were made were: a spray rail was built into the hull (we welded a spray rail onto the **Patterson**) and added trim tabs controlled from the pilothouse (we later welded the tabs in place).

Nineteen seventy-six was America's Bicentennial and the year of Blount's 200th-built boat. Luther Blount planned a big christening ceremony and wanted the wife of the governor of Rhode Island to christen the **Miss**. Blount was unhappy when we would not agree to this since we had made plans to have my daughter, Casey, do the honors. The ceremony included a fife and drum marching band in colonial dress, a musket salute was fired off, there was a Coast Guard boat with its fire hose shooting water up into the air, and local TV was present. The reason Blount wanted to have the governor's wife take part was that he needed a political favor to get the property south of his shipyard rezoned, and he needed all the help he could get. Blount eventually was able to get the rezoning approved for use to operate his dinner cruise boat.

We went to Blount's to bring the *Miss* to Bay Shore and when we arrived, we where told to go home and wait a few days until the seas from a storm just passing settled down. The forecast was for the wind to go northwest, and I thought that would knock down the seas, and we would be in the lee of Long Island. We departed and had a nice trip down Naraganset Bay. When we got out in the open water of Block Island Sound, it was a different story. The seas were high and close together; the boat was great, but you had to go slowly and hang on for dear life. We had to pull into Point Judith and tie up the *Miss* for a few days before continuing the trip to Bay Shore. (Always listen to local sailors.)

-47- ✸**Traveler** (second) ON 583473   Radio WYF7801

TRAVELER (second) (circa 1980)   Ed Mooney photo

Built in 1977, one year after the *Miss*, by Blount Marine at Warren, Rhode Island for Fire Island Ferries, Inc. (Ed Mooney and Frank Mina). (We gave Blount a deposit on October 31, 1976.) She was the sister ship of the *Captain Patterson* and *Fire Island Miss*. Length 75', beam 18', draft 5.2', GT 59, NT 39, 3 Detroit 12V71TI, 595 hp each, Twin Disc MG 514, 2-to-1 gears turning 4-blade 34" x 32" props on 2.25" shafts, 32 volt starting and lighting, light ship speed about 24 knots, total of 800 gallons of fuel in two tanks, dry exhaust out the stern, steel hull, aluminum cabin, two decks, 298 passengers. When first in service, she made most of the Fair Harbor weekend trips.

FIRE ISLAND TRADER (2001)   Ed Mooney photo

Built in 1971 in West Sayville, New York by Clifford Varin as the clam dredge *Kyle S. Lane*. Length 62.8', beam 18', draft 4.2', GT 33, NT 23, two 6-71 engines, 165 hp each, two 2" shafts, Allison hydraulic 1.5-to-1 gears, 26" x 22" 4-blade props. FIFI bought her from Edward C. Schildt in April 1980 for $15,000 for use as a freight and garbage boat. Ed dredged on Blue Points Oyster Company's company-owned bay bottom and sold them the clams. The boat looked like a mass of rust as she lay out on the end of a long, badly damaged pier, south by Charlie Hart's in West Sayville. Upon closer inspection, the rust from the topside ran down on the hull, but the /" steel hull was in good condition coated with epoxy coal tar. FIFI removed all the deck gear used to dredge clams and built a flat deck forward of the pilothouse to hold one 34-yard garbage compactor. This arrangement was used on our 1981 to 1985 Fair Harbor garbage contract.

The winter of 1980-81, the boat was completely stripped to a bare hull and rebuilt with the pilothouse located on the starboard side, eight feet above the deck so the captain could see over garbage containers. The engines were converted to lay-downs so they fit under the deck, allowing for a flat deck from bow to stern. This way, two containers could be carried, and each could take about ninety yards of un-compacted garbage. A hydraulic crane was added to the port side, and she made a great freight boat (no passengers are carried). She has been used to take Ocean Beach, Fair Harbor, Atlantique, and Point O'Woods garbage to Bay Shore. Before 1980, we used 37-yard cone packers. Prior to that, we used 4-yard containers that were pressed down with a dock-mounted compactor at Ocean Beach. By the mid-1990s, garbage trucks were driven on and off at Bay Shore and Ocean Beach.

✦ **Vagabond** (second) ON 607906 Radio WQZ2872

VAGABOND (second) (circa 1985)   Ed Mooney photo

Built in 1979 by Blount Marine in Warren, Rhode Island as a freight boat for Fire Island Ferries (Ed Mooney and Frank Mina). Length 75', beam 21.5', draft 5.2', GT 74, NT 50, two Detroit 6-71N engines, 175 hp each, small injectors (55 mm), rated at 1,800 rpm for twenty-four-hour-a-day use, two props, 36" x 30" 4-blade on 2.25" shafting, Allison MH 3-to-1 gears, steel hull and cabin, aluminum pilothouse, one working deck with the pilothouse on a second deck, freight capacity of 60 tons.

The price was so high ($360,000) that it was decided to also license her for 225 passengers at an extra cost for seats, life jackets, heads, holding tank, and other equipment needed on a passenger boat on a run of more than a half hour. With her slow speed, she was used for passengers on Sundays for Atlantique or our short run to Kismet. She was also used for night charter sails. She was built to safely go through ice. This called for a heavy hull so her maximum speed would be ten knots or hull speed. She is loaded at Maple Avenue dock and leaves at 10 A.M., going to almost every stop, and many days going to Point O'Woods with items that they can't take on their ferry. A Hiab hydraulic crane in our vessel design worked out to be one of the smartest things we ever did in our freight operation.

VAGABOND (second) (circa 1985)   Ed Mooney photo

-50- ✦**Fireball** (second) ON 634661   Radio WYR6038

FIREBALL (second) (1981)   Ed Mooney photo

Built in 1981 by Blount Marine in Warren, Rhode Island for Fire Island Ferries (Ed Mooney and Frank Mina). Built as a passenger ferry for service from Bay Shore to stops from Kismet to Ocean Beach. After 1984, she was used in service at Seaview and Ocean Bay Park for Westferry Inc., the new company that bought out Zee Line. The **Ball** is a copy of the **Patterson**, **Miss**, and **Traveler** with only minor changes.

-51-   ✦**Firebird** (second) ON 670012   Radio WSR9873

FIREBIRD (second) at west terminal (1999)   Ed Mooney photo

Built in 1984 by Blount Marine in Warren, Rhode Island for FIFI (Ed Mooney and Frank Mina). Length 85', beam 20', draft 4.8', GT 72, NT 44, 1,785 hp total of three engines, 12V71TI

Detroit, three shafts 2.25" diameter, three props, 34" x 32" 4-blade, two decks, 395 passengers. This was the first aluminum hull for FIFI. She's a copy of the *Patterson* class vessel, built ten feet longer and two feet wider with the same engine arrangement, the side doors located the same distance aft of the bow to give the boat the same docking arrangement as the *Patterson* class boats, ten feet of cabin was added aft of the freight door, the engines were placed the same distance from the stern so we could interchange shafts and props, the *Bird* is six tons lighter and three knots faster than the steel hull ferries of the *Patterson* class, and she can carry 100 more passengers. When new, with about half a tank of fuel and no passengers, she made twenty-six knots. As with all our other ferries, she was built light, and nothing is installed or carried on board that is not needed.

Her performance delighted all of us, except Luther Blount. He had just finished his newly-designed 65' high-tech ferry, made with aluminum frames and lightweight foam covered fiberglass on the outside. The ferry had two 12V71TI Detroits and was designed to carry 150 passengers. The ferry was a lightweight vessel, and Blount expected her to run away from the *Bird.*

The high-tech boat was ready for sea trials the same day we were there for the *Firebird* owner's trials. Luther made a $5 bet with me, just before going out for our first sea trial, that his boat would be faster. It was a long, close race, but we were just a little faster. When we got back to his shipyard right behind him, he was gone; when I got to the office, Luther had left the $5 for me.

The *Bird* makes less wake, planes off quicker, and stays up better in deep water than the steel hull 75-foot boats. She was built a little light around the strut and prop area, and some cracks developed. A few frames were added to that area, and we have not had a crack since then. The struts also cracked, and we replaced them with struts shipped up from Gulf Craft. We also liked the fact that she uses a little less fuel than the steel hulls, and the engines run longer between overhauls. She worked out so well that we made two copies of her at Gulf Craft, the *Voyager* and *Explorer*, and seventeen years after building the *Bird*, Blount Barker built the *Flyer*, another copy with a new series of engines.

The first year we used the *Bird*, she set a record in our fleet for the most passengers carried in one year. (We always use a new boat as much as possible the first year while her engines are under one-year warranty.)

-52- ★**Stranger** (second) ON 684623 Radio WSK8527

STRANGER (second) at Patterson, Louisiana (1985)   Ed Mooney photo

Built in 1985 by Gulf Craft, Patterson, Louisiana, for Fire Island Ferries (Ed Mooney and Frank Mina) as a passenger ferry. Length 65', beam 17', draft 4.25', two engines, 12V71N Detroit Diesels, 450 hp each, Allison MH gears, 1.5-to-1, two props, 28" x 26", 4-blade, 2" shaft size, aluminum hull and cabin, two decks, 150 passengers. The primary run is Saltaire terminal, Bay Shore, to Saltaire.

Dick Ivey was her longtime captain on weekends. The layout is a copy of *Zeelion*, two decks forward, one deck aft, bottom designed by Gulf Craft. The hull of *Zeeliner*, after a Coast Guard dry dock inspection, required extensive repair, more than was practical on an old boat; she was stripped of all usable equipment and sunk as a fish wreck. We trucked engines and equipment out of the *Zeeliner* to Gulf Craft to be used in the *Stranger.*

The *Stranger* is used year-round and as the winter boat, keel cooled with dry exhaust, no water to drain or freeze. The lower cabin is heated with bus heaters using engine-cooling water.

Johnny Maderara, engine installer at Blount's, delivered the boat from Patterson, Louisiana across the Gulf of Mexico to Fort Myers in Florida, up the Caloosahatchee River to Lake Okeechobee through locks of the St. Lucie Canal to the East Coast, up the East Coast to Bay Shore, a 1,900 mile trip. The Gulf Craft-built boat delivered by Johnny had nothing to do with Blount; Johnny delivers boats as a sideline. He knew Gulf Craft was building the boat because Blount lost the bid when his price was well over 15% higher than Gulf Craft. I would have given Blount the contract if they were within 10%, the amount saved in delivery cost, airline cost, and travel time.

-53-   ✦**Evening Star** ON 697080   Radio WSA7434

EVENING STAR (1990)   Ed Mooney photo

Built in 1986 in Patterson, Louisiana for Fire Island Cruises (Frank Mina and Ed Mooney), a sister corporation of FIFI. Length 113', beam 28', draft 5', two 12V71N Detroits, 55 mm injectors, 420 hp, each engine rated at 1,800 rpm for continuous duty, 3-to-1 gears, 3" shafts, 36" x 35" 4-blade props, two Delco 60 kw at 1,200 rpm, gen-sets driven by 6-71 Detroits, aluminum hull and cabin, 400 passengers, four decks, two bars, heat and air conditioning, full galley, two convection ovens, large refrigerator, steam tables, dishwasher, tile heads below the main deck forward. We ran eleven years without working on an engine, not even a minor repair.

The *Star* made the trip from her build site near Morgan City, Louisiana, 550 miles across the Gulf of Mexico to Fort Myers, Florida, across lake Okeechobee to the east coast of Florida into the Atlantic Ocean, up the coast to around Norfolk, Virginia for fuel, and out again into the Atlantic to Fire Island Inlet to Bay Shore, about 1,900 miles.

The *Star* was not built for or used in ferry service, but she was operated by FIFI and did run numerous trips to the beach for parties, weddings, and other charter events. The *Star* operated mostly in Great South Bay, but did sail in New York Harbor for special events, after-prom nights, weddings, and so on. In 1992, she went to Boston for the Tall Ships events on the 500th anniversary of Columbus Day. We even sent her to Hilton Head, South Carolina for the winter of 1992 to try to keep her busy off-season. It started to get busy about the time we had to get her back to Bay Shore for her season. It's a tough business; too much work followed by a long winter of no sails or income, but lots of expense.

After ten years of service, each year making a few less trips than the year before, I decided to sell the *Star*. In October 1997, I put an ad in *Boats and Harbor*, a trade paper for the commercial boating industry, and had instant responses. Again, most of the people who looked at her wanted to buy her as soon as they sold their boat, or in one case, sell two boats. Skeets Winner of Wilmington, North Carolina drove up, looked at her, and made an offer. He stated that he had the money and could close in a week. He left on a handshake and said he would wire up a 10% deposit when he got home. After he left, I called a friend in Boston who knew Skeets, and he told me that Skeets had the money. Within ten days, I had the money in escrow, and a day or two later, the *Star* was on the way to Wilmington, North Carolina, with Captain Rich Kline, Mike Mooney, Dave Kahler, and Mike Miller.

Although I got less than I wanted for the *Star*, we immediately cut the expense of owning her, including mortgage, insurance, heat, repairs, and labor. The boatyard property next door, now called Maple Marina,was going up for auction (Frank Mina had gone bankrupt and lost the property to the bank), and the sale of the *Star* gave me enough money in the bank to bid. The bid was held in March of 1998, and I was well outbid by Ned Hurly.

-54- ★**Voyager** ON 961188   Radio WAL7934

VOYAGER (1990)   Ed Mooney photo

Built in 1990 at Gulf Craft in Patterson, Louisiana for Fire Island Ferries (Ed Mooney) for ferry service from Bay Shore to the western end of Fire Island, mainly Ocean Beach. She's a copy of the *Firebird*. Length 85', beam 20', draft 4.8', International GT 126, NT 82, three 12V71TI Detroit Diesels, 1,785 hp total, 34" x 32" 4-blade props, 2.25" x 19", 10"-long shafts, two decks, aluminum hull, 389 passengers. When the boat was finished at Gulf Craft, 1,900 miles away by water, a FIFI crew of Rich Kline, Dave Anderson, Vic Klipp, and Michael Gleason flew down with toolboxes, charts, and personal items. They sailed 550 miles across the Gulf of Mexico to Fort Myers, Florida, then up the Caloosahatchee River and across Lake Okeechobee to the St. Lucie Canal, then out the inlet into the Atlantic Ocean to Norfolk, Virginia for fuel, and from there took a straight course to Fire Island Inlet.

-55-   ✳**Explorer** ON 974101   Radio WAU3844

EXPLORER (1991)   Ed Mooney photo

Built in 1991 by Gulf Craft in Patterson, Louisiana for Fire Island Ferries (Ed Mooney) for use as a passenger ferry. Length 85', beam 20', draft 4.5', three engines, 585 hp each, Detroit 12V71TI diesels, reduction gear twin-disc MG 514C, 2-to-1, three props, 34" x 32", 4-blade, shaft 2.5", aluminum hull and cabin. On her sea trials, light ship, she made a speed of twenty-six knots (about twenty-nine miles per hour). She is a copy of *Voyager* and *Firebird*; they cruise at about nineteen knots at 1,800 rpm, which is using about 70% of their horsepower. At this rating, we have had higher than standard engine life between overhauls. The lighter aluminum hull and longer waterline length give us this extra speed, and these boats use less fuel than the steel hull ferries. Ports served are Bay Shore to Fire Island communities, Kismet, Saltaire, Fair Harbor, Dunewood, Atlantique, and Ocean Beach.

-56-   ✳**Fire Island Flyer** (second) ON 1110461   Radio WDA5135

Built in 2001 by Blount Barker in Warren, Rhode Island as an all-aluminum, 398-passenger ferry for Fire Island Ferries (Ed Mooney). She was a copy of the *Firebird* Blount built in 1984, 85' x 20', two decks, three Detroit Diesel, 8v2000, 645 hp, 1,000-gallon fuel tank, electronic controlled engines, keel cooling and dry exhaust, Twin Disc 5141, 2-to-1 gears turning 5-blade 34" props on 2.5" shafts. Up until this boat, FIFI used Detroit, 71 series, 2-cycle engines in all its new vessels, 6 and 12 cylinders, turbocharged and no-turbocharged. As of January 2001, the 71 series could not meet Federal exhaust emission standards and therefore could no longer be installed in new vessels, but could remain in existing use. The *Flyer* had to meet new USCG regulations, which required greater fire protection, fire doors to the stairwells, alarms, smoke detectors, and more fire insulation.

FIRE ISLAND FLYER (second) (2001)   Dave Anderson photo

-57-   ★America ON 1125089   Radio WDA8290

AMERICA (2002)   Dave Anderson photo

    Built in 2002 in Bridgeport, Connecticut by Derecktor as an all-aluminum freight vessel for Fire Island Ferries (Ed Mooney), 85'x 23.4', twin Series 60, Detroit Diesels, 400 hp each at a continuous duty rating of 1,800 rpm, keel cooled, dry exhaust, 2.5-to-1 Twin Disc gears, 2.5" shafts turning 4-blade 36" x 34" props. Pitman, hydraulic deck-mounted crane and hydraulic stern ramp. While designing and building the *America*, we added 150 passengers to her USCG certificate when she is not carrying freight. *America* may never be used in passenger service, but when the unexpected happens on a Sunday or holiday, she will be ready to help out.

AMERICA leaving Bay Shore off-season (2002)   Ed Mooney photo

Saltaire Ferries

-58-   **Susie R** ON 116157
   Built in 1886 in Brooklyn, New York as a fishing boat. 40' x 13.2', GT 10, NT 8, wood hull, gas screw. Used by Fire Island Beach Development Company to transport prospective buyers of lots at Saltaire.

-59-   **Stranger** (first) ON 207661
   Built in 1895 in New York, New York. Home port Patchogue, New York. 78.6' x 12', GT 27, NT 23, one Standard, 50 hp, gas engine, screw prop. Built as a yacht owned by John T. Wrigley. Converted yacht, rosewood paneling, velvet curtains, marble bathrooms, most elegant ferry on the bay. Saltaire's second ferry, and served for many years, beginning about 1910. *(Listed in 1927 MVUS.)*

STRANGER (circa 1915)   Shirley Patterson Collection

-60- Eladio ON 201237

Beyond the wreckage you can see the ferry *Eladio* where some seventy people rode out the great storm.

ELADIO at Saltaire dock after September 1938 Hurricane   1977 Saltaire publication

Built in 1902 in Astoria, New York. 65' x 12.4', GT 22, NT 17. One of the first passenger ferries to Saltaire in 1910 or 1911, she was owned by Fire Island Development Company and later owned by the village of Saltaire. Captain Herbert Patterson, superintendent of ferries for the village of Saltaire, purchased the **Eladio** from the Hartford Insurance Company for $700. The **Eladio** was tied up at Brewster's Shipyard in 1949. *(Listed in 1929 and 1937 MVUS, she had 36 hp; listed in 1946 and 1949 MVUS as owned by village of Saltaire as passenger ferry with 125 hp diesel.)*

-61- Saltaire ON 219549

SALTAIRE (circa 1930)   From *Fire Island Tide* publication

SALTAIRE (circa 1930)   Shirley Patterson Collection

Built in 1919 in Wareham, Massachusetts by Cape Cod Shipbuilding for the village of Saltaire. Length 73.5', beam 19', GT 68, NT 46, wood hull and cabin, passenger ferry, two crew. In 1937 she had a 64 hp engine; sometime later, it was replaced with a 160 hp engine. The captains were Herbert Patterson and George Adams. Reported to be a sightseeing vessel in 1950. *(Listed in 1929, 1935, 1937, 1941 MVUS owned by the village, and listed in 1949 as owned by Boat Sales Inc. of Wareham, Massachusetts, 250 passengers with 330 hp diesel.)*

-62-   **Saltaire II** ON 246082
Built in 1929 in West Sayville, New York for the village of Saltaire. 40.2' x 11.7', GT 14, NT 12, one 160 hp engine, wood hull. *(1937 MVUS has the **Eladio** and **Saltaire** as Saltaire's only ferries. 1949 MVUS has this ferry listed as plain **Saltaire** with the above number and owned by the village of Saltaire.)*

-63-   ✸**Saltaire III** ON 255412   *Fire Island   PT 3685*

SALTAIRE III (circa 1953)   Ed Mooney photo

110

Built about 1943 by Elco in Bayonne, New Jersey as a US Navy PT boat, 85' long with three V-12 Packard gas engines. After World War II, she was converted at Cape May, New Jersey into a ferry. She was cut down to just under 65' to register her as a motorboat, which had simple regulations at that time. The three Packards were replaced with one 200 hp surplus Gray Marine 6-71 diesel, concrete was poured in the stern below the lower deck to trim down the stern. She then had a draft of six feet and was slow. Also, with two decks and high out of the water, she was difficult to handle in the wind. She was painted all gray (often called Big Moe) and difficult to load. I am sure it was a big disappointment to the village and the passengers riding on her when just about every boat in the bay passed them by.

Patterson had to take **Saltaire III** as part of his Saltaire Ferry contract of 1950 and had to pay off its debt ($15,000). He had her painted white. In 1952, she was made into twin screw by adding another Gray Marine diesel, and the concrete was removed, making her a better ferry. She helped Patterson handle peak travel loads until better, faster boats were built.

With her name **Saltaire**, we had difficulties getting passengers going to Ocean Beach to get on since they did not want to go to Saltaire. Her name was changed in 1954 to **Fire Island**. When we called to her on the radio as "**Fire Island**," the Fire Island Coast Guard Station would answer, so we had to call to "Ferryboat **Fire Island**" to prevent the Coast Guard from answering.

Later, the upper deck was removed and the lower deck raised to the guardrail height, making her into a single-deck boat. With removable seats, she was used as a freight boat, much needed at that time. Still later, a 1,000-gallon tank was mounted on the deck, and she transported gasoline to Kismet to be sold by Patterson at his gas dock. Someone informed the USCG of this dangerous operation, and it was quickly ended.

Patterson sold the vessel to Guy Lombardo to take dinner patrons from his Freeport, Long Island restaurant to Jones Beach Marine Theater, in which Guy was involved at that time. The boat was poorly maintained by Lombardo's captain, and her certificate was removed by the USCG until safety violations were corrected. The boat lay at the Jones Beach Marine Stadium dock for a few years.

-64- ✦**Fire Islander** ON 260685   Radio WJ8548

FIRE ISLANDER (circa 1958)   Ed Mooney photo

Built in 1942 in Miami, Florida as a Navy air/sea rescue boat #C9501. Reported to be owned by Bill Levitt of Levittown fame, brought up from Florida to Freeport by Fred Scopinich and his cousin, rebuilt into a ferry by Freeport Point Shipyard by the Scopinich family for Captain Patterson in 1951. Length 63', beam 14.4', GT 51, NT 39, 750 hp, two decks, 150 passengers, double-planked wood hull and cabin.

The *Islander* entered service in 1952 with the upper portion of her hull cut down from about fifteen feet aft of the bow to the stern. The engines were in the stern, driving connecting shafts forward under the lower passenger deck to a V-drive. On the ends of the drive shafts were large universal joints, one of which broke while underway, and the loose end whipped around, ripping up the deck and seats down below aft (luckily, there were no passengers in the area). Shortly after this happened (1961), the engines were moved forward to mid-ship, the V-drives were removed, and the gears connected directly to the prop shafts.

The evolution of the *Islander* continued: bulkheads were installed forward and aft of the engines to make an engine room, passengers then boarding mid-ship over the engine room (boarding used to be at the stern), a pilothouse was added well forward of the open pilot station, the old, mechanical Capital gears were replaced with Allison hydraulic reduction gears, and a 6-71 diesel was installed between the 6-110s since the 6-110s did not have enough power to maintain speed with a full load of passengers. (These changes took place over a twenty-year period; there was little money available for capital improvements and to pay bills.)

The *Islander* ended service in 1991, and she was stripped of all machinery and equipment and sunk in the Atlantic as a fish reef in 1992.

Seaview Ferries

-65-   **Fire Island** ON 210297

FIRE ISLAND (circa 1936) reported to have serviced Seaview about 1934   Courtesy of *Fire Island Tide*

Built in 1912 in New York, New York, 138 GT, 99 NT, 99.8' long, 23.3' beam, draft 4'3", diesel, 190 hp, 350 passengers, sailed from Babylon, owned by South Shore Navigation Company, owner B.W. King *(1947 MVUS has owner Poor Navigation Company, Boston.)*

-66- **Mary** ON 236558

Built in 1929 in Ipswich, Massachusetts. At 43.4' x 12.5', she was 48' long, GT 13, NT 10, one Buda, 85-hp gas engine, wood hull. Bought by Tonis Zegel and rebuilt (1936) as a charter fishing boat and also used as an Ocean Bay Park ferry. She was used also as a ferry to West Fire Island when an attempt was made to develop the island in the 1930s. Captain Zegel sold the **Mary** to the Navy in 1942. A newspaper story about the 1938 Hurricane and Saltaire tells of Tonis Zegel and his boat **Mary** as being the first vessel to get to Saltaire after the storm passed. A note sent to me from Brud Zegel states: "My father came home from Ocean Bay Park to Bay Shore in the **Osceola** when it was still rough. He came home, and he and I went to Maple Avenue, Bay Shore. A couple of newsmen and some others wanted to go to Saltaire, especially a girl (with a French name) who said her mother was in a house at Saltaire. My father and I left Bay Shore with about ten people aboard (one being a captain of the Saltaire ferry). No word had yet reached the mainland of the damage suffered. When we reached Saltaire, my father didn't know where we were until we recognized the **Eladio** in the basin. Wreckage had been washed into the bay, and in daylight, Saltaire looked like a lumberyard after a tornado. So the real story is that the **Mary**, my father, me as mate, and about ten people were the first to the beach that night. Incidentally, the girl's mother had drowned."

Another story has **Electra**, owned by Chris Veryzer, as the first boat to Saltaire after the storm, to bring over the mayor.

-67- **Osceola** ON 206373 *South Bay Trader*

OSCEOLA (circa 1950)   Ed Mooney Collection

Built in 1909 in Tottenville, New York. 50.4' x 12.6', GT 13, NT 9, wood hull. Tonis Zegel used her for gunning (duck hunting) and fishing when not in passenger service to Ocean Bay Park and West Island. Later, she was used for freight to Seaview and the Park. The first engine, a 35 hp gas Buda, was changed to a 150 hp gas Speedway, and after Word War II to a Detroit Diesel, 6-71, about 200 hp. Copper sheathing was added to her bottom for winter ice service. Working well in ice, she could pass the **Maid** in heavy ice since she had four-foot less beam and did not have to push as much ice out of the way. She was not a big freight boat and was loaded and unloaded by hand. When large loads of building material had to be taken to Seaview or Ocean Bay Park, it was loaded on a small scow and towed by the **Osceola**.

The **Osceola** was sold to Dick Block and Billy Leyrer about 1968 for use as a freight boat to Dunewood, with the expectation of buying or taking over the Fair Harbor run from Gus Pagels. They renamed her **South Bay Trader**. Very little freight went to Dunewood, and they sold her along with a small scow in 1969 or 1970 to a fish company in south Jersey. Dick Block relates that they towed the scow with the **Osceola** from Bay Shore to Manasquan Inlet, New Jersey. While in the ocean, the barge started to take on water. They had to transfer a gas-powered pump from the **Osceola** to keep her afloat, and they had to patch a plank that had come loose. He stated that the new owner wanted the engine and gear and was going to scrap the 61-year-old hull.

ARTEMIS (circa 1954)   Ed Mooney photo

Built in 1931 in New York, New York as a rumrunner; one of the Greenpoint fleet of "Nick the Greek." Length 55', beam 11.3', draft 3.6', GT 14, NT 10, two 1.75" shafts, wood hull and cabin, one deck, reported to have had two Liberty aircraft engines converted for marine use, 400 hp each. The vessel was later converted to carry passengers, and in 1958 that number was set at 59 (prior to that date, she carried more).

This rumrunner was reported to have almost been captured going up a creek to unload when she was surprised by authorities. She backed down and turned around in time to get away, but not before getting bullet holes in the stern. She is reported to have a speed of 35 knots, the fastest of all rumrunners (one report had her at 50 mph; I don't believe she had the horsepower needed for that speed).

Captain Elmer Patterson owned and operated the *Artemis* with her big gasoline engines as one of the two fast ferries in Great South Bay, between Seaview and Bay Shore. While Captain Patterson was in the Navy, the boat was acquired by Gil Smith, whose ancestors at one time owned all of Fire Island under an English grant. Gil Smith in turn sold her to Snyde Zegel, who continued service to Seaview and the Park during World War II.

The *Artemis* had two Hall Scott 6-cylinder gas engines, dry exhaust mufflers straight up on the cabin top over the engines, and she could be heard miles away. The engines were later replaced with two Gray Marine 6-71 diesels of 225 hp each.

Billy Leyrer and Dick Block bought the *Artemis* in 1968 and renamed her *South Bay Courier* for their new company, Fair Harbor Ferry Company, to run to Dunewood. They ran in 1968 and 1969, with hopes to buy out Gus Pagels and take over his run to Fair Harbor. Billy and Dick were broke and out of business at the end of 1969, and Fire Island Ferries bought the *Courier* in 1970 and sold her in 1982. *(Listed in 1935, 1937 MVUS as owned by John W. Ellis and with 1,420 hp.)*

SEAVIEWER (circa 1960)   Ed Mooney photo

Built in 1942 by Elco in Bayonne, New Jersey. The hull was begun as a rumrunner and finished as a ferry by Zee Line Ferry (1950). Length 55', beam 11.2', draft 3', GT 11, NT 7, two 6-71 Detroit diesel engines, 200 hp each, two props, 26" x 20", 4-blades, shaft 1.75", wood hull and cabin, one deck, cruising speed about 17 knots, 81 passengers. The exhaust went straight up and out the cabin top into truck-type mufflers (the exhaust could be heard miles away). This arrangement was used by many ferries at that time. With the engine setup of a dry exhaust and keel cooling, no seawater had to be drained in the winter or sea strainers cleared of seaweed. The constant problem with wet exhaust, heat exchanger-cooled engines is that the cold seawater enters the hot exhaust pipe and erodes and cracks the pipe, leaking water and exhaust into the engine room, and the engines suck in the dirty exhaust. Ports served were Bay Shore to Seaview and Ocean Bay Park, Fire Island. She was one of the boats Fire Island Ferries bought from Zee Line and was sold on July 9, 1986 for $25,000 to Jack McCormack for use on the Finger Lakes in upstate New York. She was reported to be in Newport, Rhode Island in 2000 with the name *Rumrunner II*.

-70- ✦**Zeeliner** ON 277200 Radio WK5003 Military # C36231

ZEELINER (circa 1965)   Ed Mooney photo

ZEELINER after engines were changed to 12v71N   Ed Mooney photo

Built in 1942 as an air/sea rescue boat for the US Navy (the 1942 Navy contract cost for a complete 63' air/sea rescue vessel was about $122,000). Bought by Zee Line in 1956 for $6,150, all running gear except engines. Converted into a ferry and first used in 1958 (owner Tonis Zegel). Converted at Brewster's Shipyard and by the Zegel family at their Bay Shore terminal at a cost of $29,000 plus their labor. Length 63', beam 14.6', draft 4', GT 44, NT 34, two props, 26" x 26", 4-blade, two 2" shafts, wood hull and cabin, 167 passengers, four engines, military war surplus tank twins. A tank twin is composed of two 6-71s set side-by-side driving into one gear case, connected to one reverse reduction gear; the tank twin developed 450 hp. The heads and blocks were turned to have the exhaust on the outside over the top of the blowers; the bell housings had the starters on the outside. Each engine had its own governor with an outside rod joining the governors together. (Patterson bought a new set - one unit of two engines - for $550 about 1962.)

The tank twins were replaced (1980) with two new 12V71N with Allison MH 1.5-to-1 gears. They were new engines that they obtained at a good price; they were an older model without cooling below the intake ports. Detroit then had a replacement model out with cooling below the intake ports. FIFI changed the blocks at a later date due to the fact that they had a short life between overhauls. The pistons and liners ran hot, the block warped, ring life was shorter, and when buying used engines, you stayed away from the older, no-cooling-below-the-intake port block.

Ports served were Bay Shore to Seaview and Ocean Bay Park, Fire Island from 1958 through 1984. The *Zeeliner* was owned and used only one year by FIFI (Westferry), 1984. USCG inspection requirements for hull repairs were too costly to undertake, costing more than the boat would be worth when the work was completed, and we would still have an old boat. FIFI removed all machinery and equipment in November 1984 for use in the *Stranger*. The *Zeeliner* was dismantled and sunk as a fish wreck in the ocean off Fire Island in 1985.

ZEE WHIZ hauled at Main Terminal (circa 1987)   Ed Mooney photo

Built 1964 at Freeport Point Shipyard, Freeport, New York by the Scopinich family. (They were famous for building more than thirty rumrunners with speeds near thirty knots, even when loaded with liquor. They also built fifteen Coast Guard boats to catch rumrunners; the rumrunners were always built to run faster.) The *Whiz* was built for Zee Line Ferry, the Zegel family, as a passenger ferry to service Seaview and Ocean Bay Park. The naval architect was Richard Taubler. Length 65', beam 16.7', draft 4.8', GT 73, NT 56, three Detroit 6-110 diesel engines, 431 hp each, three 2" shafts, 28"x 26", 4-blade props, double-planked wood hull, wood cabin, two decks, 150 passengers. If run for long periods over 1,700 rpm, this model engine was subject to cracked heads, stuck injectors, or holes blown in a piston. The heavy one-piece head required four people to lift it off and on and often someone would hurt his back. The wing engines were replaced with late model Detroit 12V71N, leaving the center 6-110 for several years until it was replaced with the smaller Detroit 6-71 to gain space between engines and to remove the 6-110 that was no longer being manufactured. The time was right to take out the 6-110 engine, since it had a knock and had to be rebuilt.

Captain Patterson provided the bottom drawings of the *Fire Island Belle* to the Zegel brothers. They widened the boat out at the chine, and they built the boat heavier. The boat had seating for over 200 passengers, but after 1958, the USCG regulations limited new wooden and non-metal boats to 150 passengers. The *Zee Whiz*, along with the Zee Line operation, was bought by FIFI (Westferry) in 1994.

ZEELION (circa 1970)   Ed Mooney photo

Built in 1966 at Freeport Point Shipyard by the Scopinich family for Zee Line as a passenger ferry for service to Seaview and Ocean Bay Park, with the same hull design as *Zee Whiz*. Length 65', beam 16.7', draft 4.8', GT 79, NT 62, two 12V71N Detroit diesel engines of 478 hp each, two props, 28" x 24", 4-blade, two 2" shafts, double-planked hull, wood cabin, two decks forward, one deck aft, limited to 150 passengers by being built of wood. Sold to FIFI (Westferry) in 1984 as part of a complete package of Zee Line Ferry. When the USCG would not allow a vessel made of wood or plastic to carry more than 150 passengers, Zee Line Ferry made a copy of the *Whiz* with two engines and one deck aft of the engine room to carry freight; then they no longer needed the *Osceola*. The aft seats were removed for the freight operation and replaced for passenger service on Friday afternoons, Saturdays, and Sundays.

Fair Harbor Ferries/Cherry Grove Ferry Inc. Vessels

-73-   **Zuzu** ON 227002   *Souvenir*

ZUZU (circa 1926)   Warren James Collection (he is one of the little boys in the photo)

Date built unknown. Her official number would have her built about 1923; the official numbers (ON) seem to advance in proper sequence, starting about 1910. Length 36' (was longer), beam 13.5', GT 14, NT 10, 20 hp diesel, 50 to 75 passengers. Owner *(1929 MVUS)* Captain Charles J. Smith. Passenger boat to Fair Harbor, reported to have served there from 1923 until 1934 when Pagels took over the run. Prior to 1938, owned by Ernest Grassnik, who renamed her *Souvenir*, and used her as his freight boat to his grocery store at Fair Harbor. Eddie Lipinski bought the store and boat, then sold the boat to Eddie Robbins, who used it as a freight boat while Lonelyville was being developed. *(Listed in 1935 MVUS with a 32 hp engine, and listed in 1941 MVUS as Souvenir.)*

-74-   **Atlantic**   ON 201919

ATLANTIC (circa 1960)   Ed Mooney photo

Built in 1905 at Week's Shipyard, Amityville, New York. 59.7' x 20.5', GT 25, wood hull. Originally a side-wheeler that ran twenty years from Amityville to Hemlock Cove and Gilgo Beach on Jones Beach. First engine found in MVUS was a 26 hp single screw. Owner Gus Pagels, Cherry Grove Ferry Inc. Home port Sayville, New York. Gus Pagels bought her in 1927 for $1,500 from W. G. Conley and converted her into a 180-passenger ferry and ran from Sayville to Cherry Grove in the 1920s and early 1930s. The gas Speedway engine was replaced in 1949 with a 6-cylinder Cat diesel, D-319. She used very little fuel; Gus claimed less than five gallons a round trip. She was a slow boat, about fifty-five minutes one way to Fair Harbor. The *Atlantic* was the vessel used from Bay Shore in the March 1, 1935 contract with Fair Harbor Development Company, Inc. During the week, Gus carried a lot of freight on the *Atlantic* while she also carried passengers; there were times the passengers sat on the freight. I found a letter from the community association asking Gus not to load the passenger boat with freight. When she was hauled on Brewster's railway in 1968 for an annual drydock inspection, a plank fell off the bottom, and the inspector saw more bad frames that were covered over by an inner hull. She was at the end of her sixty-three years of life and was dismantled in 1968 and towed out in the Atlantic, south of the Fire Island Lighthouse, and sunk to become an artificial fishing reef.

-75- ♣**Cherry Grove** ON 231536   Radio WJ6897

CHERRY GROVE operating from Sayville to the Grove before moving to Bay Shore for the
Fair Harbor and State Park runs (circa 1934)   Luke Kaufman Collection

Built in 1932 in Sayville, New York by Gus Pagels for his Cherry Grove run. Length 42.8',
beam 14', GT 14. Her gas Speedway engine was replaced with a Chrysler Royal in 1941, later (around
1951) that engine was replaced with a 6-71 diesel engine of 225 hp, wood hull and cabin, one deck.
Service from Sayville to Cherry Grove, and in the 1940s from Bay Shore to Fair Harbor and Fire
Island State Park. She was a slow boat and did not get much use after the *Isle* and *Isle II* were added
to the Fair Harbor fleet by Gus. FIFI acquired this vessel as part of Gus's assets in the 1972 sale to
FIFI. FIFI did not use this boat, and in February 1973, she was sold to Barry Barton as a freight boat
to the Pines and Grove.

-76-   ♣**Running Wild** ON 231475   Radio WJ7189

RUNNING WILD (circa 1955)   Ed Mooney photo

Built in 1932 at Bergen Beach, Brooklyn, New York as a rumrunner, but registered for coastal
trade (as most of them were; some rumrunners were registered for mackerel fishing). Length 54', beam
12', draft 3.8', GT 14, NT 9, one deck, wood hull, V-bottom forward, wide flat stern that would rise
when in a following sea (the wave coming from behind you). This would cause the stern to lift with
the bow down in the sea. The bow is then deeper than the rudders, and the bow steers the boat in
whatever direction she was headed; she ran wild. Most boats with a deep V-forward and sharp entry
run well into a head sea, but are hard to steer and keep on course in a stern sea. Reported to have had
one Speedway gas engine in her early years and replaced with two Chrysler gas engines, which were
replaced in January 1951 with two 6-71, 200 hp diesels. Her stability letter of May 1958 was for 82
passengers. FIFI bought the *Running Wild* in 1972 from Pagels as part of the Fair Harbor ferry system

and used her for Fair Harbor service, selling her in November 1977 to George Hendrich, National Seashore Ferry, Inc., for Watch Hill service after he had leased the boat for two years.

-77-   ★Isle of Fire   ON 276311   Radio WJ9703   *Martha Washington*   Military #C22600

ISLE OF FIRE at Fair Harbor (1973)   Ed Mooney photo

Built in 1944 at Terminal Island, California by Harbor Boat Building Co., for the US Navy as an air/sea rescue boat. Length 63', beam 15.4', draft 4', GT 45, NT 35, double planked, V-bottom, light framing, two 2" monel shafts, 1958 conversion, two Detroit 6-110 diesels, 270 hp at 1,800 rpm, light ship speed about 20 knots tops, Allison hydraulic 1-to-1, M gears, 22" x 17", 3-blade props, two decks. Gus Pagels paid $2,860 for this hull, and $3,160 for hull #36278 from Norfolk Naval Shipyard in March 1957. Naval architect Richard Taubler prepared the drawings and engineering, and the Scopinich family at Freeport Point Shipyard converted her into a ferry. I found one invoice dated October 22, 1957 for $11,669.64 signed by Mirtos Scopinich and a past due invoice dated November 1958 for $4,169.64 for work on the *Isle*. A stability test was conducted on May 5, 1958 in Bay Shore for 160 passengers. She entered Fair Harbor ferry service in June 1958. At that time a wood boat, if she had the stability, could carry one passenger for each 18" of seating. FIFI bought the *Isle* as part of the sale of Gus Pagels' assets in October 1972, and used her in Fair Harbor service until she was sold in 1990, having made 168 round trips her last year. She needed more power when carrying a load, but she worked well for thirty-two years of ferry service. She was in use as a research vessel out of City Island, New York, when Ernie Villing worked on the engines in 1998.

Someone left a newspaper article and picture dated May 2, 2004 on my desk of her with only her pilot-house out of the water. The article stated that she sank in Connecticut and would be re-floated the next day. That's been a very long life for an ASR.

ISLE OF FIRE at carpenter's shop (circa 1987)   Ed Mooney photo

121

ISLE OF FIRE II leaving Bay Shore Marina (circa 1973)   Ed Mooney photo

Built in 1943 in Miami, Florida for the US Navy as a 63' air/sea rescue boat (hull C-9461). The *Thumper II* was bought by Gus Pagels from Thomas W. Murray of Wilmington, Delaware in December 1962 for $17,000. Length 63', beam 15.4', draft 4', three Gray Marine 6-71 diesels with Twin Disc 8708X mechanical, 1.5-to-1 gears, three 2" diameter shafts, double-planked wood hull, wood cabin, two decks forward, one deck aft of the engine room, 150 passengers. FIFI bought the *Isle II* as part of Gus Pagels' Fair Harbor ferry system in 1972. The *Isle II* continued to serve Fair Harbor and Atlantique until 1975, when she was sold to Davis Park Ferry Company Inc. of Patchogue. They renamed her *Matabanks* and used her for the Watch Hill run. She was later sold to Sayville Ferry where she was used on the Barrett Beach and Sunken Forest runs. Ken Stein sold her to Jack McCormack for use on the Finger Lakes, upstate New York, where she ended her travels after she could no longer pass a dry dock inspection. She was stripped for her parts and engines. She was not a popular boat with the passengers or crew. The bottom was warped out of shape, the pilothouse was mid-ship, and she had a high loading area that required steps (some of our other boats also needed dock steps).

Dunewood Ferry

-79-   South Bay Master

SOUTH BAY MASTER (1979)   Dick Block photo

Built in Louisiana as a crew boat for oil rig service in the Gulf of Mexico, converted in the Morgan City area (1969) for Dick Block and Bill Leyrer for Dunewood service. 65' steel hull, two

Detroit 12V71N diesels. Average speed ferry, about eighteen knots light ship, but lost speed with more than half a load of passengers. She also drew too much water for the bay. She was used only for the second and last year of their Dunewood service. At the time that Bill and Dick ended ferry service, a hurricane damaged and destroyed many crew boats in the Gulf of Mexico, so the *Master* went right back there into service. Dick Block believes she later ran into an oil drilling platform in the Gulf and sank.

Kismet Ferries

-80-   **XL** ON 27026

Ferry XL (circa 1944) [note the air/sea rescue boat on right]   Artie Weis Collection

Built in 1903 in Bay Shore, New York by Clifford Weis, Bay Shore Boat Co. 43.5' x 14.6', GT 14, NT 13. In 1922, she ran to Fire Island State Park from the head of Watchogue Creek behind the "Carlton Opera House" for a round-trip fare of 50¢. The *XL* was owned and operated by Cliff Weis and served as the Kismet ferry to the restaurant owned by Cliff and his two brothers and their father. The *XL* also ran to West Island, Fire Island State Park, and Camp Cheerful, a camp for handicapped children near the park that used the park dock. Cliff also chartered her out for bay fishing and charters to other ferry companies when they needed extra boats. Cliff ran many trips for Patterson from Ocean Beach in the late 1940s and through the 1950s. She was a slow, mostly open boat that carried no more then sixty-five passengers, which was not many when the passengers waiting in line was a block long, but every boat helped. Grumman and Republic tested new planes over the nearby Atlantic Ocean, and if one went down, the ASR in the photograph above picked up the pilot. *(Listed in 1927 MVUS, with a gas engine, and the owner was Leander Jeffrey. Listed in 1949 MVUS, she had a 115 hp gas engine.)*

-81-   **Kismet** ON 219913

KISMET (circa 1930)   Artie Weis Collection

Built in 1920 in Bay Shore, New York. Used by Clifford Weis, his father, and his brother to operate Kismet ferry service. The boat also made stops at West Island and Fire Island State Park. 43.4' x 16', GT 14, NT 10, one 40 hp gas engine, wood hull.

-82-   **Mischief** ON 229993

MISCHIEF behind Cliff Weis's house (circa 1940)   Artie Weis Collection

Built in 1930 in Brooklyn, New York as a rumrunner. Length 48', beam 12.6', two Chrysler Royal gas engines, 262 total hp, wood lapstrake hull, one deck, 48 passengers. In the late 1930s, she was owned by Bay Shore Boat Company, the Weis Family, and they used her as a Kismet ferry. In the 1950s, she was used as a Babylon to Fire Island State Park ferry, owned by Clyde and Mattie Best. Bill Ranch was the captain for many years when she sailed from Babylon and Captree to Fire Island State Park.

Other Ferries to Fire Island

-83-   **Miss Captree** ON 269656   *Bayberry Mist*
Built in 1941 in Stamford, Connecticut. Length 60.4', beam 15.6', GT 14, NT 9, two GM 6-71 diesels, 90 passengers. She ran from Captree to Fire Island State Park after the 1954 Captree Bridge was built and ended that service in 1964 when the bridge over the Inlet was finished to the new enlarged and renamed Robert Moses State Park with its large parking fields. She was then sold to Davis Park Ferry and renamed *Bayberry Mist*. *(Listed in 1960 MVUS as owned by Clyde Best.)*

-84-   **Miss Fire Island** ON 276617   *Highlander*
Built as a Navy target towboat, converted in 1948 to a ferry. Length 65', beam 13'3", GT 12, NT 8, two GM 6-71 diesels, 200 hp each, wood hull and cabin, two decks, 137 passengers. Ran from Captree Boat Basin to Fire Island State Park. Last located at Duck Key, Florida.

-85-   **Avocet II** ON 227143
Built in 1925 in Honga, Maryland. 39.3' x 9', GT 10, NT 6, gas engine, 32 hp. Owner M.A. Sumner, 23 Southard Lane, Babylon. She was used for service to Fire Island State Park from Babylon prior to 1945.

-86-   **Bellmore** ON 223874

BELLMORE (1938)   Ed Mooney Collection

Built in 1924 in Bellmore, New York. Owner Chas. S. Stevens. 38.2' x 14.2', GT 14, NT 9, gas, 40 hp, wood hull. Ferry to Jones Beach prior to 1928 before the bridges and beach road. Ran service to Fire Island State Park from Babylon in the 1940s to early 1950s.

-87-   **Captree Spray**

CAPTREE SPRAY (circa 1969)   Ed Mooney photo

Blount built about 1964 to carry people from New Jersey to the New York World's Fair in Flushing, New York, 65' x 33', steel, single screw Detroit diesel 8V71, 3-to-1 gear, two decks, sightseeing and charters along and to Fire Island. She was chartered a few times by local ferries, but was slow and so wide that she didn't fit at many of the docks.

-88-   **Captree Mist**   *Silver Star*

CAPTREE MIST (1986)   Ed Mooney photo

Blount built in 1964, 65' x 33', steel, single screw, Detroit diesel. She was used for charter trips to Fire Island from Captree Boat Basin. She also made a few backup Fire Island ferry trips to Bay Shore for Fire Island Ferries. Captain Federico bought the *Mist* from Casco Bay Lines, Portland, Maine and removed a heating system to reduce her draft.

-89- **L. R. Brandsford** ON 206141
Built in 1909, Quincy Point, Massachusetts, home port Patchogue, New York. 51.7' x 15.4', GT 24, NT 14. Built for fishing. May have sailed to Ocean Beach.

-90- **Elenor** ON 230478
May have sailed to Ocean Beach for John Wilbur.

-91- ✦**Second ASR Hull of Gus Pagels's** Military #26600
Built in 1943. In 1957, Gus paid $2,860 for it and sold it to Zee Line Ferry. The hull was in bad condition and would require more repair than it was worth. About 1959, Zee Line sold it to Al Olson, who actually bought it for Patterson since Zegel and Patterson did not get along at that time. FIFI decked it over as a flat deck uninspected barge and carried loads of building material to Fire Island. She did tow better than most barges and was higher and kept a load drier in a head sea.

-92- **Nancy Lee**
Reported to have been an early ferry in the bay to Point O'Woods or Ocean Beach.

WATER TAXIS

Water taxis are not ferries, but they have transported people to Fire Island for as long as people have had to go over and back. Most operators went into the business since it looked like easy money and they enjoyed running boats. Unlike ferries, water taxis have until recently had a short business life. It's a demanding business, working nights, the season is short, engines wear out quickly, insurance costs are high, and someone has to answer the phone twenty-four hours a day.

I arrived in Bay Shore in 1948 on the *Socks*, a thirty-eight foot Chris Craft built in 1929 with a 600 horsepower gasoline engine that went into the water taxi trade. The *Socks'* owner was out of business at the end of the season, and Cliff Weis bought her. He replaced the big gas engine with a 6-71 diesel and was in the water taxi business part-time. Cliff sold her to Dick Gunther, who also had another water taxi at one time. Dick was a painter at Brewster's Shipyard and could put his paintbrush down and make a trip during the day. Bill Brewster also owned and operated a water taxi for a few seasons.

SOCKS water taxi (circa 1960)   Luke Kaufman photo

Bob Henning, captain on the freight boat *Fire Island Maid* from 1953 to 1957, went into the water taxi business part-time about 1955. He became so busy that he left the ferry company to pursue the trade full-time with his boat *Johnny*. When he looked over the last two years of business, he found he and his wife were on call or working twenty-four hours a day, plus new engines were needed, and there were fuel costs, insurance, boat and prop repair, which made it no longer fun or profitable for two working people. Bob sold his boat and house and moved to Florida.

Gene Worthly operated the Point O'Woods parking terminal in 1948 and used a Chris Craft open speedboat as a water taxi. I made a trip with him one summer day, and when we docked back in Bay Shore, he pushed sawdust under the boat with a net (the dry sawdust would flow with the water into the leaking seams where it would swell up and stop most of the leaking).

Tommy McNama had the wooden skiff *Nina* and later an aluminum boat, and he, too, went out of business.

In the 1990s, Vic Klipp organized a water taxi business of four boats before selling out to Dave Sanders, owner and operator of South Bay Water Taxi, the largest and longest surviving operator in that business.

Water taxies (2004)   Ed Mooney photo

In March 2004, Fire Island Ferries Inc. bought the assets of South Bay Water Taxi from Dave Sanders and re-named the new business Fire Island Water Taxi.

POWER AND ENGINES

Sail

Although steam came into common use as boat power by the 1850s, sail power was still in use until cheaper, lighter, smaller gas engines, and later diesels came into use. At first, many sailing vessels making long hauls, such as ice from Maine, coal from Norfolk, Virginia, brick, lumber, etc. Sails were used for most of the trip, and the engine was used when docking or when they had light winds.

When I first arrived in Bay Shore, the captain of the Point O'Woods ferry was Hank Rhodes. I was told that his grandfather was captain of a schooner used in coastal trade around New York City, Islip, Point O' Woods, Bay Shore, and other East Coast ports. Islip schooner captains Hank Haff, Nathaniel Clock, and Urias Rhodes became famous as sailing masters on America's Cup J-Class boats of the New York Yacht Club.

Steam Engines

In July 1812, five years after Robert Fulton made his famous two-day trip up the Hudson River to Albany with the steam-powered *Clermont*, Fulton started ferry service between New York City and New Jersey with the steam-powered *Jersey*. His boats were about eighty feet long and thirty feet wide. Each ferry had two distinct double-ended hulls connected by a "bridge" with a paddlewheel between the hulls. Fulton and his partner, Robert Livingston, were given exclusive rights to operate steam ferries on the Hudson River. Fulton died in 1815, and the exclusive rights monopoly ended in 1824.

Steam engines were not new as a power source; they were used to pump water out of coal mines in England well before they were used in boats or trains. The early engines burned wood in a boiler to make steam at about only thirty pounds per square inch (psi). The steam was used to move a large piston, which moved a rod connected to a walking beam on top of the vessel. The beam drove a rod and crank that turned two paddlewheels, one on each side of the vessel.

Over the 120 years of steam-powered ferries, steam engines improved: boiler pressure was raised to 110 psi, and a smaller piston and shorter stroke could then be used. This higher pressure steam, when released from the first piston, still had pressure and was directed to a larger diameter second piston on the same shaft with the same length stroke. These were known as compound engines. Later steam engines had a third and again larger piston added to use the steam that still had pressure, and were known as triple expansion engines. Wood as a fuel gave way to coal, and coal gave way to oil.

These changes came very slowly. Low-pressure steam engines and boilers continued to be manufactured and installed well after the compound engines were in use, and coal continued to be burned into 1950. Steam engines would continue on as a major source of power until about 1926, when diesels started to replace steam engines as new ferries were built. Diesel electric was in use on ferries in San Francisco Bay in 1920. Steam engines (Skinner Uniflow) were still installed in newly-built New York City ferries in 1950.

Screw propellers were in use during the Civil War, but it was not until 1888 that New York City had its first screw propellers on a ferry, one on each end. Extensive tests were run to compare a side-wheeler ferry to a screw-propelled ferry by operating ferries on the same run (both owned by the same company so it was not a race). The ferry company had a large operation and wanted the best boat design for future new construction. They also ran the double-ended ferry with a prop on each end, and then with one prop removed. The drive or prop shaft went from end-to-end of the boat. It wasn't long after this that screw propellers on each end became the choice of propulsion.

Up until 1886, most ferries were built of wood and a few built of iron. About 1888, steel started to be more readily used, and sidewheel use was on the way out in the building of new ferries.

The early Surf Hotel ferries were steam sidewheel, and later steam, screw propelled. Being smaller, passenger-only vessels, most of them were made of wood and were not built by or for Sammis. All the ferries were single-ended.

Diesels and gas were not yet in common service in 1895 when Point O'Woods started service. They used steam and a propeller.

Gasoline Engines

Gasoline engines were smaller, lighter, and safer, and replaced steam on smaller vessels around 1900. Steamboats required a large boiler, storage for wood or coal, and someone to keep loading fuel onto the fire in the boiler, making steam. The engine also needed a supply of clean fresh water; all this required a large engine room and storage space for wood or coal close to the boiler.

The automobile age and their mass-produced gasoline engine led to an engine easily converted to marine use by adding water-cooled manifolds, a water pump for cooling, marine gear for forward and reverse, and engine mounts. Some companies manufactured the complete engine while others adapted a ready-made automobile engine; many engines were noted for hard starting. Gasoline engines are still in wide marine use today in pleasure boats since they are much cheaper, lighter, smaller, and cleaner with less odor than diesel. However, they use more fuel for the same horsepower, and if the gas leaks into the bilge, the fumes are explosive.

Karl Pausawang of Sayville made a two-cylinder gas engine and had exhibited it in the New York Boat Show of 1928.

Diesels

The first use of a diesel engine for propulsion in marine use was in 1903 in a canal boat built in France. That same year, a diesel was used for propulsion of a larger vessel on the Volga River in Russia. In 1912 was the beginning of large diesel-powered ocean-going ships. As a comparison, steam engines are only about 10% efficient while diesels are about 75% efficient (energy from fuel burned).

Although Captain Robinson installed a large slow-turning 140 horsepower Atlas diesel in the ferry **Ocean Beach** in 1929, diesels were not in common use in the bay until after World War II, when inexpensive, military surplus came on the market. About 1948, the surplus Gray Marine diesel 6-71 (71 cubic inches per cylinder) started to replace existing gasoline engines, and they were installed in almost every ferry in Great South Bay. A few exceptions were the **Mischief** with two Chryslers on the state park run, Fair Harbor's slow **Atlantic**, then with one Chrysler and later replaced with a Cat diesel, and the **Running Wild** had two Chrysler gas engines until the 1950s when she had two 6-71s replacements. The 1950s also saw the end of the gas Hall Scott Invaders in the **Artemis**, **Margaret**, and **Miss Ocean Beach**.

Gray Marine 6-71 diesels were removed from landing craft, complete with a marine reduction gear, and installed without changes. The price for one was very low as were the readily-available surplus spare parts. They used less fuel, which cost less than gasoline, and had about the same horsepower as the Hall Scott.

The basic 6-71 diesel engine was developed about 1936 by General Motors for buses and became widely used in trucks, generators, pumps, boats, and cranes. The original 6-71 was designed for 165 horsepower. For military use during battle, 225 hp could be developed by using a 90-millimeter injector with a governor that had a battle setting. If you used the battle setting for more than ten or fifteen minutes on a regular basis, you could expect to end up with one or more of the following: a hole through a piston, a stuck injector, timing gear failure, a broken crankshaft, broken flywheel bolts, broken vibration dampers, shot reduction-gear bearing, stuck rings, burned valves, blown head gaskets, or cracked cylinder heads.

Many of these engine problems occurred on Sunday afternoon when engines were pushed hard and long at the governor battle setting. If the boat could continue to run on her remaining engine or engines, she continued in service at a slow speed, often doing the shorter Kismet run while the Kismet boat replaced her on a longer run. Monday morning triage decided the repair priorities to get all the boats back in service by Friday afternoon.

Detroit Diesel research and development engineers worked on all these problems to retain their lead in sales of diesels in this horsepower range. The 71 series, 71 cubic inches per cylinder, was manufactured in cylinders of 3, 4, 6, 8V, 12V, 16V (two 8V blocks bolted together), and a 24V (two 12V blocks bolted together). Detroit kept most of the parts interchangeable, such as pistons, liners, heads, injectors, exhaust valves, pumps, starters, etc. They designed a new cylinder block called High Block to get more air into the cylinder through a larger, longer intake opening. It required soft iron rings on the top of each cylinder, and O-rings at each water and oil port, plus a one-piece seal set in a groove instead of a one-piece head gasket. Now it is rare that we get a leak between the cylinder head and block.

Detroit Diesel corrected burned valves with a higher-grade valve and better valve seat. All currently manufactured 71s have four exhausts per cylinder, helping the engine remove exhaust faster and allowing more air in for clean burning and developing more horsepower. Timing gears were switched from cast iron to steel. Pistons were changed many times over the years as were piston rings to get longer ring life and a better seal at the top of the piston to improve compression. Injectors had their injection pressure increased, and the small injector valve that controls fuel release was improved to stop low-speed smoke from drippy injectors.

Early engines used vibration dampener of steel and rubber that failed at high-speed use, leading to broken flywheel bolts and later, a broken crankshaft. We have had engines run with a broken crank, but they shake and may not restart.

The Twin Disc marine gear on all the early engines were shifted by mechanical means. The captain applied force from the pilothouse, except on the *Queen* and other ferries over sixty-five feet long, where an engineer stood between the engines near the gear and directly moved a long handle on the gear for forward, neutral, and reverse. He also moved the throttles at the captain's direction.

The throw-out and pilot bearing failures in the old Twin Disc gears was solved by using an extremely high-melting temperature grease. Detroit Diesel built the 71 series, a two-cycle engine or a power stroke each revolution, which was lighter, smaller, and cheaper than its competitors and continued in worldwide use in the ferry trade.

When we built the *Captain Patterson* in 1972, we had to decide on the engines. The first set of plans Patterson had drawn up called for two V-12 Cummins. After a little study and looking at the engine in the 85-foot Coast Guard boat, we decided it had problems: too heavy, too big, not enough horsepower with just two engines, and the cost would be greater than three Detroit 12V71. We had already used Detroits for twenty-three years and knew how to keep them running. The 12V71TI would be new to us, but they performed well, and we used the same model engine in the next eight boats we built.

With the demand for more horsepower, Detroit developed the 92 series in 8V, 12V, and 16V. The first 8V engines had rear main bearing problems that were corrected, and this series was meant to replace the 71 series, which it did not since users like us did not want to change our basic fleet engine.

The 71 series is so widely in use throughout the world that parts and used engines will continue to be readily available. Detroit has a great parts distribution system worldwide. If a local dealer doesn't have the part in stock that is desperately needed, they can get it for you the next day from a major distributor, or they may even have it flown in from the factory and add the cost to your bill. Replacement parts for these engines have been manufactured and competitively sold at a lower price for years by manufacturers and dealers other than Detroit, and with the great number of Detroits in service, they will continue to do so for many years.

For over thirty years, Detroit outsold Cat, Cummins, Volvo, or any other diesel in its horsepower range. Detroit began to lose some of its market share in the 1990s as Cat and other companies developed better, cleaner engines. About 1997, Detroit joined with MTU, a leading German engine manufacturer, and in 1998 jointly made and marketed a 2000 series made in the United States and a 4000 series made in Germany to replace production of the two-cycle Detroit engines. January 2000 was the end of production of the 71, 92, and the larger Detroit 149 series, all two-cycle. They were no longer able to pass new highway exhaust standards.

Gas Turbine

Gas turbine use in ferries has the advantage of lightweight, very small, smooth, long life between overhauls, and high horsepower output, but they are expensive and use lots of fuel at low speed going to and from the dock in the harbor. They are being used on longer runs on larger ferries where people will pay a premium to save time. Some of the builders are General Electric, Caterpillar Solar, Lycoming, and Rolls-Royce.

FARES

Prior to 1978, a Suffolk County Court Judge signed county ferry license renewals and fares (for many years, it was Judge Frank L. Gates). The law was then changed requiring the county to hold public hearings for the license and one for the fares. As I read back through Bob Royce's files, it reminded me of all the abuse we took at the public hearings; people stated: the fares were already too high, inter-company rents were high, parking revenue should go to ferries, increased company wealth by buying new ferries, poor off-season service, train connections, selling cheaper tickets to Ocean Beach and Saltaire homeowners, speeding and traffic on Maple Avenue, parking of Fire Island visitors in uptown parking lots, etc. In addition, many people spoke about things that had nothing to do with the ferries, but there are not many open public forums in town to speak your piece. It was not a pleasant evening!

OCEAN BEACH FERRY
SCHEDULE 1·9·3·5
EFFECTIVE JULY 1ST, 1935

DAYLIGHT SAVING TIME

TRAINS LV PENN STA.	BOATS LV BAY SHORE	BOATS LV OC'N BC'H	TRAINS LV BAY SHORE
5.10 A. M.	6.35 A. M.	M 6.00 A. M.	7.06 A. M.
9.15 A. M.	10.30 A. M.	6.50 A. M.	7 57 A. M.
	12.00 N.	8.10 A. M.	9 19 A. M.
K 12.31 P. M.	K 1.50 P. M.	K 1.30 P. M.	2.54 P. M.
K 1.35 P. M.	K 2.50 P. M.	x 2.55 P. M.	4.09 P. M.
3.45 P. M.	4.55 P. M.	K 3.50 P. M.	6.02 P. M.
x 4.47 P. M.	x 6.00 P. M.	6.00 P. M.	7.45 P. M.
x 5.39 P. M.	x 7.00 P. M.		

		SUNDAYS		
8.45 A. M.	10.00 A. M.	8.00 A. M.	9.15 A. M.
	11.00 A. M.	A 2.20 P. M.	4.58 P. M.
10.40 A. M.	11.55 A. M.	4.40 P. M.	6.23 P. M.
1.49 P. M.	3.25 P. M.	6.50 P. M.	8.08 P. M
4.07 P. M.	5.30 P. M.	7.30 P. M.	* 8.51 P. M.
4.50 P. M.	7.40 P. M.		
	8.20 P. M.		

K - Saturdays Only   x - Daily except Saturday
M - Mondays Only   A Train at Brentwood 3.54 P. M.
* - Except September 1st

Special Schedule on July 4 and Labor Day
SUBJECT TO CHANGE WITHOUT NOTICE

131

After the judge turned the rate increase and license renewal over to the county, we had to petition the county about six months in advance with our new rate proposal, provide certified financial statements for the last two years, have the rates published in three local newspapers, and appear before the county transportation committee made up of county legislators.

The County Budget Review Office studies our proposal and presents a full written report at least two weeks before the hearing to the committee. The committee holds an open meeting for anyone to speak on the license or fares, and then they vote to reject, pass, suggest changes, table, or reschedule. When the committee approves the rate or license, it is scheduled for the next General County meeting in Riverhead or Hauppauge to be voted on. It's never easy, and at times delayed until after we have sold more than half of our 40-trip books of tickets for the year at the old rate.

FARES 1924-2001

One way	Year
$.25	1924
.35	1935
.50	1938
.75	1948
.85	1950
1.00	1961
1.25	1966
1.50	1969
2.00	1977
2.25	1979
2.50	1980
3.50	1981
3.75	1982
4.00	1984
4.25	1985
4.50	1987
5.00	1988
5.25	1991
5.50	1994
5.75	1996
6.00	1998
6.50	2001

FIRE ISLAND FERRIES, INC.
99 Maple Avenue, P.O. Box 5311, Bay Shore, NY 11706-0224
www.fireislandferries.com

OCEAN BEACH

SUMMER 2002

SUMMER 2002

JUNE 21 thru SEPTEMBER 3

Leaves Bay Shore	Leaves Ocean Beach
MONDAY thru THURSDAY	
Use Saturday Schedule July 4,5 & Sept. 1	6:00am
7:00am Use Sunday Schedule Sept. 2	7:35am
8:15am	8:45am
9:25am	10:00am
11:00am	11:30am
12:15pm	12:45pm
1:30pm	2:00pm
2:45pm	3:15pm
4:15pm	4:45pm
5:30pm	6:00pm
6:45pm	7:15pm
8:00pm	8:30pm
*9:05pm	*9:35pm
*10:15pm	*9:50pm
	*10:45pm
* Trips Will Not Run Sept. 3	
FRIDAYS & July 3rd	6:00am
7:00am	7:35am
8:15am	8:45am
9:25am	10:00am
11:00am	11:30am
12:15pm	12:45pm
1:25pm	2:00pm
2:00pm	2:30pm
3:00pm	3:30pm
4:00pm	4:35pm
5:00pm	5:30pm
6:00pm	6:30pm
6:45pm	7:15pm
7:30pm	8:00pm
8:00pm	8:30pm
8:50pm	9:20pm
9:50pm	10:20pm
10:30pm	11:00pm
11:50pm	12:45am

Leaves Bay Shore	Leaves Ocean Beach
SATURDAY & SUNDAY	
Use Saturday Schedule July 4,5 & Sept. 1	
Use Sunday Schedule Sept. 2	
7:00am	8:10am
9:15am	9:45am
9:55am	10:25am
10:45am	11:15am
11:15am	11:45am
11:55am	12:25pm
12:30pm	1:00pm
Saturdays ONLY ← →	1:30pm
1:00pm	
1:30pm	2:00pm
2:00pm ← Saturdays ONLY	
2:30pm	3:00pm
3:30pm	3:40pm
4:10pm	4:40pm
5:10pm	5:50pm
6:20pm	7:00pm
7:30pm	8:05pm
8:55pm	9:30pm
10:10pm ← Saturdays ONLY	
	10:50pm
***Saturdays ONLY ← → *** 1:00am	
*** Special $12.00 One Way cash fare ***	
** or $6.00 with a ticket **	

Village of Ocean Beach website
WWW.OBVILLAGE.COM

SMOKING ON BOATS PROHIBITED BY LAW
CONSUMPTION OF ALCOHOLIC BEVERAGES
ON BOATS IS PROHIBITED

Phones: (631) 665-3600 or 666-3600

NO FREIGHT CARRIED ON PASSENGER BOATS

Passengers may carry 2 pieces of hand luggage, 25 lbs. total, free of charge for each ADULT FARE paid. Luggage carried into the passenger compartment must be stowed under the seat in front of you. All other bags, etc. must be carried in the luggage section. A limited amount of space may be available for excess luggage and other small items and will be assessed a fee double the freight boat rate. The tariff imposed for shopping carts $3.00+, and luggage carriers $3.00+, and excess baggage are in effect at all times on all trips.. All other items including large canoes, plants, lumber, furniture, bicycles, wagons, bedding and heavy baggage MUST BE SHIPPED ON THE FREIGHT BOAT, which leaves Bay Shore at 10:00am Monday through Saturday. No lumber will be accepted on Saturdays.

No bicycles permitted on passenger boats.

FI Ferries is not responsible for lost or stolen items on any boat or dock.

FARES

ADULT, One-Way (except 1:00am)	$ 6.50
ADULT, One-Way 1:00am	$ 12.00
ADULT, Round-Trip (except 1:00am)	$ 12.50
ADULT, 40-Trip Ticket book	$195.00
CHILD, One-Way	$ 3.25
CHILD, Round-Trip	$ 6.00
CHILD, 40-Trip Ticket book	$ 95.00
INFANTS (under 2)	No Charge
Seniors & Handicapped w/ Suffolk Cty. ID card ONLY, One-Way	$ 5.00
Shopping Carts & Luggage carriers	$ 3.00+

ALL DOGS CARRIED AT CHILD RATE AND MUST BE LEASHED AND UNDER OWNER'S CONTROL AT ALL TIMES ON BOATS AND ON TERMINAL PROPERTY

CREW OF FIRE ISLAND FERRIES, INC.

Crew and former crew at Saltaire terminal 50th anniversary, May 3, 1998

Many interesting people have worked on the ferries, some for only one season and others for a lifetime. Fire Island Ferries has had over 1,400 people in its employ over the past fifty-seven years.

I'll try to mention some of the more memorable people who spent time in the trade and left an impression behind. I have already talked about Elmer Patterson, Bill White, Ed Davis, Gus Pagels, Al Skinner, and Tonis Zegel.

Deckhands, from 1948 through 1952, were paid a weekly salary of $48, and captains were paid $65 to $75. We worked an average of 10 hours a day, 6 days a week, with no overtime paid.

Most of our present captains started out as sixteen-year-old deckhands, worked three summers and weekends in the spring and fall while in school, and at nineteen years old (now minimum age to sit for the test), they took the captain's exam. At one time, you could get a license at eighteen years old. Most of our help went on to college and became lawyers, doctors, engineers, accountants, teachers, etc. After getting a college degree, many continued to work weekends in the summer, and for the last few years, we have had about twenty-two part-time summer captains. Working on the ferries has always been a sought-after job with more applicants than job openings, and we could choose the best of them.

I first met Jess Garrett when I was eighteen, and he was over seventy. Jess was the father of Captain Harold Garrett. (Harold was the father of deckhand Donald Garrett and grandfather of Jennifer Garrett of the Evening Star Division.) Jess was a ship's carpenter and all-round handyman, who lived all his life in Bay Shore, rode a bike to work, and was a pleasant old fellow to work with.

I loved to have him tell stories of the "good old days." He had a bike shop on Main Street in Bay Shore when it was still a dirt road. He cut salt hay on West Fire Island with horses that had pads on their feet to keep them from sinking into the soft, wet soil. The hay was loaded onto small scows that were about fourteen feet wide and forty-five feet long. The hay was used as a packing material as well as winter feed for animals. Jess died in 1952.

Captain Harold Garrett, senior captain, worked for Captain Robinson for twenty-five years and made the last trip for the Ocean Beach Ferry Corporation on April 30, 1948 and then made the first trip to Ocean Beach for Captain Patterson the next day. (During Word War II, Captain Garrett was a Navy tugboat captain.) His knowledge and experience during the difficult early start-up years of Fire Island Ferries may have made the difference between success and failure. Harold died in 1956 while having a heart valve replaced.

Some of the facts about events occurring prior to my arrival in 1947 came from Captain Garrett as well as from old Harry Wilson, who was even older than Jess. Harry was the engineer required by regulation on the *Queen*. I remember one story that he told of the winter of 1918 that was so cold that the water mains froze underground, and they couldn't get anyone to dig down and thaw the frozen pipes.

Patterson had me work one winter day with Harry, rebuilding one of the *Queen's* old 6-71s. After putting in the liner kits, I figured we would put on the head since it was still early (when I helped Al Olsen, we would put an engine together in a few days or sooner if it were summertime and we needed the boat). Old Harry said we were not going to put the head on. The next day, Captain Patterson had me go back to work on the freight boat so Harry got one of the other crewmen to help him. A complete 6-71 overhaul, pistons, liners, valve job, rebuild blower, bearing, could be done in one week by two men; Harry took three months to do the two engines. He didn't want to be laid off for the winter, and Patterson didn't want to lose him since there were no engineers around to take his place in the summer. Harry worked as the *Queen's* engineer until about 1952 when he retired and was replaced by Bill Madsen.

Bill was by far the best all-round engineer I have ever met. He not only was fast at rebuilding diesels, but he was great with electric, hydraulic, welding, engine installation, pumps, but most important of all, no one was better at troubleshooting. Bill was also a prankster and practical joker, never too busy at the end of a day to pull a trick, such as silver soldering a quarter to a large nail, putting the nail into a dock board, and laughing as people tried to pick it up. He also placed stones in Frank Smith's hubcaps, and another time crawled under Frank's car, tied a heavy line from his axle to a pole, and watched Frank try to pull away. Once during a heavy snowstorm when the *Flyer* was soon due to dock, noticing the snow was drifting near the car of the captain of the *Flyer*, Bill enlisted the help of a few co-workers and completely covered the car so it could not be seen. During another snowfall, Bill jacked up Billy Berka's car just enough so that it would not get traction, and when Billy tried to drive away, the wheels just spun. Madsen and a few others pretended they were trying to push the car, and Madsen kept yelling not to give it so much gas, and then he had Billy get out of the car so he could show him how to drive in snow. Madsen got into the car, we gave him a push off the blocks, and he drove the car out the long driveway with Billy running after him.

Bob Henning, captain of the freight boat *Fire Island Maid*, also liked to play practical stunts. The crew unloaded Clem Hill's cement blocks on the Ocean Beach dock and piled them so high that Clem's helper, Joe Stretch, had to find a tall ladder to get to the top blocks. The freight crew did the same thing in Bay Shore with the wooden Dugan breadboxes. The next day, when they asked the Dugan truck driver how he got them down, the driver told them that he knocked them down with his truck. On a hot summer day on the return to Bay Shore, Bob would drop the anchor out in the bay, and the crew would go for a swim. In those days, ice cream was packed in dry ice, and soda fountain coke syrup was shipped in one-gallon glass jugs with metal screw-on tops. Bob sent a crewman to John and Ann's ice cream parlor for the jugs while he chopped up the dry ice so it fit through the top of the jug. With dry ice, some bay water, and the top on tight, he threw the glass bottle into the basin while I was still nearby on the upper deck of the *Belle*, and there was an explosion and flying glass. No one was hurt, but glass landed on the *Belle's* deck. He then decided to set one off underwater. In need of a weight, he looked in the Ocean Beach waiting room where Patterson stored all sorts of old stuff. He found an odd brass thing with gears and levers, tied it to a new bomb, and threw them into the basin where it went off like a small depth charge. The funny part was when Patterson couldn't find his mechanical diesel engine synchronizer, and no one would tell him where it was. Another time, Bob found an inner tube at the beach, cut it so it was long with each end open, tied a knot in one end, and used a hose clamp to fasten it to the *Maid's* exhaust on the overhead. He started the engine and the inner tube expanded like a giant sausage, but did not blow out as he had hoped. There was never a dull moment with Madsen or Henning around.

Fred Freiermuth, known and remembered as "Fireball Fred," was a great painter and worker, and was also at the forefront of unusual happenings. He found a body out in the bay on a trip, rescued people off a burning yacht, had a steady stream of complaints about his wake, and once ran the *Flyer* from Kismet to Bay Shore with all three engines wide open, no passengers, and no reason to do it except to see how long it took (he blew out two engines on the trip). After Fred left FIFI, he worked for Zee Line and then Sayville Ferry where he was captain of the ferry *Beachcomber*. The Sayville crew called him Fireball Fred, and after a while, he told the guys he had not run that boat for a few years and not to call him Fireball Fred anymore; they promptly renamed him "Beachball Fred."

Luke Kaufman and Dave Anderson were working as captains for Zee Line Ferry when FIFI bought that company, and along with Doug Zegel, at that time working for FIFI, managed the Seaview, Ocean Bay Park ferry, and west side parking. Doug, a son, and a nephew of the Zee Line owners, had left Zee Line a couple of years prior to the sale to work at FIFI. Luke has one of the largest collections of ferry and Fire Island pictures I have come across. He is also an artist who can create any drawing when needed; his drawings are used on FIFI ferry shirts. Luke, in addition to being a full-time captain, oversees the painting of all our vessels.

Many of our captains worked for FIFI during their summer college break and went off to their future occupation when they got their degree. We kept a smaller crew when the summer ended. As we grew, we did keep on a few who are still here: George Hafele, John Allen, Ed Schaluch plus Fred Goldaker and Don Guinta left for other occupations and returned to FIFI.

Captain Tom Lenehan, after high school, went off to enroll in a local college, but sat in his car near the admitting office for a while, decided not to enroll, and returned to work at the ferry company.

Captain Dick Ivey worked full-time for the State of New York and part-time for FIFI for over 30 years.

Captain Harry Manko, a great cartoon artist, went off to Wall Street.

Captain Jeff Mansfield became a maritime attorney and is now in California.

After Bill Madsen left, I tried a few other mechanics who did not work out so I put an ad in the paper for a diesel mechanic. A woman came by to apply for the job for her husband, who at that time was working for Mercedes Benz in Brooklyn, and he did not know she was applying him for the job. She told me he was well trained in all fields, diesels, electric, and welding. I then hired Adolph Muller, who was born and trained in Austria as a diesel mechanic during World War II and who served in the German Luftwaffe. He was wounded when his plane was shot down while landing in Italy. He was sent to a hospital in Germany where they released him as the Russian Army was about to take the area. Adolph and his wife then went to Brazil, then Canada, then the United States. Adolph was great, everything his wife said he was, and everyone loved him. Years later, Adolph did not return to work after suffering a heart attack.

Chief Suydam retired from the US Coast Guard and worked freight on the *Maid.*

Captains Jack Romeyk and Tom Lenehan started work on the same day, May 4, 1957, as sixteen-year-old deckhands, and both were active captains in 2004 with 47 years of continuous service. They both go back to the days before we installed radios or had radar and were trained to operate with a stopwatch and compass. They may be the only FIFI captains who would now leave the dock without a working radar. They were there when long work days were the norm, and you were paid by the day or week; no time clock or time cards! Shortly after Captain Romeyke received his license, Patterson had him running a ferry. Romeyke stated he was surprised Pat made him an operating captain so quickly, and I asked Jack why he thought that. Jack's reply was that Patterson was always yelling at him. I explained to Jack that that was normal - he always yelled at everyone! Jack is the one captain you want running a ferry in thick fog or gale winds. Jack loves to drive and does long-distance trucking to pick up parts for FIFI.

Freight captain Tom Lenehan, after getting his license, ran passenger ferries, but when there was an opening for a freight captain, he quickly took it and has been number one freight captain for over 35 years. Freight is a labor-intensive part of the ferry operation. We like the freight to go from the delivering trucks right onto the freight boat or on waiting pallets on the dock to be then loaded on with forklift trucks or pallet jacks. Lumber is first taken off the truck with a forklift and then loaded on with an onboard hydraulic crane.

Don Guinta, Dianne Villing, and Eddie Schaluch are constantly on the phone with: Is my (whatever) on the freight boat? What time will the freight get to (any stop)? Why did you send my (whatever) back and not accept it? I only have ten of my eleven items and where is the missing item? We get items every day labeled only with a name and an address of "Fire Island." If we don't recognize the name for a destination, we try to get the driver to find out from his boss which one of the sixteen communities on Fire Island it's going to. Lost items, broken packages, freight returns, large near-future freight, prices, billing, COD, FedEx, UPS, etc. keep the phone and radio going full-time in the summer.

Captain Tom is a master at keeping all in order, and every effort is made to leave at 10 A.M. The busiest freight week of the year is just before Memorial Day weekend. Stores and restaurants stock up for the first long weekend of the season, builders try to finish new houses as promised, the owners of a new or recently purchased house are moving in along with new beds, refrigerator, linens, everything needed for a summer house at the beach.

HISTORY OF FIRE ISLAND FERRIES, INC. (1947 TO 2004)

Ocean Beach Improvement Company began to sell building lots in Ocean Beach in 1908, and provided free ferry service for its customers. When the hamlet grew and the lots were sold, the developer no longer provided free service. After obtaining a county license, anyone could run a boat as a public ferry to temporary piers or pole docks at the bay front. (The pole docks were removed in the winter because of ice and storms.) There was no established ferry service with uniformity of rates, schedules, or landing places. There were few if any residents after the end of the summer season, and no reason for maintaining service in the winter months. When emergencies arose, year-rounders called the local US Coast Guard for help to get to the mainland.

In 1918, the original developer, John Wilbur, constructed an inland boat basin and rented it to ferry operators and private craft. One of these ferry owners was Captain Azariah Robinson. An *Islip Press* article of December 13, 1928 states that Robinson had run the ***Traveler*** to Ocean Beach for the past eight years. This, however, did not solve the problems of uncertain schedules, fares, and dangers from unscrupulous competition.

The village grew rapidly, and in 1921 the homeowners decided to become an incorporated village under New York State Village Law. At that time, Ocean Beach was serviced by a number of individually owned gasoline powered boats converted into ferries. Captains hustled to get fares, and there were disputes on the docks at Bay Shore and Ocean Beach. Competition was so keen that captains forcing another ferry out of the channel often endangered the public. This situation continued for five years and was of considerable concern to the village board.

On March 6, 1922, the New York State Senate and Assembly enacted a law, signed by the governor, "an act to authorize the village of Ocean Beach to maintain and operate ferries and borrow money to acquire or purchase ferries." The village had the right to acquire, lease or charter, provide, maintain, and operate a ferry or ferries, together with the necessary terminals.

The village decided Robinson alone could discharge and load at Ocean Beach. This action also required a county license, signed by a county judge, after obtaining signed letters permitting the landing in Ocean Beach by the village and a letter from the town of Islip for Maple Avenue dock.
As the village grew, the boats provided by Robinson were not adequate, and in 1927, the village

board determined to require better boats and service. The board advertised for bids for a franchise, requiring bidders to state the number and type of boats offered, capacity, schedule, fares, and freight rates. The best bid received was from Robinson, who by then had formed a corporation. The board issued a ten-year exclusive franchise to the Ocean Beach Ferry Corporation, headed by "Cap" Robinson. This franchise required almost year-round service and required a Suffolk County license. Robinson rented use of the boat basin from the private owner as a ferry terminal and paid the rent for exclusive tenancy of ferry service. The basin was also used by private boats, much to Robinson's objection. This franchise gave Robinson exclusive ferry service rights to Ocean Beach from 1927 to April 30, 1937.

Captain Azariah Robinson (called Ed or Cap) was born in 1884 in Westhampton Beach, New York. His wife, Virginia, was born in 1883 in Brooklyn, New York. They had one child, a son, Ernest, born in 1904 and who died at the age of nineteen in 1923. The Robinsons lived on the second floor over the Maple Machine Shop at his Bay Shore terminal, just south of the present west terminal building (Ball parking field).

Ocean Beach freight and passengers were loaded and unloaded just outside his door. In the summer season, he and his wife lived at Ocean Beach, feeding and housing his early morning boat crew who stayed at the beach overnight. Sometime before losing the Ocean Beach run to Captain Elmer Patterson, Robinson had moved to Garden Place, Bay Shore, about two miles from the dock. I did not know Robinson personally, but did see him often by his boats. Everyone who worked for him or who knew him held him in high esteem.

In 1934, John Allgeier attempted to operate a ferry into Ocean Beach in defiance of the exclusive landing right issued by the village. Robinson sought the aid of the Supreme Court of Suffolk County to restrain Allgeier, and the court issued a permanent injunction restraining him from interfering in Ocean Beach ferry service.

When the ten-year franchise was about to expire in 1937, the village again publicly advertised for bids for a further franchise. Bids were received, Robinson's was determined to be the most advantageous, a public hearing was held, and a new franchise was awarded to Robinson to end on April 30, 1948.

Robinson's ferries were the *Traveler,* which ran from 1920 until 1941, the *Pathfinder* from 1925 to 1928, the 75-passenger *Chesapeake* from 1925 to 1929 (then she became his freight boat and Sunday afternoon backup boat until 1948) as well as two converted rumrunners, the 85-passenger *Margaret* and the 75-passenger *Miss Ocean Beach* (both of which he acquired to compete with Captain Patterson's fast ex-rumrunners that ran out of Seaview and Ocean Bay Park).

In 1927, some of the residents of Ocean Beach subscribed to preferred stock to finance the building of the 250-passenger ferry *Ocean Beach*, which was built in Patchogue for Robinson in 1928-1929. The stock provided for a 7% annual dividend and for voting power if dividends remained unpaid. In twenty years, dividends were never paid, and Robinson virtually single-handedly operated the management of the company, never consulted the stockholders, or held a stockholders' meeting.

Lovebird Runs Into the Vagabond

In the summer of 1937, Captain Robinson on the *Lovebird* ran into Captain Patterson on the ferry *Vagabond*. Patterson was at first held at fault, probably for not maintaining course and speed, and his license was suspended.

The following is the decision by Judge Galston of the United States District Eastern District of New York, on January 20, 1938 when Patterson brought action against Robinson, and Robinson brought a counteraction against Patterson:

June 26, 1937, 1:30 P.M., bright sunny day, little wind. Patterson, master of the ferry *Vagabond*, left the basin at Seaview to go west way to Bay Shore. When Patterson passed by the Ocean Beach Basin, he could see the ex-rumrunner *Lovebird* at her berth in the basin. As the *Vagabond* proceeded along toward black can number one (now number eleven), she overtook the ferry *Ocean Beach*, passing her about 150 feet off her port side. As he passed the *Ocean Beach*, he noticed that the passengers on that boat where standing up and looking astern. Endeavoring to see what they where looking at, he also looked aft and saw the *Lovebird* coming up directly astern of the *Ocean Beach*. The *Vagabond* was making from sixteen to eighteen miles an hour cruising speed, when suddenly she was struck on her starboard side by the *Lovebird*, causing her to lie on her port side with water coming in on that side. At the time the vessels hit, she was headed due north along East Fire Island. The *Lovebird* skidded off the stern of the *Vagabond* and kept on going into deeper water, going down the channel about 200 feet before turning.

The damage to the *Vagabond* was to her starboard quarter. Patterson, the master, made an excellent witness and in no sense was shaken under cross-examination. He had heard no whistle from the *Lovebird*, which was confirmed by McCabe, the mate on the *Vagabond*. McCabe had had the wheel for a while after Patterson took her past the basin and up to the time they passed the ferry *Ocean Beach*. At that point, McCabe went out to collect fares, and Patterson took the wheel.

I accept Patterson's version of how the accident happened, supported as he was by the testimony of passengers on his vessel, who were impartial, rather than the testimony given by the master of the *Lovebird* and his supporting witnesses, for in describing the course of the *Vagabond*, they tell an improbable story.

It is incredible that in attempting to pass the *Ocean Beach*, the *Vagabond* should have cut across the course of the *Ocean Beach* at an angle of 45 degrees, heading directly for the East Fire Island beach. There is not the slightest explanation of why such a foolhardy maneuver should have been adopted by Patterson. He had absolutely nothing to gain by following the course indicated; it was not the usual course. There is not a suggestion that necessity, immediate or remote, should have caused him to cross the bow of the *Ocean Beach* so closely and at such an angle. There was plenty of water, a wide channel, and every reasonable aspect of the matter leads to the conclusion that Patterson did exactly as he testified and as he had done on other occasions. On the other hand, it is much more probable that the failure of the *Lovebird* to slacken speed (she was making, on her own admission, at least thirty miles an hour) and cut too closely to the barrel buoy caused her to run down the *Vagabond*.

Incidentally, it may be noted that the *Lovebird* witnesses do not agree on the question of whether the *Lovebird* passed within or outside that buoy. Robinson, the master of the *Lovebird*, said he passed it very closely on the inside within a matter of a few feet, so that in running up the beach toward East Fire Island, he had the barrel buoy on his port hand. Davis, also on the *Lovebird*, said that the *Lovebird* passed closely to it on the outside. Captain Harold Garrett, in charge of the *Ocean*

Beach, couldn't recall which side of the barrel the ***Lovebird*** passed, nor did Koch, a passenger on the ***Lovebird***, though he said the ***Vagabond*** passed very closely to it. Hendrickson, a deckhand on the ***Lovebird***, said that she passed inside the barrel buoy. Incidentally, this witness testified that at the time that Robinson gave his one whistle, the ***Vagabond*** was only 100 or 125 feet ahead of the ***Lovebird***. This witness particularly reveals the improbability of the accuracy and truth of the ***Lovebird*** story because he said the three boats were traveling practically on parallel courses and that when the ***Vagabond*** made the alleged change in course, she was only 200 feet off the ***Lovebird's*** port side.

Accepting then, as I do, Captain Patterson's version of the accident, I find that his libel must be sustained, and that of the Ocean Beach Express, owner of the ***Lovebird***, dismissed. If this opinion is not in sufficient compliance with the rule requiring findings of the facts and conclusions of the law, submit findings of the facts and conclusions of law in accordance therewith.

US District Judge Galston

I found another letter, dated March 28, 1938 from the law office of Purdy, Mason & Lamb to Captain Elmer Patterson (they represented Patterson in this case). They had received a letter from the Honorable Daniel Roper, Secretary of the Department of Commerce (the Department of Commerce was in control of the Coast Guard at that time), in which Roper reversed the decision of the director and granted Patterson's appeal completely. The effect was that the Secretary held that Patterson's license suspension was reversed and that the license should never have been taken away and that this would not leave a mark on Patterson's record. Robinson had to pay about $500 in damages.

Patterson Awarded Ocean Beach Ferry Franchise

When Robinson first had the village franchise, he was younger, and he had two associates, Henry Kuever and Clarence "Babe" Morriss, who were both active in the operation of the ferry company. Mr. Kuever died, and Mr. Morriss entered military service, leaving Robinson to carry the entire load of a steadily growing ferry system. During World War II, it was difficult to obtain operating crew and materials to repair the ferries. Government regulations were a constant source of trouble, and these conditions weighed heavily on Cap. Cap also wanted higher fares and freight rates. In the summer of 1946, World War II was over, and some of the old crew returned from military service to the ferry company and a new mayor and board of trustees took office. Robinson stated to members of the board and the village attorney that he could not stand another season of ferry operation and intended to quit at the end of his contract. The mayor advised Cap to turn over some of his duties to his younger employees, some of whom had been with him for many years. Since Cap had always done everything himself, he did not take their advice.

To ensure continued ferry service, one or more of the younger boat captains, who were thoroughly familiar with the ferry operation, did approach Cap to see what proposition he was willing to make to them. The village attorney, Leroy B. Iserman, spoke with Cap while making many crossings with Cap running the boat and also at his Bay Shore terminal in an effort to have him work out some proposition whereby he could turn over the heavy work and responsibility to younger men. Each time Cap was evasive.

After the summer of 1946, due to Cap's attitude, the board of trustees held frequent sessions to discuss the future of ferry service. They were concerned with the increase in activity and population of the village. Robinson operated the large, slow *Ocean Beach* and two smaller ex-rumrunner speedboats, which frequently broke down and also ran overcrowded on trips during rush hours. Robinson had made no attempt to improve his boats over the years.

Again, at the end of the 1946 summer, Robinson told board members that he was not interested in renewing the franchise when it ended in 1948. The opinion of some people at that time was that Cap didn't think anyone would bid, and he could then renew the franchise under more favorable terms: he would not have to remove his gas engines and install diesels, and he wanted his rent lowered while fares and freight rates increased.

Faced with this situation, on February 18, 1947, the village published a Request for Bid with the terms of a new ferry contract in local newspapers as well as in three New York City newspapers. This was done more than one year in advance of the winning bidder's start-up date of May 1, 1948. Copies of the bid were sent to local boat operators who might be interested. A copy of the bid was also sent to Robinson by the village attorney, who again, along with board members and other friends of Robinson's, tried to convince him to take in younger men, thereby continuing to operate after nearly twenty-six years of service. But after the bid advertisement appeared, Robinson repeated to the mayor, trustees, and village attorney that he did not intend to bid.

Fire Island Ferries Inc., founded by Captain Elmer Patterson, Ed Davis, and William White, was incorporated on April 14, 1947 for the purpose of bidding on the ferry contract for service to the village of Ocean Beach on Fire Island. They were the only bidders and therefore awarded the bid in May of 1947 when Captain Azariah Robinson, the leaseholder and Ocean Beach ferry operator for twenty-seven years, failed to submit a bid on time, believing no one else would bid.

The Notice for Bidders of February 18, 1947 gave bidders three months to prepare and submit a bid to be opened on May 17, 1947. It also called for the resume of the principles submitting the bid. Fire Island Ferries Inc. was the only bid received.

I found a copy of the bid package submitted by Fire Island Ferries, Inc. from the office of Fowler and Kendrick, counselors at law in Riverhead, New York. This, along with many other documents, were among seven boxes of papers given to me by Robert Royce, the longtime attorney for Fire Island Ferries and Fire Island Terminal, when he retired and closed his office in 1997. The bid provided facts regarding stories I had heard, but for which I lacked dates or proof of the events.

The bid contained this resume for the president of Fire Island Ferries: Edward H. Davis, thirty-nine years old, born in Rockville Centre, New York. His first summer at Ocean Beach was in 1918 when his family rented a cottage, renting again in 1919-1920. In 1921, his family built a house in Seaview; it was the fifth house built in the Seaview hamlet. He spent a good part of those summers on the family powerboat, gaining a working knowledge of the bay and small boat handling. During summer vacation of 1922, he worked for Ocean Beach Ferry Company as a deckhand on the ferryboat *Chesapeake*. During the summers of 1923 and 1924, he was a deckhand on the Ocean Beach ferry *Traveler II*, where a more thorough knowledge of handling freight and passengers to Ocean Beach was acquired. In 1925, having been licensed as an operator of motor boats, Mr. Davis served during the seasons of 1925, 1926, and 1927 as captain of the *Chesapeake*. In 1928, Mr. Davis was licensed by the US Steamboat Inspection Service as a second-class pilot and served as associate master of the motor vessel *Traveler II*. During the fall, winter, and spring of 1928-1929, he helped to install the machinery and complete the construction of the motor vessel *Ocean Beach*.

The fall, winter, and spring of 1929-1930, Mr. Davis was a test engineer on the first high-speed diesel engines built in the US. In 1929, he also became a licensed chief engineer of motor vessels (needed on vessels over sixty-five feet). He returned to Ocean Beach Ferry Company in the spring of 1930 and spent the next seven years as master and pilot of boats serving Ocean Beach on a year-round basis. He also raised his license to first-class pilot, required at that time to captain a vessel over sixty-five feet long.

Mr. Davis left Ocean Beach Ferry Company in 1937 to work for Cummins Diesel Engine Corporation as a marine diesel sales engineer, serving in this capacity until 1942 when he was promoted to district manager in charge of East Coast operations of Cummins. One of his responsibilities was to supervise the installation and sea trials of various types of vessels built for the Army, Navy, and Federal Maritime Commission, and he was deferred from military service for this purpose throughout World War II.

It will be noted from the above that Mr. Davis, having spent most of his life at Ocean Beach, is fully cognizant of the problems involved in operating ferries to Ocean Beach.

Submitted with the bid in 1947 was the resume of the executive vice-president: Elmer D. Patterson, forty-one years old, born in East Marion, New York. He first came to Fire Island in 1911 as a small boy to live during the summer at Saltaire. His father, Herbert M. Patterson, was the captain in charge of the Saltaire ferries for some twenty years. While in school, Elmer Patterson worked summers as a deckhand on the Saltaire boats. When he was nineteen years old, he was granted an operators license by the Steamboat Inspection Service, and then captained a Saltaire ferry, the *Eladio*, for four summers. In 1927, Mr. Patterson graduated from the engineering school of Pratt Institute as a mechanical engineer and went to work for Bethlehem Steel in Pennsylvania, leaving three years later to return to his first interest, Great South Bay and its ferries. He acquired a first-class pilot's license and a chief engineer's license.

(Mooney Note: Vessels longer than sixty-five feet were required to have a chief engineer in the engine room to shift the gear into forward, neutral, and reverse, and change engine speed when signaled to do so by the captain by way of a telegraph, consisting of a set of cables that moved levers on a large dial above the engineer's head near the gear shift and throttle. As the captain moved his levers in the pilothouse, it also rang a bell at the engine room dial to get the engineer's attention. The engineer moved his lever at his dial that rang at the captain's telegraph, indicating that he had complied with the captain's orders.)

Upon his return, Patterson spent the first two summers working as engineer on the Ocean Beach ferry *Traveler II*. He spent the next two years serving as engineer on Point O'Woods' ferry *Point O'Woods III*. He supervised the conversion of that boat from a yacht to a diesel ferry in 1934.

After Patterson's many years in the ferry business, he was convinced that the courteous and considerate service rendered at Point O'Woods, combined with a short running time, would present an attractive service if offered to Seaview.

Captain Patterson initiated a new type of high-speed ferry with the ex-rumrunner *Vagabond*, later adding the ex-rumrunner *Artemis*. The bid application states "both these boats incorporate the ideas and designs of Mr. Patterson and are considered the finest boats of their type." With these boats, he operated a service into Seaview until the start of World War II. During the war, Mr. Patterson served as a lieutenant commander in the US Navy's Bureau of Ships in Washington, DC. In this position, he was personally responsible for materiel maintenance, alterations, and battle damage of minecraft vessels. He also served as a consultant on matters of design, building, and outfitting of all minecraft vessels, a fleet of approximately 800 vessels. Mr. Patterson was placed on inactive service in March 1946.

The bid also included the resume of the third partner: William White, forty-nine years old, born in Rockville Centre, New York. His business experience was entirely confined to banking, successively employed by Kountze Brothers, Guaranty Trust, New York Trust, and Nassau Bank. During this period, he attended the American Institute of Banking at night, taking courses in all phases of banking and commercial accounting. (Mooney Note: At the time of the bid preparation, Mr. White was a New York State bank examiner, a position he held ten years or more while an active owner of Fire Island Ferries.)

Fire Island Ferries' bid also stated the following:
     A. If Fire Island Ferries is awarded the franchise, with needed village approval, it will procure a license to operate from the County Court of Suffolk.
     B. Fire Island Ferries now owns or controls vessels capable of transporting 562 passengers for a single trip between the mainland and Ocean Beach. One vessel, the twin-screw *Point O'Woods III*, was decided upon as the best large shallow water boat now available on the entire East Coast, and if awarded the franchise, we plan to increase her capacity to above 350 passengers, and to replace her present diesel engines with diesels of greater power. Mr. Patterson has served as engineer in this boat, and at that time it made the trip from Bay Shore to Point O'Woods in thirty-eight minutes. The second boat, *Vagabond*, easily carries 100 passengers on the Ocean Beach run. In order to avoid any question of overloading, she will be limited to 85 passengers. With diesel engines, she will easily make Ocean Beach in less than thirty minutes. The third boat, *Doris*, twin-screw, is inspected and licensed for 127 passengers. If awarded the contact, we intend to rebuild and re-engine her to make Ocean Beach in forty minutes. (Mooney Note: I have not found any mention of *Doris* again in any search of material.)
     C. As required by the bid, all vessels will be diesel-powered.
     D. As required by the bid, all vessels, we estimate, will make the one-way trip in no more than forty minutes.
     E. Fire Island Ferries' terminal will be Maple Avenue dock, until such time as suitable land is available for the company's own terminal. In no event will a terminal be acquired by FIFI and used without the consent of the village board. The company aims to eventually establish additional high-speed service between Ocean Beach and Babylon. (Mooney Note: Babylon had much better rail service to and from New York City. Electric trains ran to Babylon and diesel from there ran east.)
     F. FIFI will pay a yearly rental of $3,000 for the basin and facilities at Ocean Beach and an annual franchise fee of $500.
     G. Special trips outlined in Schedule A will be between $10 and $20.
     H. FIFI will maintain reasonable and adequate ferry service between Bay Shore and Ocean Beach, at least in a manner not less frequent than that furnished the village during the seasons of 1946 and 1947. Fire Island Ferries will cooperate with the village board in the scheduling of trips. In June, July, August, and September, if, during daylight hours, equipment is available to run a trip desired by the board, it will be put in the schedule for one week. At the end of that time, an analysis of that trip will be done to either cancel it or add it permanently to the schedule. It is the intention and aim of management of FIFI to strive for hourly scheduled service during daylight hours of the summer season.
     I. The management of Fire Island Ferries Inc. has spent months of careful study of all boats available and suitable for the shallow waters of Great South Bay. Leading naval architects have been consulted, as well as naval designers of the Bureau of Ships, and it has been concluded that the sixty-three foot aircraft rescue boats, if adapted to ferry service, would be the most desirable type of boat obtainable. It is, therefore, the intention of Fire Island Ferries Inc., if awarded the franchise, to acquire two of these boats and rebuild them to use as fast twin-screw diesel ferries into Ocean Beach. They

will be inspected boats, and the number of passengers carried will be determined by the US Coast Guard.

The required financial statement was brief since they had not been active. It showed $53,000 in cash, and estimated appraised value of $62,000 for three boats. Liabilities were $50,000 notes payable to First National Bank and Trust Company in Bay Shore, New York, capital stock common $25,000, preferred $15,000. Equipment, when reconditioned, *Vagabond* $25,000, to carry 85 passengers, *Doris* $30,000, to carry 127 passengers, and *Point O'Woods* (to be renamed *Fire Island Queen*) $60,000, to carry 350 passengers.

Fares and freight rates were outlined in Schedule A, and were about the same rates as Ocean Beach Ferry charged in 1947, some of which were: one-way fare 75¢, ten-trip ticket $5 (with the company absorbing the 15% tax), individual monthly commutation ticket $10 (tax included). A few examples of the freight rates were: 40¢ per 100 pounds, moving van load of furniture $25, chair 15¢ to 25¢, lumber (Mooney Note: In the future, this would be a major source of work with little income) $2.50 per 1,000 board feet, bag of cement 20¢, 300-pounds block of ice 40¢ (Mooney Note: At that time, about half a truckload of ice a day went to Ocean Beach), milk 15¢ a case of twelve quarts, and a case of bottles of beer or soda 15¢. Annexed to the bid was a $10,000 performance bond.

Fire Island Ferries Inc. submitted the sole bid on the due date of May 17, 1947. Robinson was at the bid opening and examined the FIFI bid. On June 12, 1947, prior to the scheduled public hearing of June 21, Cap Robinson handed the village clerk a letter with the same bid terms that Fire Island Ferries had submitted on May 17, in order to renew his franchise.

Cap had been paying $2,000 annual basin rental and now offered $3,000. In his letter, Cap stated that he held a county license, and that he owned the following vessels debt-free: *Ocean Beach*, 250 passengers; *Margaret*, 85 passengers; *Miss Ocean Beach*, 75 passengers; *Chesapeake*, 75 passengers; 12' x 40' barge of 20-ton capacity. If awarded the franchise, he would acquire another 75-passenger diesel-powered ferry, bringing his capacity up from 485 to 560 passengers before May 1, 1948. He owned a Bay Shore terminal for fifty cars under cover, 135 cars outside with steel fence and watchman; freight receiving station; freight storage warehouse; ticket and administration office; washrooms; 500' of private docking; complete machine shop; crews' quarters at Ocean Beach. (He pointed out all the above because Fire Island Ferries did not have a Bay Shore terminal and would have to operate off Maple Avenue dock.) He would have $300,000 insurance by Hartford Insurance Company, and post a $10,000 performance bond, and he would apply for a ten-year renewal of his franchise.

The village had no choice but to reject his bid since it was weeks late. A petition of 200 village homeowners in support of Cap Robinson was presented to the village at a public board meeting June 29, 1947. The petition stated that "just because Cap was a little late in presenting his bid, he should not be thrown out after twenty years of service." Friends of Robinson's wanted all the bids discarded and new bids submitted. Cap Robinson was at the meeting, but made no explanation for his late bid.

The board, composed of Mayor Edwin F. Thayer, trustees Anna Pichard, Curt Wimmer, Wilbur Bullard, John R. Riley, and village attorney Leroy Iserman, rejected the petition. The entire Fire Island Ferries bid contract was read at the village meeting, and the board voted unanimously to award the contract to FIFI. The board rejected Robinson's bid letter because of his repeated statements that his company was through with the ferry operation, because he did not bolster his personnel with younger men, he did not offer adequate boats or improved service, he did not propose to operate with diesels, he did not submit a bid on time, and it would be unfair, un-business-like, if not illegal, to consider his bid after he had had the opportunity to inspect and study Fire Island Ferries' bid.

There were a few changes from the bid to the final signing of the franchise on August 2, 1947 by Mayor Edwin Thayer. The franchise pointed out that the village had publicly advertised the bid, that the bid had to be filed with the village not later than midnight May 17, 1947, that FIFI was the only bid received, a public hearing was held in the village on June 21, 1947 at 2 P.M. as required by law, residents stated their opinion, all who desired to be heard spoke, the board considered all the facts and circumstances, and the board then granted a ten-year exclusive franchise to FIFI, beginning May 1, 1948.

Additions that were noted in the franchise and not in the bid or were different than the bid were: the ferry company shall own or control vessels to transport, in one direction, not less than 500 passengers, 50% in a running time not to exceed forty minutes, and 50% not to exceed one hour. In the event that traffic increases, the ferry company shall acquire and place in service additional vessels powered by diesel motors. The ferry company management shall be the sole judge as to whether it is safe at any time to operate a boat on a scheduled trip. Children under the age of five years shall be carried free of charge when accompanied by a passenger. Members of the US Coast Guard, while in uniform and on duty, shall ride free of charge. The board of trustees has the right to lower fares if the cost of living goes down, and the ferry company has the right to raise them if the cost of living goes up due to inflationary conditions, making the ferry company unprofitable.

If agreement of the parties can't be reached, arbitration will be used to settle the conflict. (Mooney Note: Keep in mind, only sixteen years earlier, the US economy was in a depression, and two years prior to the writing of the agreement, World War II ended and price controls were removed; the ferry fares remained the same, with little increase for many years.)

Terms of special trips remained as in the bid, but were spelled out in more detail. The ferry company was to pay freight and express only and not pay COD. It spelled out all the freight regulations that we use today, fifty-seven years later. The franchise was granted to FIFI because of the training and experience in ferry operations of its management, Davis and Patterson, and the management couldn't be changed without written approval and consent of the village board. The ferry company was to acquire a scow for the transportation of bulk and heavy merchandise. The ferry company could service other places, but in no event could this service interfere with service to Ocean Beach.

That gave FIFI one year to obtain the equipment needed to start service on May 1, 1948, when Robinson's lease would expire.

Captain Patterson purchased the **Point O'Woods III** from the Point O'Woods Association at a favorable price because she had some rot in her stem, a fact he made sure everyone was aware of. The large, old Winton diesel engines were replaced with Gray Marine military surplus diesel engines, and the newly named **Fire Island Queen** started service on May 1, 1948.

The **Fire Island Maid**, formerly the **Viking Sr.** out of Freeport, was a very shallow draft fishing boat (surf clams) that was converted into a freight boat with plans to add a second deck for passengers. The second deck was never added, and she carried only freight to Fire Island destinations until 1984 when she was sold to Sayville Ferries to be used as their freight boat. Captain Patterson owned the rumrunner **Vagabond**, and used this boat as part of his share of investing funds. Her gasoline engines were replaced with Gray Marine surplus diesel engines, and she, too, started service on May 1, 1948. She was renamed **Fire Island Miss**. A contract to build the **Fire Island Belle** was also signed shortly after the village contract was awarded in June of 1947. Wheeler Boatyard of Clausen Point, New York built the **Belle,** and she was delivered in June of 1948.

145

The **Belle**, **Queen,** and the **Miss** were hard-pressed to handle the rapidly increasing Ocean Beach traffic load, especially the holiday and Sunday exits. Captain Patterson hired other vessels from Bay Shore, **Running Wild** (Captain Warren James) and **XL** (Captain Cliff Weis), a Babylon fishing boat, and a Davis Park ferry from Fred Sherman of Patchogue to handle the peak period traffic. The diesel engines broke down constantly, which only added to the weekend problem. Although service was somewhat limited off-season, service was provided in all weather, despite the fact that radios and radar were not used on the local ferries at that time.

During the start-up years of 1948-1950, Fire Island Ferries had financial problems as well as a legal problem with Captain Robinson and his old Ocean Beach Ferry Company. A lengthy court case over the right of the village to contract with only one ferry company was settled in favor of Fire Island Ferries and the village in January 1950.

Cap started legal action pursuant to "Article 78 of Civil Practice" in late July 1947 after the contract was awarded to Fire Island Ferries on June 29, 1947. He wanted to be allowed to continue service after May 1, 1948, but Judge Ritchie would only renew Cap's cross-bay county license through April 30, 1948 because after that date, he no longer had village rights to use the ferry basin. His suit against the village claimed that they did not have the legal right to grant an exclusive franchise for the use of the ferry basin to only one company, which was just the opposite of the case Cap won years earlier, when another operator tried to use the village basin.

Justice Froessel, a county judge, wrote an opinion that the village could issue a franchise. In 1927, the village board had granted Robinson an exclusive franchise, and only after that did the county judge grant Robinson a county license. FIFI now had the contract, and just as important, the county license. The attorney for the village was Leroy B. Iserman, a longtime village summer resident; FIFI was defended by Stanley Fowler.

Cap Robinson, not being a property owner in Ocean Beach, could not bring an Article 78 action against the village, so he had village resident George Stretch, Sr. (father of Bob, George Jr, and Joe), enter the lawsuit with him. Before the new exclusive franchise granted by the village was to go into effect, Robinson and Stretch appealed to the Appellate Division of the Second Department, and Justice Froessel's decision in favor of FIFI and the village was unanimously affirmed. Robinson also appealed Judge Ritchie's order ending his county license on April 30, 1948, with no success.

Robinson and Stretch made application to the Court of Appeals to prevent the new franchise from going into effect on May 1, 1948 and to permit Robinson to continue ferry service and use the village ferry terminal. Judge Fuld refused, but did agree to hear the case at a later date.

A few days before the new franchise was to begin, Robinson again made an application to the Suffolk County court for an extension of his license, and this application was again denied by Judge Ritchie.

The Court of Appeals handed down a decision, reversing the two lower courts' decision, holding that the village had no statutory authority to grant an exclusive franchise or right to operate a ferry to Ocean Beach; that right belonged solely in the court of Suffolk County. This confusing ruling led to a two-and-a-half year court case. The Court of Appeals refrained from deciding whether or not the village had the right to lease its own ferry terminal exclusively to one ferry company. At the time this decision was handed down, FIFI was in operation for over a month.

The Court of Appeals' decision did not give Robinson's Ocean Beach Ferry Company any rights of its own; it declared the exclusive franchise to FIFI invalid. Letters between the village attorney, mayor, and Patterson questioned what this meant.

On July 10, 1947, Robinson asked Judge Froessel to annul FIFI's franchise. The Supreme Court, Part One, Nassau County, dismissed the petition.

On September 25, 1947, Judge Froessel upheld Ocean Beach Ferry (Robinson) and ordered the franchise to be reviewed.

On November 17, 1947, the Appellate Division of the Supreme Court, the village, and FIFI asked for an appeal and for dismissal, but were told to prepare for court on May 1, 1948.

The following documents or letters were found in old files:

March 12, 1948 letter to Ed Davis, then president of FIFI, from village Attorney Iserman, stating "get Bay Shore landing rights from the town of Islip and the county license; you have the Ocean Beach landing rights. Get going!!"

May 1, 1948, Fire Island ferries began to operate under the new franchise and to occupy the village ferry terminal.

June 14, 1948, FIFI told it must continue to operate, bound by its license.

June 24, 1948, Supreme Court, Suffolk County, Judge Hooley orders review of June 29, 1947 franchise for renewal and extension of Robinson's ferry franchise; denied.

The summer season of 1948 was in full swing with larger crowds and more freight than had been seen in the past. Robinson made public threats that he would attempt to run ferryboats into the village-owned ferry terminal in defiance of the rights of the village. He did not have a cross-bay license to Ocean Beach. Fire Island Ferries had the county license, providing diesel boats of greater capacity, including a new diesel speedboat, *Fire Island Belle*, and service had improved over that provided the year before by Robinson. On June 17, 1948, the village board leased the village basin to FIFI for ten years at $3,000 a year. The lease signed on July 7, 1948 replaced the franchise the court had trouble with, but contained all the language of the franchise, which had been declared invalid by the Court of Appeals; the document's name was changed from "franchise" to "lease."

After the lease was executed and in force, Robinson's attorneys, Morris Rockman and Milton Pinkus of Hempstead, New York, brought suit to have it declared nullified on the ground that the village had no legal right to make the lease. Robinson's attorneys continued legal action based on the idea that Robinson had some right to use the village basin. Justice Hooley denied Cap's petition and restrained him from interfering with the use of the ferry basin.

On October 20, 1948, Robinson's attorney, Milton Pinkus, wanted a hearing on the county license.

On March 1, 1949, Judge Hill gave hope to Robinson with a favorable decision that the "village exclusive lease to FIFI for the Ocean Beach Basin interfered with the county court," but Judge Hill refrained from directing the village to permit Robinson to use the basin.
In March 1949, at the county court in Riverhead, re-argument by Robinson. If Robinson could

find another dock at Ocean Beach and show public necessity, county could issue him a license.

In March 1949, Robinson's application for license from Judge Ritchie was denied, ordered re-hearing and re-argument denied.

On March 7, 1949, Appellate Division, Supreme Court New York, Second Department, Brooklyn, the matter was remitted to special term for trial.

On March 18, 1949, Appellate Division, Supreme Court, Second Department, court order for trial, Brooklyn Courthouse, at a later date (no date given at that time).

In the spring of 1949, Robinson brought action in New York State Supreme Court against the village, former board of trustees, and Fire Island Ferries, Inc., alleging conspiracy to wreck his business of operating a ferry. It was reported at a March village board meeting that Cap was heard to remark that if he could not operate in the summer of 1949, he intended to sell his boats and quit, but he didn't.

In April 1949, Robinson made a motion for re-argument to the Court of Appeals, which stated the appeal had to be submitted without oral argument and returnable on April 8, 1949.

On July 11, 1949, Suffolk County Supreme Court, Justice Hooley dismissed Cap's petition on its merits.

In August 1949, the village attorney received a Notice of Appeal from Robinson's attorney, Milton Pinkus, to be heard in October in the Appellate Division.

Judge Hooley's secretary fixed the date to hear argument in the case for November 23, 1949. (FIFI had now operated for two summers.) The opposing attorneys met with Judge Hooley in early December, and letters were written back and forth between all attorneys.

In January 1950, the Appellate Division passed the case back to the Court of Appeals. The appeal date was set for February 27, 1950, but the case was ended on January 23, 1950.

From letters of March 17, 1950, between Pinkus, Fowler, Iserman, and the village clerk, Miss Yates, it appears they reached the end of this long dispute, and Cap Robinson's case was closed; Robinson would no longer appeal.

Cap Robinson tried by legal means to get back the Ocean Beach ferry run from May of 1947 until January of 1950. I don't believe he ever had a chance. He did not present a bid; when he did bid, it was four weeks late. He did not agree to have diesel ferries by May 1, 1948. He operated with an exclusive franchise for twenty years, and when he lost the franchise, he claimed it was illegal to grant one.

The cost of all this included village and FIFI attorney fees (the village conducted most of the defense), FIFI also lost time and money, but Robinson lost the most because he was out of business. The end was March 23, 1950 when Robinson had to pay the $56.35 court cost for denial of appeals.

Many letters were written between the attorneys, the village, FIFI, and the courts. Court dates were set and delayed, judges had different opinions, emotions ran high, and many Ocean Beach residents backed Robinson, their longtime friend.

Cap gave up and sold his boats. The *Ocean Beach* went to Florida, where it was destroyed in a fire. Al Olsen, on a prearranged deal, bought the *Chesapeake* and then sold it to Patterson. The *Miss Ocean Beach* went to Sayville Ferry and was renamed *Fire Island Pines* and later *Flying Hornet*. The *Margaret* was sold to Dick Block and Billy Leyrer, and renamed *South Bay Challenger* and served Dunewood in 1968 and 1969.

During the two summers that Robinson tried to regain the Ocean Beach run, he worked for Zee Line as a captain on the *Margaret* and *Missy*, then being used by the Zegels to Seaview and the Park. The court case was difficult on Cap, and he died a year after the final judgment at the age of sixty-seven.

The bid raises some questions: What happened to the *Doris*? Also, I know Patterson considered Babylon for its frequent train schedule, and it's not that much further to Ocean Beach than from Bay Shore, but I don't think a suitable terminal could be found. They stated they would use Maple Avenue dock until suitable land was available. It appears that White and Patterson began buying and rezoning the present Main Terminal in 1951. On May 14, 1953, service from the present Main Terminal started, five years after the May 1, 1948 start-up date to Ocean Beach.

At the bid date and start-up date, Ed Davis was still president of FIFI. The only story I have heard of his leaving was that he would not put his share of money into the business. Patterson had to have Mr. Davis legally removed, and Patterson became president. I had heard from more than one person that when the new *Fire Island Belle* arrived in Bay Shore at the end of June or first week of July 1948, Patterson and Davis had a heated argument over who would be captain for the first trip to Ocean Beach. After twenty-five years of working for Patterson, I know he always got his own way, and he made the *Belle's* first trip to Ocean Beach.

In early July 1948, I was at Flynn's Ocean Bay Park dock on a Sunday afternoon with the water taxi *Socks* when the *Fire Island Belle* pulled in with Captain Patterson in command. The *Belle* was new and only had a temporary certificate for eighty-five passengers, who were loaded on, leaving at least a hundred on the dock. At the same time, he also left people behind in Ocean Beach, leaving him no choice, under the Ocean Beach franchise, but to give up service to the Park. The Seaview Ferry Company continued its operation of the Ocean Bay Park run.

Starting about 1951, construction on the beach exceeded anything seen in the past. Summer houses were being built at a rate that led to the need for more vessels, some of them being the old *Chesapeake*, ex-rumrunner *Fire Island Flyer*, surplus World War II air/sea rescue boats *Fire Islander*, *Fireball*, *Firebird*, ex-state park ferry *Roamer II*, a cut-down PT boat *Saltaire III* renamed the *Fire Island*, two barges, and the self-propelled barge *Turtle*.

The village of Saltaire operated its own ferry service beginning in 1922, three years after the village's incorporation. For a twenty-nine-year period, the village owned and operated five ferries, not all at the same time: the *Stranger*, *Eladio*, *Saltaire*, *Saltaire II*, and *Saltaire III*. After World War II, they bought a cut-down PT boat with one diesel engine, which was both slow and unsightly, named *Saltaire III*. I believe the village board was embarrassed and voted to have their ferry operation run by professionals. In 1951, the village signed a contract with Captain Patterson to operate ferry service, and Saltaire Ferry Inc. was formed. It was operated by FIFI, but had its own crew, boats, and set of books.

Part of the contract called for a ferry to replace *Saltaire III*. Patterson converted an air/sea rescue vessel with two V-12 gasoline engines mounted in the stern with V-drives into the ferry *Fire Islander*. The *Islander* was extremely fast with its gasoline engines, and Patterson had to remove his posters stating "Ride the Safe Diesel Ferries." (Gasoline in the bilge is explosive; diesels are much safer.) The competition, Ocean Bay Park and Seaview Ferries, still had gasoline engines at that time. The *Islander* consumed twice as much gasoline as a diesel vessel, and the cost of gasoline was twice as much as diesel. After about two years, two new Detroit Diesel 6-110s replaced the Hall Scott gasoline engines. They provided marginal power for the fully loaded *Islander* and broke down often. The *Islander* provided service to Saltaire for about thirty-three years and was replaced by the *Stranger* in 1985.

Fire Island Ferries took over service to Kismet after the Weis family left; at one time, they owned most of the commercial establishments in that community. Kismet grew rapidly during the 1950s and 1960s. The ferry docked at the entrance to the Kismet boat basin until Patterson bought the bay front north of Kismet Inn and Kismet Out, where he installed his own ferry dock.

When Dunewood development was started in 1958 by Murray Barbash, all the material and workmen were transported by FIFI, and when passenger service started, it was combined with Kismet and ran from the Main Terminal.

In 1965, Patterson outbid Gus Pagels and won the Atlantique bid from the Bay Shore Marina, which carried a high volume of middle school children. I don't believe anyone knew he was bidding on the contract, and the *Queen* served this run well.

***

He was called Captain Patterson, Elmer, Pat, Cap and, at times, unkind names. I first met Captain Patterson in 1948 when he was about forty-two years old, a handsome bachelor, well educated, and articulate. At that time, I was eighteen and taking care of the water taxi *Socks* and its 600-horsepower Curtis Conqueror converted aircraft engine. Pat liked to talk about engines, and shortly afterward, I started to work for him as a deckhand and mechanic's helper. Pat's life revolved around his ferries and engines and Fire Island.

Pat had nice blue eyes, and I am sure everyone told him that because he always wore a light blue sweater or a light blue windbreaker and a blue cap. For many years, Patterson lived at 46 Park Avenue, Bay Shore with his parents, and during the summer, he lived in Ocean Beach.

For the first ten years of his ownership of Fire Island Ferries, Pat drove an old car, never took a vacation, never spent money on anything for himself, and reinvested everything back into the ferry company or ferry terminal. He bought some of the early boats himself and sold them to Fire Island Ferries, Inc. after converting them into ferries. In the thirty-three years he worked for his ferry company, he never went far from Bay Shore or his boats, except once when he and his first wife, Marion, drove to Florida to pick up a poodle, and they were back in about five days. He had no children or hobbies, and he wasn't interested in sports or travel. Marion died in the 1960s.

I don't believe he was ever interested in money for himself, only in its value to improve or buy a ferry or terminal. Pat was able to see ahead and plan for the future, always getting another boat in service just as it was needed. He was great at putting out misinformation or withholding his next move when it was to his advantage. He appeared to be a hard person, but when he was old, he told me that he did that so people, passengers as well as crew, would not always ask for favors or exceptions to company rules.

Pat never backed down from anyone. He yelled at everyone with equal vigor. He didn't mind having a heated disagreement with anyone, be it Gil Clark, the town of Islip, old man Zegel, Spence Newins, who was owner of the shipyard to the south of the Main Terminal, all our neighbors to the north on Aldrich Court and Shore Lane, and particularly he screamed at his captains and crew. Captain Harold Garrett of the *Fire Island Queen* had to tell Pat that if he had anything to say to the *Queen's* crew, he was to tell Garrett, who would talk to them; Captain Garrett didn't want to lose any more crew who quit when Pat yelled at them.

It didn't take much of a problem to have Patterson get beet red in the face and neck and start to yell, kick stones, throw things, and threaten people. One day he fired his deckhand, and the kid started to walk away. Pat yelled, "You're not fired until tonight."

He had no patience. I helped him pick up a blower off the shop floor to put it on a workbench. There was an empty oilcan in the way on the bench so he grabbed it and threw it across the shop. I have never seen anyone get so mad so quickly over nothing, and then just as quickly return to normal.

If the wind blew from the north for a long time, a lot of eelgrass gets into the Ocean Beach basin and stays there until the wind comes out of the south, which it usually does every day by mid-morning in the summer. There are times when it can make turning around in Ocean Beach a little slow when the props get loaded with weed. On a Sunday afternoon in 1950, with the weeds about two feet deep in the basin, Pat was on the dock and started yelling as only he could to hurry up and move the boat ahead into her loading position. The *Belle* just inched ahead with all the weeds on the props, and he yelled even more. I docked the boat, told him to run her, and went to John and Ann's for lunch since we had a one-hour layover. Pat came in shortly afterward, sat down next to me, and said to ignore his yelling and to make the next trip. This was before we had south bay outside strainers on the cooling water intakes, and the seaweed had blocked the intake pipe to the inside strainers. They were plugged solid and had to be cleared before I could sail; it was a hot, dirty job. We have much less eelgrass in the bay now (2004) than in the 1950s.

Pat yelled at customers as well. I heard a story of him yelling at Eddie Fisher, the singer, and when he was asked if he knew who he had yelled at, he said he didn't know, and he didn't care.

At the time Patterson sold his interest in FIFI, he lived on Saxon Avenue in Bay Shore, and he spent his summers at his Kismet house near the ferry dock.

During the twenty-four years I worked for him, and the next ten years after he retired, he did not appear to age one bit, but after being ill for six months, he aged to become an old man. When I went to visit him in a local nursing home, I walked by his room and saw an old man in bed, but didn't recognize him. I went on to the next room, and then realized that I had passed his room. Despite Pat's poor short-term memory, he and I recalled all the good old days. He also told me that he was sorry that he made his help work so hard (we worked six days a week, and many ten to twelve-hour days plus some much longer days with no paid overtime). Pat died on August 3, 1982.

***

Ed Mooney, Frank Mina, and John Van Bree bought Fire Island Ferries Inc. from Captain

Patterson on January 15, 1971, along with a three-year option for Fire Island Ferries to buy Fire Island Terminal Inc., which option was exercised in January 1974. John Van Bree retired in 1975.

This closing took place in Bob Royce's upstairs office on Main Street, Bay Shore. Van Bree's attorney, Ruby Kaufman, began by asking Patterson why the payments had to be made by the three partners with money they had to pay income tax on first, rather than have Fire Island Ferries make the payments in a leveraged buyout. This type of buyout made sense to everyone except Patterson, who started to gather his papers together to leave; it would be his way or no deal. It was his way, and I was faced with ten years of being broke, making principal and interest payments to him with after-tax earnings.

We also signed a three-year option to buy Fire Island Terminal; this purchase would be a leveraged buyout with Fire Island Terminal earnings buying Pat's stock. Without this option, I was not too sure I would have bought FIFI. My attorney, Jack Weiss, advised me that it was not a good deal as we would be buying all debt and past liabilities of the company, including lawsuits, not knowing of any pending liabilities I had bought into.

The spring of 1972 began the program by Fire Island Ferries to replace its old ferries with more modern, cost-effective vessels, beginning with the *Captain Patterson* followed by the *Fire Island Miss* in 1976, *Traveler* in 1977, *Vagabond* in1979, *Fireball* in 1981, *Firebird* in 1984, *Stranger* in 1985, *Voyager* in 1990, and *Explorer* in 1991. These nine vessels replaced sixteen obsolete ferries, providing better on-time service, moving more people with less crew.

Captain Gus Pagels, owner of the ferries to Fair Harbor for forty years, sold his four vessels and the Fair Harbor dock to Fire Island Ferries at the end of the 1972 season. After buying out Fair Harbor Ferries, FIFI had a large fleet of ferries to take care of, and Bill Brewster did his best to haul out a ferry when we had a problem or inspection, but we decided to get a boatlift for the slip Patterson had built for a lift before he sold the company. After looking at a few lifts around Long Island, in 1976 we decided to buy a 60-ton Acme. Twenty-three years later, we sold it and bought a new Acme 85-ton lift. (At 60 tons, we were at our limit when lifting the 60-ton *Vagabond*.)

In 1974, Fire Island Terminal entered into an agreement with the village of Saltaire to operate its parking field.

About 1982, the Zegel brothers offered their whole operation, boats, docks, and parking for sale. They had many offers, but they wanted all their money at the closing and would not hold a note or mortgage. They were over to see us many times to tell us of another great offer they had received (but not of a sale). The Seaview Association tried to get a group of investors and sell shares, but no one invested. The Ocean Bay Park Association tried to buy it, but again there were no investors. Then, both Seaview and Ocean Bay Park combined to try and buy it, but no shares sold. This went on for well over a year, and the boys wanted to retire, but did not have a firm offer until Mooney and Mina gave them one.

Westferry incorporated on September 15, 1983 to buy Zee Line. And finally, on February 10, 1984, Zee Line Ferry sold all their Seaview and Ocean Bay Park assets to Westferry Inc. (Ed Mooney and Frank Mina,) owners of Fire Island Ferries and Fire Island Terminal. This sale included the parking field on the west side of Maple Avenue and the Seaview and Ocean Bay Park docks at Fire Island.

On February 5, 1985, Westferry Inc. real estate was merged into Fire Island Terminal, and the boats merged into FIFI.

Fire Island Terminal (Ed Mooney and Frank Mina) bought 108 Maple Avenue, the Ball parking lot south of Zee Line Terminal, from Marty Bushard in 1985. It was a mess: broken bulkheading, big potholes, garages falling down, sunken abandoned boats, metal indoor parking building and main two-story building ready to fall down. We cleaned up most of it that winter.

In 1986, Penataquit Shipyard (Ed Mooney and Frank Mina) bought 118 Maple Avenue (a restaurant) from Ellie Corcaran and leased it to Il Garafano as a restaurant. When the operator got behind in the rent so that he could no longer pay it, he left, and we tore down the building and added the property to the south parking lot. On December 29, 1986, Penataquit Shipyard bought Bay Shore Marine Basin from Gibson and Cushman Dredging, owner Mr. Kenneth Carrode, and cleaned it out to make more parking, more boat slips, and more room for outdoor winter boat storage.

On April 4, 1989, Ed Mooney traded the shipyard (the old restored Bay Shore Marine Basin) to Frank Mina for Mina's ferry and terminal stock, ending the eighteen-year partnership.

At the end of 1994, FIFI stockholder Ed Mooney created an Employee Stock Ownership Plan (ESOP). The first FIFI ESOP payment was made on July 1995 with seven years of payments for 35% of FIFI stock. The plan gives an employee, after five continuous years of over 1,000 hours per year, a vested interest in stock, based on their salary. Upon retirement, their stock value is paid to them over a five-year period.

All of the employees of Fire Island Ferries Inc. are qualified to do more than one job, and many could probably leave and earn more money elsewhere, but there is more to a job than money. I believe many employees have stayed on all these years as I have because each day brings new, sometimes unexpected challenges, and Fire Island Ferries continues to operate as a family of people dedicated to delivering good service.

I plan to continue to collect pictures and data of ferries that went to the west end of Fire Island.

CAPTAIN EDWIN J. MOONEY
FIRE ISLAND FERRIES, INC.
99 MAPLE AVENUE
P.O. BOX 5311
BAY SHORE, NEW YORK 11706
PHONE (631) 665-3600
FAX (631) 665-7656
WWW.EMOONEY.COM (for purchase of additional books)
WWW.FIREISLANDFERRIES.COM (for ferry service information)

CAPTAIN EDWIN J. MOONEY

Born in 1929, Edwin Mooney grew up in Teaneck, New Jersey, the son of a policeman, and one of six children. He spent most of his childhood outdoors, hiking, camping, involved in the Boy Scouts, playing sandlot baseball, delivering papers after school, collecting newspapers and metal for the war effort, cutting grass, and shoveling snow. While in high school, he worked part-time in a boatyard and took care of a neighbor's boat.

In 1948, Ed Mooney graduated high school, left Teaneck, and ended up in Bay Shore, Long Island, working on the water taxi *Socks*. He started work on the ferries a week later, getting his captain's license by the end of the summer.

In 1949, he was captain of the *Fire Island Maid*.

In 1950, he became captain of the *Fire Island Belle*.

Captain Mooney married Pat Brown in April 1951.

He was drafted into the Army for the Korean War in May 1951, received one year of infantry training, and after arriving in Germany, he was transferred to an Army engineer boat company in France for a year.

After two years of military service, Captain Mooney was back on the *Belle*, one week after returning home from France.

He has two sons and a daughter and nine grandchildren.

Captain Mooney became President of Fire Island Ferries in 1971 and Chief Executive Officer in 2000.